The Way of God

It Just Is

SHER GILL Galib

Grosvenor House
Publishing Limited

This book is published by
Grosvenor House Publishing Ltd
Link House
140 The Broadway, Tolworth, Surrey, KT6 7HT.
www.grosvenorhousepublishing.co.uk

A CIP record for this book
is available from the British Library

Paperback ISBN 978-1-80381-331-8
Hardback ISBN 978-1-80381-332-5
eBook ISBN 978-1-80381-333-2

First Published: 16-10-2014

Website: www.shergill.uk.com
Email: beingasaint@gmail.com

SHER GILL Galib

CONTENTS

INTRODUCTION

The Way of God is for the Seekers, who want to feel the presence of God here and now. In simple words, the flow of Spirit will open as you read along. If you have spiritual discipline; there is nothing you cannot know or understand. All religions point to the fact that God is within; we fail to feel its presence because we fail to follow 'The Way of God.'

The first chapter explains how to follow the way of God. The Way of God is an eye-opener for true Seekers. It answers common questions and help the Seeker to find the truth. The way of God is simple; somehow, we make it complicated. God is 'The Soul,' and so are you. We create the barrier and say, 'I cannot do it.' I don't think I can use simpler words than these: **Just do it.** We are the children of God, who loves us dearly and is waiting for us with open arms.

I have experienced the presence of God and so can you. Each chapter is unique and has a clear message to let you feel how close you are to God. You will feel as if God is talking to you. Once you know the way of God, you will be the centre of all universes. There is a tremendous amount of God-knowledge infused within each chapter. There is a history of known world prophets and religious track records. One chapter explores aliens, conveying information on their good looks and how they are beyond our physical judgement.

The physical universe is explained in-depth, including knowledge of all of earth's fellow planets and how they affect our astrology charts. The way of God explores how we experience the 'wrath of God' due to these planetary and karmic effects. You will be surprised to learn; 'where does this knowledge come from? It is within us all the time. You may find the key to opening this treasure and being part of great silence.

THE WAY OF GOD

This subject is very close to my heart. I don't think many people understand what it means. We go around the subject and only want to know what it means from the surface level. Most people are aware that if we apply the whole philosophy of God, it will not benefit us on a material basis. Many years ago, I advised someone to go for the whole instead of the parts. This person knew me very well and replied, I know that you will be the future Master, so it is okay for you to be this serious.

But at present, it does not suit me. I said, fair enough if that's what you believe. Mind you: this person is still struggling today. The clear message is that I am God and so are you. Now the question is, 'Are you? Unless and until you understand this concept, you will never have any serious spiritual success. God; You must know my way; how and why I created this world and all the universes. To say that this is schooling for the soul is an understatement.

You are part of this schooling. You are the student; you are the teacher. You are part of the universe and you are the universe. You are learning within this universe and at the same time, you are running this universe. I am the experience and I experience myself through each of you. The whole of creation was made for a purpose. There is not a single atom that is worthless. I have given you free will to live on your terms and suffer accordingly.

Many species are known to be dangerous to humans. For example, hearing the word *snake* or seeing one in the garden causes many people to shiver. In the past, you were one of them too. You never know how many people you have bitten and died from your poison. Rats are known to spread disease and mosquitoes can spread malaria. The bees sting but they provide us with the gift of honey.

Salt and chilli are for other experiences. The day you understand my way is the day that all your questions will cease. Your questions and complaints are the results of not knowing me - God. You pray to me for others to change mentally to please you. This is not going to happen. Praying means you do not understand my way.

You never know; the other person may be acting under my instructions to polish your state of consciousness. Or the interaction between the two of you could be a significant experience for both; it cannot be altered to please you. This world, atmosphere, people and animals will not change to satisfy you. You better change yourself and learn to adjust accordingly or suffer.

I am God, 'Are you?

The only difference between you and me is how you understand this sentence. Sher; recently a person came to see me and said he requested Spirit to make one of his relatives behave 'gently' towards him. No change of this kind is going to happen. You see, this is where we all go wrong. You never know how difficult a time you may have given this soul in the past. Or it could be a new account to be settled in the future. I am not very proud of my family, apart from my grandparents.

All others were stationed at a perfect place to strike with their spikes at every opportunity. Hell was created around me to test me from every angle you could think of. I lived within this hell and continued to recite God's word. I did not let them affect my spiritual goal.

Others I have interacted with were experiencing life from a different angle than I was. They may not be aware of what purpose they were used. This is what I said in my discourses on disciple and discipline. These discourses came from my personal experiences. One of the virtues of God is that God does not react. Therefore, do not expect God to punish someone because they have done something wrong to you.

Leave the execution to the person appointed by God, the lord of karma, for any action. The punishment will occur when all the learning conditions are perfect for that soul. There is no such experience that I have not been through. You must learn to let it be. This applies to you and all others. You must take every situation as the will of God. Silence is golden. It can help us to go through challenging experiences with ease.

Sometimes we make situations worse than they are or are supposed to be with our lack of command over physical actions or spoken words. It may be suitable for some to have a silent fast once a week. It can help calm down your mental activity and while you are silent, Spirit may begin to flow more freely. I am going to give you a spiritual exercise to practice. It has never been offered before. Do not take this exercise as an ego boost. If you do, you did not understand my message in this discourse.

Just for a day, think of yourself as being in the position of God.

If you were God, considering every situation during the day, good or bad, 'What would you do? 'How would you react? You will be surprised to learn the answers to these questions. God does not respond to any situation. It does not matter how bad things may be; God does not suffer either. In the physical sense, someone hurts you; God gets hurt because you are part of God. But hurting someone else also hurts God because the other person is part of God too.

With this knowledge, I am sure you will not hurt anyone. God experiences every situation through each of us. Every action hit God directly. We are being used as foliage on the surface but continue to complain. You are an individual; who can explore the universe as a soul; you are also part of God's experience. Now you know; to what extent we underestimate ourselves and walk into the traps of Kal.

This happens when a young person enters a relationship trap that uses sweet alluring talk or back-stabbing and leaves their family. Sometimes it may take many years to learn that it was a trap. On realisation and returning, the family accepts the person again with open arms. In the same way, God is always waiting for you, no questions asked, because he knows that it is all part of the learning process.

You may conclude that God is neutral and does not respond to any situation. God is beyond the emotional state and you have acquired the same qualities. 'Can you imagine the state of consciousness you have just accomplished? The word unfoldment has been used by Paul Ji quite often to express that there is no thing or situation a soul does not know of as part of God. But during its journey into the lower worlds, a soul must unfold to every available situation for training.

To attain full knowledge, we need to experience the totality created by God and become the assistants of God. Many different logos have been used, such as 'A Way of life.' These logos change every decade but we cannot twist the teachings to satisfy our minds. Over the last forty years, we have seen the results; they have not been very fruitful. The 'Wind' can blow in one direction only for a limited time.

God is omnipotent, omniscient and omnipresent. God has been and will always be the same, total and the whole of totality. It is we who have been sent into the lower worlds for schooling. The training ground has been prepared for your experience or enlightenment. So do not expect changes to suit your preferences. I would instead give you a hard and distasteful medicine to swallow. All these goody-goody talks or writing has been our failure. I do not wish to see anyone fail who believes in me.

It is not you who has failed. I will take it as my failure; if I cannot correctly convey the message of God. There are no other teachings I am aware of that give the message of God in this manner. Many of the world's spiritual leaders would not know, what I am talking about here. They lead the masses to prayer, which means their followers directly or indirectly beg for something. Instead, they should guide their congregations to work off or balance their karmic load for a better future.

Most of these leaders are interested only in financial gain in their accounts at the expense of their followers. That is their reward for the hard work they do for their followers. I do not ask for money from anyone or accept any donations. But some people feel that it is their religious obligation to give donations. My reward from you will be your spiritual success, as you have become 'the master of your universe.' Please put yourself in the shoes of God.

You will come to know how flexible you have become. You will let go of whatever it may be. Be yourself and do not interfere in any situation created by God. You are flexible, you are forgiving, you are silent and you are neutral, as is God. You will experience total calm within yourself. Absolute happiness is an understatement. You will be sitting within the spiritual pool created by God and your knowingness will be beyond description.

This will be the first time you will experience what you have heard many times over the last forty years. **You live in this world but are not a part of it.** Before it was just a saying but now you will be in this experience. You must create this situation to experience the scheme of God. 'Guess what? You cannot even guess what you are going to experience.

Try to maintain this state of consciousness daily. I will not be surprised to hear from you one day, 'I am the Master.' My spiritual goal is accomplished. God wants us to become the knowers of truth and feel part of it. Now consciously say:

I am it and it is me and we are one.
Now I know the one,
To whom, no one knows but now it knows **me.**

God; people try to know me by reciting the verses of the religious text. These verses are all talking about religion but not about God. By repeating and trying to understand the verses, you can or will become like the priests or scholars who wrote them but you will never become like me. These writings are only for guidance. I live within those pure in their hearts and down-to-earth, as I am.

I live within those who approach me directly through the Master. Your problems will never solve and your cries will never be heard until you begin to listen to me and are conquered by the Spirit. At the moment, you are very similar to a wild horse. That will not let anyone sit on its back until the horse trainer breaks it. You may struggle if you wish; I have given you 'free will.' But until you say to the Spirit, 'Please do whatever you wish to do with me; I am at your service,' you will struggle.

Now, you are not practising the concept of 'letting it go.' Or maybe you are letting it go but simultaneously holding onto everything. These two points do not go together. You are a raw material like clay, which needs to be moulded to take any shape. A toy can be made or it can be shaped into a brick. Let me mould you in the form of a toy, a brick or flexible, as I am.

And all will be yours and you will open the gates of heaven to others to let them know who I am and where I am. I am so close to you, as I am God. God has given this message to you through me, as I am the open channel for Spirit and so are you. Make the most of your time. It is never too late. After reading this discourse, you can moan and groan or act happy-go-lucky. The ball is in your court.

Spirit loves you, as you are part of it.

DWELLING WITHIN

We always seek God in temples or churches when it is sitting right within us. No one wants to know this truth because we have no insight into it and are taught this way. We can only lead others if we have personal experience. When we are in trouble or in desperate need, we go anywhere to pray. We have reached a point in Kali-Yuga where we feel God is miles away and out of reach.

We have lost this connection and awareness of God's inner presence and our approach to life has become materialistic. Over the years, I have come across many people who have asked, 'What God? 'Where is God? 'Has anyone seen God? 'Can you show me where God is? These people are not wrong to raise these questions. The reason for questioning the presence of God is the way they are living or life has treated them.

There are situations when a saint or a good person suffers at the hands of villains but the villains are having a good time and living a prosperous life. After witnessing such circumstances, many people will lose their faith and ask similar questions about the nature and existence of God. These situations do occur. And in some cases, this may be a lesson in disguise for the villains. Such a lesson may not materialise instantly but it will shine through in later years.

Many times, saints set up these examples to show people how to obey the will of God and let it be when they could have done anything to teach a lesson to the people involved. Saints leave the punishment in the hands of Spirit on a neutral basis. The saints do not get involved when Spirit punishes, whether instantly or in later years. They are beyond being for or against any situation. They are examples of patience and tolerance.

Jesus Christ could have escaped if he wanted to but he did not. Therefore, we know him today. Otherwise, we wouldn't know who he was in terms of history. Sikhism is full of examples. The fifth Guru, Arjan Dev, sat on a hot metal plate over a heated clay oven while the Muslim captors poured heated sand over his head. Despite the pain, he continued to recite holy chants throughout this ordeal. So, what gave him the strength to suffer without uttering a single word against the people who tortured him?

This is an example of a saint connected to the divine Spirit and had a direct link with God. Whether you see God at work or not depends on your state of consciousness. It was Arjan Dev's inner strength or connection with Spirit at work. Unless we have this inner connection, we will never be called saints. With book knowledge, we are known as priests or scholars. To be in contact with or known by the Spirit is most important.

We should try in this life or the opportunity may arise in future lives when we have earned good karma. Based on good karma, we express our individuality, which will be the state of consciousness. We come to a point in life where our spiritual mind seeks an outer teacher who can lead to inner teachings. These newfound teachings may lead the individual to have a mystical experience. This urge within leads you from one teacher to another until you are satisfied or your destiny leads you to the teachings appointed by the lord of karma.

At times, Spirit leads you under the instructions of God itself so that you can lead the people of some religion in the future. Any Master or teachings that do not lead you to the inner teachings are not worth following. Your spiritual journey will be at a standstill; another life will be wasted as if living like a vegetable. The outer teachings give insight into what to ponder when imagining the 'inner.'

Whatever you have read over the years is good. But now, it is your efforts and the responsibility of the Master to lead you to the inner. Here are the answers to whatever you have been seeking in life. Now is the time to reap whatever you have sown over the years. To become the knower of inner worlds, you must build a relationship with the spiritual Master. Otherwise, your journey or dream will be at a standstill. The basic steps are:

1. Do meditation with complete sincerity.
2. Have total reliance upon the spiritual Master.
3. Practice the presence and communicate with the spiritual Master.

Inner communication

The Master should be able to operate physically and spiritually. Physically, he is limited; he cannot be with everyone simultaneously. But spiritually, he can be with everyone, depending on the situation. Despite your meditation, you should try to maintain inner communication with the spiritual Master. I only met my guru physically a maximum of ten times over thirty years.

But I never lost sight of him spiritually; I learned that it is important to build this inner relationship. Most of the members failed on this point and tried to be known by the Master on a physical level. Perhaps that is all they achieved; they also lost that in later years. This inner communication makes it easy for the Master to teach the Seeker; spoken words are not used and the mind is also set aside.

The silent language is very powerful. It is beyond the reach of any physical means and the teachings are given directly to the soul. It will be a natural process for the recipient but could become a phenomenon for the average human mind. This inner communication will lead you to become the master of your universe. Once this communication is established, you will operate from the level of sun and moon worlds in the astral plane.

This state of consciousness must contact the spiritual Master during the spiritual exercises so that he can lead you to the inner or higher planes. A person with this ability can roam freely in the upper regions. As a regular visitor, you have built your authority, as the lords of these planes recognise you. Now you can communicate with the spiritual Master and all the lords of higher planes.

You have become the authority and can take others with you on an inner journey. You can help someone stuck in these planes; at the mention of your name, they will be set free. This communication will lead you into the presence of Satnam Ji. Once you have self-realised, you can roam freely of your own volition. Now it is time to explore the worlds of being.

You have the blessings of Satnam Ji. During the daytime, your effort will maintain this state of consciousness. It becomes easy for the Master to take you on dream travels at night-time, as you are an open channel for Spirit. Once this process is continuous for over twenty-four hours, 'Can you imagine your progress? This can lead you to God-realisation and into the presence of God. You have proven this 'Reality' to yourself.

Without this inner channel, nothing is possible. Due to this communication, all the secret teachings are made available. These secret teachings prepare the Seeker for the highway to the higher world. You will notice that your material and emotional life begins to slip to the side and your soul shines out and is reflected in your aura. Others will see and wonder what it could be. All the inner worlds beyond the physical come into focus through this inner vision.

The inner worlds are as real as the physical world is natural to our physical senses. The surrender to the Master also happens on the inner level and the outer follows. 'Who is interested in the outer when everything is alive at the inner? The presence of the Master or Spirit is felt when the inner is active. Nothing is possible unless we leave our physical shell. This inner strength is responsible for overpowering negative habits, such as alcohol or hard drugs or controlling depression.

The inner is also responsible for the origin of mystic powers. To the saints, such powers are normal. But to others, they are miracles. Once you are successful at the inner level, it is also known as soul travel. Many other achievements are natural, among them healing and telepathy. With this inner connection, reality shines and the illusion disappears.

ARE YOU A GARDENER?

This is a self-analysis for any spiritual Seeker. 'Are we doing enough concerning our state of consciousness? We are responsible for maintaining the highest ethics to be an example to others. We are the representatives of true and pure teachings in this world. Many years ago, when we joined this path of spiritual freedom, we were taught some basic principles to follow. This includes keeping our thoughts pure and simple.

It also means working toward balancing the five passions of our minds. These passions are the cause of our excessive desires and future sufferings. A gardener who looks after their garden ensures the soil texture and the seeds; they want to plant are suitable. Once the seeds are planted, they are watered at regular intervals and the first petals appear. It does not take long for a seedling to grow into many branches.

The gardener is watchful for any weeds growing alongside the plant to have good crops. If weeds grow, the gardener ensures to eliminate them. The weeds growing alongside the plant will use part of the strength of the soil supporting the plants. The plants growing alongside the weeds will not be as healthy or fruitful as expected. We must drop lots of physical baggage if we need to travel into the other or inner worlds.

Such baggage is constantly pulling us down, similar to the effect of gravity on planet Earth. To train the soul, all desires help to provide the pull to keep us anchored to this world. After all these years of following, we have become too relaxed and forgotten our true goal: to free ourselves forever from the wheel of eighty-four. One basic principle to accomplish this freedom is; to learn to set free others.

We must set free all around us as part of our family or friends. When sincere in the teachings, we try to follow all the dos or don'ts to succeed. Working on our weaknesses is a responsibility in life; otherwise, we waste our teacher's valuable time. Many people do not realise that this teaching has been designed to train individuals into sainthood. It is not a religion, which is controlled by many systems or politics up to some extent.

A few Seekers are trapped by the Kal and act their part in our teachings on political grounds. Since I have been responsible for the teachings, whoever comes my way as a true Seeker; I will do my best in the inner realm beyond limits. I will give physical assistance as much as possible; there are many limits on the physical world. Masters are not born every day. Their birth takes place under the supervision of Satnam Ji and God.

The birth may not be as dramatic as mentioned by many religions. The tales of a Master born out of wedlock to a virgin mother or appearing alongside the mother's bed are myths. The Masters are born at the right time and family where the teachings can be given when required. This child will have a guardian angel from birth. Three or four saints of different age groups will fulfil this responsibility.

The living Master does not have to die physically to pass over the responsibility. He can retire at a certain age when the next person is ready to take responsibility. The third person can be in his teens or early twenties, preparing to take the approaching responsibility. It is possible that the fourth in line has just been born or is on the way to this earth planet to take responsibility at the command of Spirit. No one has control over these individuals apart from God itself.

The present Master has no control over the giving or not of this responsibility. As this individual is born especially for this purpose, the present Master must hand over the responsibility according to the time allotted by Spirit. In turn, the next one will step in when the time arrives. This procedure is perfectly and whole-heartedly executed with the blessings and support of the departing Master.

Any assistance required in the future will be given, as these Masters are here to fulfil God's command, not create mental barriers. The master-ship will not remain in one country forever or within one race of people. It will change from one continent to the next as required by God. The master-ship staying in one place does not benefit the whole world. If it remains in one country, the people will begin to claim it as theirs to keep. This way, pure teachings automatically turn into a religion.

For the good of the whole, the present Master should pass the spiritual mantle in time to the new recipient. Due to unforeseen circumstances, Spirit will give it to the new Master in whatever country he is residing. These teachings are designed for a universal purpose, as God dwells everywhere. Now, I will bring the state of consciousness into the limelight held by our long-term members. I know some of them who have been in the teachings since the time of Paul Ji.

And definitely from the early days of Dapren. When I joined the teachings in 1976, if I recall, some were members of The **Way to God** at the time. Spending all these years on this path, they could have been as good as any saint. Since I released my book 'The Way to God,' I know who they are; sending me dirty, degrading and abusive emails. I am under the direction of Spirit and am not purposely creating any threat to anyone in this world.

After reading my book, these individuals must be experiencing some threat and are on the attack through the medium of the internet. Now the question arises, after all these years, 'What have they learned? They have learned **nothing.** I want to clarify one point about spiritual initiations. Any person who does any negative action against any individual will lose their initiations right on the spot.

It does not matter which Master has initiated you. The initiation is just an indication that an individual can maintain their state of consciousness at the level of that initiation and can strive for the next step. Since negative thoughts originated in your mind; you automatically dropped from your state of consciousness. If this state of consciousness is not maintained, you fall like a brick. On this path, you must be watchful before taking any step.

The Kal is working from all corners and is ready to trap you. To make any progress, we must be alert and not fail. To maintain this state of consciousness is our responsibility. Keep asking yourself this question: 'Am I a good gardener? God has infinite qualities; the number of qualities you have adopted or can maintain throughout your spiritual endeavours; will be your state of consciousness.

This is how we differ; otherwise, we are all the same as souls. The more qualities we adopt, the closer we are to God. One day you will realise you are receiving direct answers before even asking a question.

You are never alone; the Spirit is with you always,

SATSANG

All Seekers are recommended to attend Satsang and the spiritual meetings. It will help to build up a good spiritual foundation. The Master has written several discourses which you may read at home but if you read the same discourse in the Satsang; your spiritual awakening will be beyond what you can imagine. The reading of the discourse in the Satsang is an experience.

Holding the Satsang is important to raise positive vibrations for the whole world. If Satsang is held everywhere, it can help to bring more balance in-world activities. Positive vibrations will bring peace and prosperity. Most disasters result from imbalance, the negativity created by sinful karma.

'What is Satsang? 'Sat' means truth or true word. 'Sang' means together or union. So together, it means 'sacred union.' We get together to read and discuss the true message of the Master, which is presented through spiritual discourses. Each discourse covers different subjects, bringing truth to the Seekers. The person who attends the Satsang is known as the Seeker. Every Seeker who attends a Satsang will feel uplifting and unfold more spiritually.

Our main aim is to unfold spiritually to achieve spiritual freedom from the lower worlds. The importance of the Satsang is manifold. This is the best way to learn, much faster than reading at home. It brings spiritual discipline to the Seeker. It is also a spiritual gathering. In the place where Satsang is taking place, the vibrations are so high that most participants have different experiences.

For example; they can see the spiritual light, hear the inner sound or even see the Master taking the Satsang himself. Although he is not there physically. The number of experiences are far too many to mention. The Seekers could see the Master in his radiant form and up to three Masters can be seen. At least three Masters are present during each Satsang, so providing three chairs or other means of seating is recommended.

Satsangs can begin with minimum Seekers available but no more than twelve; if possible, exceptions in some instances can be given. The maximum number of twelve people is that each member should participate actively. They should read at least one paragraph and explain its message. If not, ask the **Teacher** to explain further so that every person understands the message conveyed by the Master.

Satsang must be held at the same time every month. Undisciplined people are not welcome, as this is not a social gathering. The Masters are waiting for you. I am sure you don't want the Masters to wait. The Masters are busier than we are in our daily routine work. The master's spiritual forms are unlimited but bringing ourselves into discipline is more important. The more disciplined we are, the more responsibilities the Master can put on our shoulders. Never forget, that we are going to be the assistants of God.

The best way to learn is to teach and take responsibility as a teacher. You will read the same discourse from a different angle. First, you were reading the discourse to understand it for yourself. This time, you want to read so that others can understand too. This way, you will experience the depth of understanding of the same discourse. This is the second stage of reading and learning.

If you follow the third stage, you will experience more depth but you will also experience the state of consciousness from which it has been written. In the next dimension of Satsang, the Master takes his followers to attend Satsang in higher spiritual planes. The Satsang classes are available in the spiritual cities on the physical plane and then progress to the astral, causal, mental and soul planes. Once the Master feels you are mature enough, he can give you the duty to take the Satsang on the physical and higher planes.

The Satsang is a way forward for spiritual Seekers.

Satsang Instructions

All members should attend Satsang at least once a month. Fix time with mutual agreement for each month. We reach our Satsang place on time. The house door or Hall should be closed five minutes before commencing the Satsang. 3 Extra seats are to be provided for the Masters.

Once all members have arrived, the Teacher will leave the room for 2 to 3 minutes during those 5 minutes. You will chant your spiritual word or Haiome silently as you are physically alone. It is called tuning with Spirit or when you feel the inner nudge indicating that you are ready, walk inside the room and feel the flow of Spirit or the inner Master has taken over. This experience for the 'Teacher' and all the participants will be different or from another dimension.

We begin with a 'Haiome' chant, for approx. Two minutes. This will help us to relax physically and raise our vibrations spiritually.

The chapter we will read and discuss today must have been read at home prior to Satsang. That way, during the Satsang, we can understand the message thoroughly.

Everyone must participate by reading a paragraph and explaining the spiritual message. If unsure, request the Teacher to explain it further or anyone can explain.

The time for the Satsang is one hour or no more than one and a half hours.

We always stay within the subject; we are discussing today.

After the agreed time, you may close the Satsang with the same spiritual chant.

May the blessings be or Sarvat-da-Bhalla holds the same meaning so that you can use either.

After the conclusion of Satsang, you may have a cup of tea. During that time, you can discuss, share or ask any questions regarding the teachings. But no social gatherings or any other topics.

Contemplate all the points we have learned. It will help refine our spiritual self to unfold further or become aware of what we already have.

DISCIPLE

'Are you a disciple? Yes, indeed you are. But at the same time, you are the future Master too. This is the point that you need to keep your focus on. Every person is a born Master, as we have all the qualities of God within us. But we have turned ourselves into the ways of Kal. There are many reasons for doing this or the bad karma we have created, knowingly or unknowingly. In either case, we are responsible for our doings. Every waking moment must be lived consciously.

Now I will give you an example. 'How can you do this? I am sure most of you have seen the movie **Silent Flute**. There was a Seeker who wanted to know the truth. The journey is from the physical plane to the soul plane. The Seeker was willing to go through any test to have the experience. Bruce Lee partly wrote it, so the journey is expressed through kung-fu or martial arts. He was attacked by several monkeys on the journey, representing the negative power.

The monkeys were trying to circle him. His Master had guided him never to let the monkeys circle him; once they do, the Master had said, they will attack you. The Seeker remembered his Master's guidance. As the monkeys tried to circle him, he turned around with them. His Master had also told him to keep eye contact with them. Once they knew that you were not looking at them, they would attack. The Seeker kept turning around and maintained eye contact with them.

After a long time, the monkeys gave up. The Seeker succeeded in his efforts. And the Master prepared him for the next step. I am sure you got the message but must make an effort to succeed in your spiritual journey. We often create the situations we face ourselves with a don't-care attitude. And many are helping the negative forces to make many circles around them in a day. This is very easily done.

You do this when you have plenty of time and indulge in self-created or natural problems. You go over and over your situation. The number of times you go over your problems is the number of circles the negative power has made around you. This is what we must be watchful for. You are a clear channel for the negative force when going over your problems. Pure Spirit cannot penetrate within to help, because you are not letting it help.

Do not let the Kal force circle around you. We all have problems. Request Spirit to resolve the issue and it will be done, provided you don't make another circle around it. Spirit will help. If not, let it be and move on with your life. Do not stand still; that is not very fruitful. Therefore, there are so many pending unsolved problems with so many followers; that people do not let go of the situations they find themselves in. We have one chapter, 'Let It Go' in our book 'The Way to God' dedicated to this concept.

I could have written a complete book on the subject if I had mentioned all the situations I have been through. Instead, I summed up the entire issue in three or four paragraphs. The less said, the better. Do not help the Kal force to make circles around you. This is the responsibility of the disciple. Early on, you set up a spiritual goal to achieve in this life. There is no looking back, no letting any situation interfere with your goal. I know you are not a failure, so do not let the Kal force fail you.

In effect, the Kal force is not here to fail you. I will take it as a blessing in disguise. The Kal force is helping you to build up your spiritual stamina. You want to graduate but do not want to pass any exams. 'How will you consider yourself qualified if you do not pass any exams? I will give you another example on the same subject. You can choose one that suits you. Many beggars come to beg for food or money in villages and in almost every house; a dog is left loose within the boundary walls for security purposes.

If the beggars got scared of dogs, they would be empty-handed all day. One day, a beggar came to our house. I kept looking at him for an unknown reason and watched him for almost two minutes. I learned something from him. As he entered the main gate, he made his call for alms. The dog became alert and came near the beggar to bark and attack. This was the learning point because something kept the dog at bay.

The beggar held a long stick under his armpit, pointing two feet behind his legs. The beggar never stood still. He kept moving his upper body continuously, a quarter of a turn to the left or right. The dog kept barking and attacking but was strangely deceived by the stick's movement. The dog followed the stick, moving from left to right in a circle. The beggar got his alms and went to the next house for the same purpose. This artful dodger deceived the dog.

You can find your way of stopping the Kal force from making a circle around you. You are never short of ideas. God has given you all the creative faculties to use, which we hardly use. I know some Seekers who are not feeling well physically. Many times, I advise them that they can do this or that. You are the first to know something is wrong with your physical body. The doctors will come to know only when you approach them.

Analyse the symptoms and work around them. There are many situations where you can use self-help remedies. I ask the same person, 'Did you do something about it? In return, all I get is a smile. I am sure that you know the answer. As a disciple, you have the responsibility to look after your body. The body is known as a physical temple because your soul resides within it. Physically, if you feel well, you can meditate better.

It will reflect in your meditation sitting if you are in pain or uneasiness. To have the best results when meditating, you should feel carefree and happy on top of the world. Feel that you are the only person on this planet because you will be in the presence of God. 'How can you meet God when there are so many obstacles? I am sure you know what kind of feelings or attitude you require when meeting God. Make your guru proud.

I am sure my guru was proud of me. He used to give me hard times when there was no need, which I do not do. That's why I used to get upset. I used to challenge him to find any fault or weakness in me. 'Can you claim this? Yes, you can. If I can, so can you. There are some examples of saints in our discourse on Bhakti marg. These people left behind all their relations and belongings to materialise their goals.

We do not have to practice this way of life and can create a balanced feeling within ourselves at home. Those saints were sitting or standing for long hours to find the focus in the spiritual eye. There is nothing that is beyond your reach. Once you know it, it will be like a toy to any child. You will not notice when you are within the physical body or outside because you have become part of the Spirit. This will be your shining moment when you say, 'I am. I am. I am Spirit!

DISCIPLINE

Discipline is the backbone of our success; every person is very much aware of this, as mentioned many times. The discipline covers most of the activities of the day. Spirit will help us to achieve our goals. The mind is responsible for our clever or misleading situations. Causal actions can drag you into unpleasant memories. The astral plane is our emotional factor and can create many unwanted obstacles that can be painful later.

The physical body only acts by following the above dictates and experiences pain. The main obstacle we find here is our mind. But with effort, we can train our minds to act as spiritual minds. Then it will have or create spiritual thoughts. I have given many examples of doing this training in the past. Some examples include regular meditation, mental fasting, doing good deeds and being in the company of good or positive people.

Never let an iota of negative thinking come into your mind. This means you have to be very alert all the time. Keep your focus on staying positive in your thoughts and actions. After a while, you will notice that you have lost focus and are wandering many miles away. Do not worry. Once you come to this realisation, forget about the lost time. Worrying about it will not turn the clock back. Make a fresh start. I have been through all this.

It may seem like a struggle in the beginning. But eventually, you will be the winner. Once your mind begins to originate spiritual thoughts, it will be out of your control because it will only have spiritual thoughts, even if you want other thoughts. I experimented with this long ago; once my mind was trained and living a positive life, spiritually and physically. I was so carried away with the Spirit that it took me a few hours to realise where I was physical.

Then I would think, I'd better make another fresh start. After some analysis, I realised I had always been in the spiritual fountain. So, 'What fresh start was I talking about? All my physical chores were looked after by the Spirit and executed to perfection. I was working on a printing machine, where all the printing details were important and I was known as the best printer. I used to feed cardboards into the machine, a two-person job.

However, I was doing it alone very successfully. At the same time, I was writing down spiritual notes that Spirit was dictating to me. These notes are still sitting in my files. I was revising our spiritual discourses as well. You may be wondering how many jobs I was doing in one go. I don't know myself. This is the beauty of Spirit. Once you are tuned into Spirit, you cross all the limits. And then, even if you try, you cannot control your spiritual thoughts. Now they control you.

Similarly, if negative thoughts control you, you may say, 'Sher Gill gives us many examples but I cannot do it.' There is nothing in this world or beyond that, you cannot do. Nothing is impossible. I removed this word from my life when I was very young, at least on the day I came in contact with Paul Ji and our spiritual journey and friendship began.

Once you are tuned into Spirit, your life will operate from a different angle.

You have never dreamed of this before. You will say, 'How did I manage to miss all this? Now you are trying to take responsibility for your life, physically and mentally. Once Spirit takes over, all your responsibilities are under the command of Spirit. All your chores are done with minimum effort and your problems begin to vanish into thin air.

Those problems still lingering in your life do not bother you as much because now you have become more powerful than them. You must train your mind to stay positive all the time. I received a very positive e-mail from Mr Raj Paul of Canada. He mentioned that he was trying his best to keep his thoughts positive and was putting effort into reading this book in his spare time. You can learn something from this young man.

He is trying to keep his mind occupied with spiritual thoughts. This is how you train your mind. To discipline yourself is the key. There are no hard and fast rules about what you should do. This is the beauty of this spiritual path. There are some dos and don'ts, as long as they are positive and spiritual. Those with no dos and don'ts in life run wild and do worse. This is the point many people have overlooked in the past. Create your strategies for disciplining your thoughts and physical actions simultaneously.

I created my ways of doing this and crossed all the limits. Most religious scriptures mention a few experiences no human being can have. With my efforts and sincerity towards Spirit, I have proved them wrong. One day, I will put these experiences in writing. Many people have not even scratched the surface of the first step. I am always around to help spiritually and physically to guide. This opportunity should not be missed at any cost.

However, I do not want anyone to do such acts that may put them out of balance. In 'The Way to God,' I mentioned in the last line of the chapter called 'God-realisation' that, 'In my terminology, you have to walk even over yourself! Many people don't even want to lose a small coin, yet they expect the sky to fall for them. You must be daring and adventuresome. You do whatever is possible in your power and leave the rest in the hands of Spirit to take over. God will not fail you.

CHILDREN OF GOD

Sometimes I wonder, we are, 'Good-for-nothings as the English saying goes. We believe that God is our father and we are the sons or daughters of God, respectively. Yet we are nowhere near having the qualities held by God. No one thinks in these terms or pauses for a minute to analyse the fundamental question: 'What we are doing and asking in life, is it worth it? We have no direction in life whatsoever. 'What are we doing?

We are puzzled and leading our lives as if others are leading or as we have been told to do by our elders. We have created the lower worlds as a battleground instead of staying in balance and enjoying the nature of having our beings here and progressing spiritually. We have a responsibility to maintain the well-being of all the universes. First; we must keep our spiritual vibrations in a balanced state.

Secondly; we must create our ability as the children of God to come and go in the presence of God. It is our right as the children of God and it has invested the ability within us. It expects us to unfold ourselves to this ability and become assistants as teachers in the lower worlds. It means helping others in what you know and acting as assistants in the higher worlds to assist the newcomers and show them around.

It is so that they can learn further, become the knowers of truth and let others know that it is possible. Once you are a frequent visitor to the higher planes and have seen the ecstasy experiences or the glittering visions of the higher worlds, you will never hesitate to leave this world. The people around you should be lucky that you are living among them. We must follow the golden rule, which is to keep silent.

I know people usually don't notice; who you are or your business. People are too busy earning their living to make the ends meet daily. We might hear the odd remark, **oh yes**; He is a good and honest man. We do not hear further than that. You cannot express yourself freely to let others know who you are. The remarks will be that he is mentally disturbed, depressed or following some cult teachings.

They will decide to leave you alone, as you are not following the traditional religion. Sometimes I wonder, 'What religion are they following? I will be glad to know if someone is following any religion seriously. If we do, we will have saints everywhere. All the religious scriptures convey the same message. All holy books are written so that, if you read or follow them seriously, you are bound to become a saint in your own right.

We are led to believe by religious leaders that we must read a page or two daily. Some repeat this process five times a day. This should bring discipline on a physical level; 'do we gain anything spiritually? Most likely, the answer is **no**. One word is good enough to meditate on properly daily. In my early life, I learned the first twenty-four words of the Guru-Granth of Sikhism, the first portion of **Japji-Sahib**.

I believe, if you contemplate on these few words, they are more than good enough to lead you into the presence of God. Based on those twenty-four words, I have managed to write five spiritual books or over fourteen hundred pages.

I often give this example to those willing to listen, which is a physical expression. The spiritual way is also the same but we try to ignore it by saying that it is not possible. We have been trained in the art of dying (death) instead of living.

I wonder sometimes, 'Why have we gone away from reality? Why have we indulged in every activity of illusion? All these worlds are 'Intact' because everything is created in balance. So 'How come we see the followers of illusion everywhere? In English, there is a saying: 'If you can't beat them, join them.' By not joining the masses, the odd person will suffer at the hands of others unless you are strong enough to face the whole world if needs be. Being alone but spiritually awakened, we are strong.

Returning to the physical example earlier, we as parents try to educate our children as much as possible to make their way in this world smoothly and successfully. One valuable point to be noted here is that we try to ensure that our children are more educated and successful than we are. The same procedure is followed for generations and throughout this world. It makes me wonder, as we are the children of God, what God may be thinking about us.

This is a physical expression as God is always in the beingness state. God sends forth its prophets to teach and make us aware of our true identity and spiritual ability. Living in the illusionary world, we are so busy solving our domestic problems. We turn a blind eye to our spiritual abilities and ignore them completely, saying they are beyond our reach. If someone is spiritually successful, we call the person a 'saint.'

With our problems, we go and sit by this saint's feet. We believe that he will sort out our problems. He is no better a person than you are; his soul is not superior to yours, apart from his awareness of reality. He has gained this awareness or unfoldment through his spiritual endeavour. I have concluded that every person in the world has given up hope of being in the presence of God. Today in the scientific world, if there was any hope, that is also fading away.

God wants to educate us as much as possible; so, we can assist in God's world just as we do in this world, helping our parents when needed. We always underestimate our abilities when we can progress spiritually more than we can ever imagine. We have similar qualities as our creator, God. Once you accomplish your spiritual goal, you will say, 'I am it and it is me! That will be the total awareness of the soul.

There is only one God. You nor I can ever be a second God. But with this awareness, you will feel close to it, as you are part of it. Of course, you are! This is the only reason to send all the souls into the lower worlds to educate ourselves to become aware that we are the 'children of God.' From now on, you better begin to act as one to be counted in the scheme of God. Now you are not the assistant of God but the son or daughter of God. As a soul, you are part of it.

GOD IS CALLING YOU

God has many ways of communicating with his creation. It is silent communication and at the same time, it is verbal too. You may be wondering what it could be. It is divine light and sound. There are so many ways by which we can communicate. This is thanks to the hard work of past saints. They spent a tremendous amount of time and brought this knowledge for us to know and have spiritual success.

The way of communication is sound. It is not one sound but several sounds on each plane according to its vibrations. There is one sound that works on all planes from God itself and right down to this earth planet. Only a few people have been successful in knowing the whole word. Most religions express part of the word according to their experience. These are the sounds according to the distinctive planes.

There are so many other sounds as well on each plane. For example, each country has its own local or folk sounds. Similarly, there are many rulers in each plane. If some aliens land in America, they will put the name of Mr Donald Trump. It will be said Mr Vladimir Putin in Russia. It all depends on the spiritual travellers' experience as a whole. You can be the knower of the whole truth or just accept what someone has written or said. **Lok** means universe or plane.

1. Physical world:	The crash of thunder
2. Astral Plane:	The roaring of the sea
3. Causal Plane:	The tinkling of brass bells
4. Mental Plane:	Running water
5. Etheric Plane:	The buzzing of bees
6. Soul Plane:	Flute
7. Alakh-Lok:	Wind
8. Alaya-Lok:	Humming sound
9. Hakikat-Lok:	A thousand violins
10. Agam-Lok:	Woodwinds
11. Anami-Lok:	Whirlpool
12. God worlds:	Hhaaioommee
13. God world:	Hum
14. God world:	Hum means total silence.

If we add all these sounds together, it becomes one distinctive sound representing all the planes of God's world. If a person chants this combined sound properly, they can have the experience on any plane or manage to raise their vibrations to the desired plane or into a **being** state. Over the millennia, only part of the 'word' has been chanted. According to their spiritual knowingness.

For the saints who managed to be in the presence of God, the sound is a straightforward 'hum or total silence.' If we travel into the worlds of duality, the word is Om or Aum. It is used in Hinduism and the people who meditate on this word can gain enlightenment or Krishna consciousness. The word Aum carries very powerful vibrations if 'attention minus effort' is applied to the spiritual eye with complete focus and chanted in rhythm.

It can raise the vibrations to the desired plane or meet the Master, opening the inner experience and enabling to see the brilliant light or hear the inner sound. As I mentioned, one complete word covers all the planes. It will suit everyone to have the full benefit. It will help to maintain a high state of consciousness all the time. It is known as 'Haiome'. To chant it properly, it will be pronounced as 'Hhaaioommee.' While chanting, the voice or sound should be raised in this manner:

OO
AI M
HA ME
H E

For the first half up to *OO*, the word is chanted by vocals and half of *OO* followed by *M*, *ME*, *E* is a humming sound. Chant this for an hour and then quit. This is, overall, the highest vibration carrier word. This will cover every plane, from the physical to God's world.

As mentioned earlier, if part of the word is used, the experience will be partial. It does not matter what word we use; it must be chanted with complete focus and in a melodious manner as if you are calling to someone you love. To materialise any success, it must be practised regularly. As they say, practice makes perfect. Once you master the rhythm of the word, then chant it a few times to raise the vibrations and open the experience.

Hhaaioommee.

SPIRITUAL FREEDOM

Spiritual Freedom is one of the most common words used today by Indian-orientated religious followers. It means 'spiritual freedom' from this world. Every Seeker's goal is to make this present life the last one in this world and not to come back again to have another incarnation. It is easily said; that freeing oneself from this world is not easy.

I have noticed that most people who use these words are fed up or going through various hardships. They do not wish to come back to this world to face the same situation again and again. Significantly few people have earned good karma in their previous lives and are ready to leave this world forever. These people feel the urge to seek a way to free themselves. As we seek a way out of this world, we become spiritual Seekers.

Spiritual Seeker

As spiritual Seekers, we must find a spiritual path or a teacher who can lead us into the kingdom of heaven to materialise our goals. To free ourselves from this world is a great responsibility. We follow a spiritual Master; who can teach or educate us on how to free ourselves from the bondage of this world. After setting this goal, I noticed that we often fail in our attempts. This is because we cannot live up to the required expectations to materialise this goal.

I have also noticed that those who are 'failing in life' use these words emotionally. They cannot execute their goal or materialise it in reality. We will not discuss karma in detail here, as it has been discussed in our previous book, 'The Way to God.' Good karma plays a significant role in this. If we do not have good karma, it is impossible to liberate ourselves from the wheel of eighty-four.

Apart from good karma, we must work on various aspects of this freedom. These are the five passions of the mind: lust, anger, greed, attachment and vanity. These aspects must be worked on or balanced to run our lives as smoothly as possible. With this balance, we won't act in any extreme way, which is responsible for creating bad karma. As long as you create serious or nasty karma, you will never achieve spiritual freedom.

There is a severe condition that many people ignore or do not wish to follow. You must set free every single person or thing within your circle before you can even dream of achieving spiritual freedom. This is where we fail. We want spiritual freedom but do not wish to let go of our loved ones. It is the attachment that keeps us grounded. As I have said many times, all our relations with people, such as mum, dad, son, daughter and others, are attached to us by karma.

Kal will create situations where we create more karma and get tangled in this karma theory. Once the karmas are balanced, you will notice that you don't have any serious relationship with anyone apart from surface communication. It is just to get along daily. Once you have reached this state of thinking, you will notice irritation or uneasiness. This is the first indication that we feel compelled to find a way to get out of this world.

You will notice that you don't have any attachment to your loved ones or property. You can leave all this behind at any time, without any notice or hard feelings. If you think or feel that you cannot escape certain things or habits, forget about your goal of spiritual freedom. Leaving your loved ones will be a huge task if you cannot let go of a few habits or things. They are more attached to you than anything else.

Spiritual freedom is a challenge to oneself to achieve in this life. It is more complex than any other work or achievement. You may not realise it but this is the total of all responsibilities put together and beyond. There comes a time in our lives when we learn; where we stand at present and become spiritual Seekers. Now the question is: 'are we, spiritual freedom Seekers? Or 'are we doing this search emotionally because we are going through some bad patch in life?

It is possible, that we want to get away from a situation or someone has talked us into it and our emotions are playing up. If your life is running smoothly and you feel some nudge within, then I think it is time to make a move. All religions claim to provide freedom from this world. When you investigate, you will find that they are run by a system designed to improve social welfare.

These are the traps set by the Kal power to entangle you more in its booby traps, from which there is no way out. It is the same with most spiritual Masters, who claim to be spiritual liberators. Many are money grabbers or in other words, pseudo-masters. You will notice they are running their systems successfully because you let them. It is a good salesman's pitch that makes them successful.

The majority of real Masters are silent or hardly known to many. When it comes to a commercial level, any religious teaching will lose its spiritual touch. It requires a combination of three to achieve spiritual freedom: spiritual education, the Master and a true Seeker. If any one of these is weak, then nothing will materialise. In my opinion, it does not matter how good the teachings or the Masters are if you cannot free others within your circle.

Then it is impossible to achieve spiritual freedom as you have failed to pass the basic requirements. It is not a game or a toy to play with. It will take sheer effort. And freeing yourself from the bondage of karma is a huge responsibility. That bondage may have been built up over hundreds of lives. These karmas will not disperse as quickly as we think. If a person is serious and sincere and puts in all the required effort, it can be achieved promptly.

If any person reads 'The Way to God' and adopts the qualities required, then I want to know who or what is stopping you from achieving your goal in this life. A person of this status becomes the knower of spiritual truth and is free to leave the lower worlds at will and any time they wish. This is spiritual freedom in reality.

MY LAST LAUGH

At birth, I cried; others laughed and celebrated my birth. Everyone picked me up and gave me love, kisses and cuddles; I felt I was in a strange land. I could not do anything; others provided for me when I cried. At my suffering, others felt joy. When they nurtured me, I fell asleep; It was peaceful and this was my golden period. At least I had the chance to re-live my old memories. I often smiled and my mum thought I was in communication with Spirit. Right, she was.

It was the best way to pass the time. 'Who wants to lie in a boring cot and act as a toy for others? They had fun and I was in pain lying on my back. Many pulled my tiny fingers but no one understood my pain. It did not take long to learn that I had landed in a world of struggle. Being so young, I had to establish my relationships. My mind could not understand who I was. They thought I was only a child but it was revealed that I was the oldest of them all in time.

They sang lullabies and laughed but it was not my language. I knew I was in a strange land. They told me who I am now but I knew I had been someone else before. I know I am a soul but they gave me a bizarre name. I thought, maybe that is who I am. One time, I was Hindu. Next, I was Muslim. Then I was Sikh. Now again, I was in a strange land. They had fun but I was confused. Time went by and my old memories began to fade.

My new name began to seem familiar. I have been enticed away from my true identity. A curtain overcame my memories and I started feeling at home in this strange land. Once, the moon and stars were so close. Now they seemed far, far away. Still, I had no fear. I played with a cat and a dog. They bestowed their pure love upon me. With their fur, I felt I was in heaven. Still, I wondered, 'Who am I and who are they? I felt love from all of God's creation.

So far, it was my golden period. I felt that I was wanted. Before my birth, my mum had cried with pain. After, she'd cried with joy. And now, she cries when I am sick. Where I come from, everyone is always happy and in bliss. After this knowingness, I felt that I was in a strange land. 'Would I ever know, who am I and where am I? One day the answer came from Kal. Welcome Home: I am your lord. May your journey be worthwhile.

In this world, I had a big account to settle. My legs trembled with the load, 'Would I ever pay back what I owed? Now it is time to decide. 'Am I a man or a mouse? If I am a man, I had to face the challenge and settle my account. If I were a mouse, I could go with the flock and have a who-cares attitude. I knew that meeting the challenge was a straight line and the sooner I finished this line, like an athlete, the sooner the game would be over.

If I followed the flock, it would be a never-ending circle. The challenge was strange and hard to follow and people might laugh. The second choice is easy. As they say, if you can't beat them, join them. You are welcomed into the family. You are happy and so are the others. Now I became the slave of five passions. I began to feel the pain; the emotions;

the anger, lust, greed and the ego. Now I was lost in this strange land.

This is my home and family; I am attached to everything more than glue. Now, 'Who wants to leave this world? At the word spiritual freedom, I laughed. My youth appeared and I felt that I was the hero and strongest. My five friends 'passions' came into play to give a helping hand. I knew I was not alone. With them, lots of other friends arrived. I thought this was fun. My marriage took place and turned into a fun fair and my emotions were high.

I felt on top of the world. Love, lust and attachments were sky-high; I wished this would carry on forever. My karma knocked on my door and a little voice said, 'I am coming to see you.' I was delighted to know that a new guest was coming. It did not take long. 'Now it is party time.' The new guest said I did not come to the party. We have an account to settle. The demands were made and I began to pay this guest back. I was giving, the guest was receiving and I felt the pain.

Yet there was pleasure within this pain. Love, greed and attachment all clouded my mind. All this taught me a lot and I became a wise man. I was the knower and philosopher of all the dictators and big boss in this world. And yet, I was in pain. I learned how to cry every moment and forgot how to laugh. Sometimes I laughed but I felt that it was another joke. A single tear of my child made me weep and a big ocean came out of my eyes.

A slight temperature in my child made me feel I would have a heart attack. My child fell on the floor and I rushed to the hospital. I felt my brain was going to explode. Yet I survived.

I began to protect my child, my family and my belongings. I was a prisoner within these walls. I began to think; I was lost in this wonderland. I was within this maze; all the paths seemed familiar. Any paths or roads I followed led me back to the centre point where I had been before. I was tired.

I gave up and said to myself, 'Who cares? And I went to sleep. I was tired of this rat race and began to analyse within myself. 'Who am I? 'What am I doing in this wonderland? The man of men appeared and said, **'I am the way and the way is within.'** 'Do you want to know the way? Come and follow me. After these years, I felt peace and bliss and remembered that I had felt this before.

He replied when you were with me last time. I sent you here to experience but were reluctant to leave and suffered at your choice. Now you have realised you are in the wrong place. But now, you are in the present moment and always have been. To me, it is now. But to you, it is a million years. Let us begin in this nowness; soon, you will be in this present moment and everlasting bliss state. Attachment intervened.

Emotions garbled within. Lust came and ego came, along with anger. They all cried and I cried along with them. I thought we were born to cry. The whole world was crying. The question came from within: 'Will I ever laugh? The Godman appeared and smiled. I looked at his blissful face and felt peace within.

'Come and follow me. I will show you the way.'

I felt joy. At last, someone had come to the rescue. He raised his hand. I heard the sound, saw the light in my body and floated above the ground. I felt I was not part of this world for the first time in his presence. This is just a glimpse; you can know more. Meditate and may the blessings be. I was over the moon. I was the same child again. The Master led me like a little child and showed me where I had been before.

The Master's love was so great that I wanted to remain a child forever. He gave me a nudge to grow up but I ignored it. I thought the time was on my side. I was part of the big tree but my colour turned yellow as a leaf and my roots began to shake. I began to tremble with fear of losing my ground. I knew that my time was close. Fear intervened and no loved ones wanted to help but waited for the leaf to drop. The ones I loved thought it was fun.

Now I was wondering if there was time. The Master appeared, smiled and said, 'I am beyond time. You can be too.' I begin to meditate. Lots of hurdles came. The mind started to act like a monkey. All the mind friends, the five passions, came to congratulate the mind on its success. I was meditating but travelling to India and Japan with the help of my mind. And without realising, I became a globetrotter. I was fighting with my loved ones, boiling with anger.

I felt uneasy and quit. Master appeared again and said, all these people are a helping hand to purify your thoughts. Give them love and let them be; they will disappear in no time. I began to realise the grudges I was holding against them. It was not they who held me back; it was my creation. The creatures of my creation were fighting within and I became the battleground. At times, I was a soldier and bandit. At the same time, I was a thief and a crook.

A vision appeared. 'I thought you were going to be a saint?
I began to give love to all and felt at ease.

The Master appeared and said, 'Show me your hands.' He looked and said, 'You need to work more.' I knew I had crossed the first hurdle but many more were to go. I meditated but nothing came as quickly as I thought. When the Master was helping, I had become a spoilt child. Now I realised I had to earn for myself. The Master appeared and said, 'I meditated for thousands of years to be where I am now. Never give up. I am always with you. You will succeed.'

I meditated and people thought I was insane. I have seen the light and heard the sound. And at the threshold, the Master was waiting for me. I felt like a little child again. The Master extended his hand and we travelled above the clouds. My effort was fruitful and I became a traveller. People came to see what I had but it was beyond their reach. To them, I was the wise old man. I knew that my time was near and they all cried. I had my last laugh and proceeded to join '**Thee.**'

To all, may the blessings be.

SILENCE THE MIND

One of the main problem for all the Seekers is how to silence our minds. We begin to meditate and take all necessary precautions to have any spiritual experience internally or externally. We prepare ourselves for this. We begin to chant the spiritual word; our sitting does not bear any fruits from our endeavour. Our mind becomes active and begins to wander around in all directions. Nothing materialises after half an hour and we get up, unsatisfied.

The same routine follows for weeks, months and years. Many people even blame the teachings of the Master and they begin to drift off and seek elsewhere. This is not the solution, as you have failed to achieve anything. I have mentioned one condition in many places. The Seeker must raise their vibrations to the level of sun and moon worlds. Once you have achieved that, only then can it become the responsibility of the Master to lead you further.

The Master can lead you into the inner worlds in no time as soon as you sit down for meditation. This way, the Seeker learns nothing. This way, you will be dependent on the Master all the time, similar to a child who cries for little things from the mother and seeks attention. Eventually, we grow up and move on with our adult lives. Similarly, if we want to become Master of our universe, we need to grow up with our efforts and find new ways to silence this wandering mind.

There is always a solution to every problem. Our mind can think about more than one subject at a time; it can think about three topics simultaneously. We learn with experience that when we chant the **word**, our mind begins to roam freely at a far distance without our noticing. By the time we realise it has been wandering; it is almost time to get up. This is where the half-hour time limit fails you. It is recommended to meditate for at least one hour.

I have found a simple solution to calm this part of the mind. Once we calm down in a particular direction of thought, we can proceed to '**deep samadhi**' or the level of sun and moon worlds, Ashta-dal-Kanwal. Once we had taken all the precautions to practice, such as our sitting position and breathing to feel relaxed, we begin to chant our 'spiritual word.' The word is chanted in a lengthy manner.

For example, 'Paramatma' becomes:
Pppaaarrraaammmaaatttmmmaaa

As you can see, it takes a few seconds;
to chant this word.

To silence the wandering thoughts during this period, we will make good use of the wandering part of the mind. As you begin to chant the spiritual word, you will use another word to eliminate wandering thoughts. Now you will be chanting two words simultaneously; you can do this. One word will be chanted verbally as usual and the second word will be silent. For example:

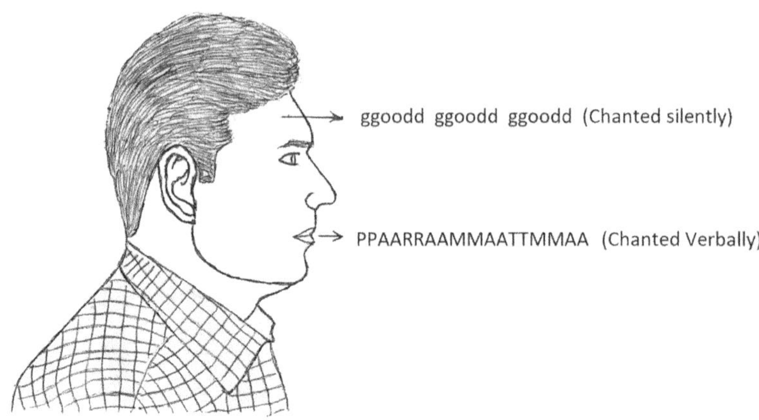

The second **word** can be any of your choices, as long as it is spiritual. Examples could include God, your Master's name or Aum. With this, you have silenced the wandering thoughts and used the mind's capability to wander positively. You will notice that you have gone into an experience without any effort. Once you have made this a habit, your every sitting will become successful. After some practice, you don't have to follow this procedure; your mind is trained to think only once. Good luck!

NAKED SOUL

A naked soul is pure and karma-less. Any garment a soul will wear that will be karma; if there is any. During the soul's journey, karma will provide two purposes, experience and the load, which will keep it in the lower worlds until it manages to free itself with the help of the Master. The soul must work off all karmas that have been created and be as pure as it was in the beginning. This time, the only difference will be the experience it has gained to become an assistant with God.

This is the soul's journey as it leaves its creator in a nameless plane, an ocean of love and mercy. It was part of God yet inexperienced. The soul comes down to the soul plane that becomes its house while it is pure. But it cannot remain there, as it has no experience of becoming an assistant within God's world. Under the guidance of Satnam Ji, the soul enters the lower world, where the soul becomes the responsibility of Lord Brahma.

Lord Brahma ensures that the soul receives the proper schooling and returns as assistant to one of the lords, Satnam Ji or the higher worlds. In the worlds of Brahma, the soul picks up the etheric and mental bodies. Then the soul is guided to the causal plane, where it picks up the causal body and eventually proceeds to the astral plane. There it becomes the responsibility of the lord of karma. This lord becomes responsible for your physical journey and he decides where to place you in the lower forms of life on the physical.

The soul is given some karma and may be placed on the physical like a little worm on the ground or a little fish in the sea. Once you have been eaten by a bird or a big fish in the sea, your karma is established with others. You have just entered the reincarnation system. For many lifetimes, it does not bother the soul. You eat and in return, you are eaten.

This situation is very similar to a small child; if a child has a physical ailment, the parents decide what treatment should be given to the child under the guidance of a doctor. The child is unaware of what is happening, so it does not bother the child as much. Once we are grown up, the fear builds up and we become more conscious of our pains. The soul comes to a point on the physical level where it leads a more active life. In danger, you can run or fly to save yourself.

You are also hunting others more vulnerable than you and the wheel of eighty-four is in full swing. You enter the animal kingdom and become more of a struggle to survive. As the saying goes, you cannot fly away but must face the music. You run away or fight for your survival. Some are unfortunate. They are caught by humans, chained and become pet animals. Here, the soul has no choice but to listen to the dictates of humans.

In this life, you serve the humans with good virtues, such as a cow to provide milk or as a horse for them to ride on and in many other ways. This is the point where you serve and the torture of humans puts good karma in your account and you progress to human form. This is the first life form where you come to know that you are living life and what you can do for yourself and others.

Although you are not that clever for many lifetimes, this participation adds experience to the soul. It is the soul's maturity and we become aware of our 'I' factor in life. This factor makes you aware of who you are as a person. You could be a believer or non-believer in God. After many lives, your spiritual mind wakes up to the spiritual call and becomes a religious person. This is another web to tie you down to the physical ground.

You favour the religion you follow and other religions seem a threat or almost enemies to you. It is not your fault. As a child, you are willing to follow any dictates from your elders or the clergy in temples. They always seem to express religious thoughts to those who attend. But at the same time, the message is not to get involved with other religions by labelling them as false religions. The religious leaders preach that our religion is the only one that can give salvation or freedom from this world.

We begin to believe this and express this to our children and they become believers of the same, which goes on forever. This is all part of the wheel of eighty-four. This is the entanglement created by the Kal for your benefit to give you a good experience. You become an extremist in one religion, which is the only way to learn the real influence. Each religion teaches different aspects of life and then you move on.

Each religion and race of people will impact the soul as an experience. I have been part of all religions and races of people. From my experience, Hindus say the only way out of this world is through their numerous deities. So, you don't know which one to follow. Most people are unaware that all these deities are only within the lower worlds. The highest point they can reach is my old friend called Brahma, so 'What will be their peak point?

It still is part of the lower planes. We can achieve Buddha, Krishna or Christ consciousness; we are still within the lower worlds. These religions have failed to express at what point the soul will have true salvation or spiritual freedom. All these religions are busy with social welfare. The needs and demands of the people are physically based. The soul and its welfare is not discussed and no one wants to know why or learn more.

On the surface, many express that they are religious; with a thorough examination, you will know they are only physical. 'How can they lead others to achieve spiritual freedom? Christians believe salvation is only through Jesus Christ. I wish that it were true. They believe that Jesus took the sins of this world on him and died on the Cross. He was the victim of the circumstances of that time and had no choice but to go on the Cross. He did not choose to go on the Cross himself.

He was sentenced to be crucified on the Cross. At present or in the past, nor will there be in future; a soul in this world could take the karma load of this world. This false statement has been made by many Masters in the past and will continue in the future. These people do not realise this violates the spiritual law. If this were allowed, there would be no need for the karmic theory and schooling for the soul.

We can serve God in some minor position with our spiritual success but we misuse our authority and make false statements. We must withstand the accounts of these statements and pay accordingly. You may have noticed in my writings that I respect Jesus very much. So, I believe; I don't think Jesus had said this himself. The ninth Sikh guru, Sri Teg Bahadur, who was alive during the reign of the Mughal Empire, went to Delhi 'willingly' on 24 November 1675.

To be assassinated by the king to save the Hindu religion and human rights. He never claimed that he was taking the sins of this world. He took this as 'The Will of God.' Later, his son Guru Gobind Singh turned the teachings into what we know today as Sikhism. If you follow the teachings thoroughly and do good karma, you can attain spiritual freedom.

Islam has its own beliefs. Islamists bury their dead because they believe that, one day in the future, all these people will wake up after death. If you look thoroughly into this belief, I don't think Islam is interested in spiritual freedom. I am not giving this information to condemn any religion. As I said before, I have been part of all these religions and love them very dearly.

My point is that they all claim their religious domain as 'the only way,' when the truth is, none of them is. They have not come to the point of universal thinking. Once you have been through all these religions, you will hold a universal thought: *I am an individual.* You will begin to search for a way out of this world. Once Seeker is ready, the Master of the time appears and teaches you how to eliminate all karmas and remove the shackles holding you down.

God and its divine light and sound and the Master of the time are pure: all else is an illusion. It is designed by Brahma to keep you grounded. Nothing in this world is a waste.

All serve the purpose of training the soul. The most precious thing or relationship we value most is the hardest to get rid of. You will be surprised to learn that most people in this world are attached to one word, **mother** and the rest are attached to money, status, country and religion.

As long as you are connected with these things deeply, you are not free. To all the saints, these relations have no significant value. You must brush off all traits, religious beliefs, thoughts and, above all, the causal, mental and etheric bodies simultaneously. We cannot take any valuables, near and dear ones or religious symbols on our journey. Once we are cremated, all the religious garments or symbols will become ashes.

It does not matter what prayers have been performed or what physical temple you have been taken to. None of them can help. All it matters is how much good karma is in your account. Good karma: these sound like very favourable words. You cannot shake them off or the lower bodies as long as the word karma is attached to your soul unless you are a saint. Saints are only born to create good karma and to take on the karma of others, to free them of their pains.

Brahma only does his duty and ensures you pass through his territory as a 'Pure or Naked Soul. Consider the last line in my book, 'The Way to God,' in a chapter called 'God-realisation.' It reads, 'In my terminology, you have to walk even over yourself.'

That is total karma-lessness or Naked Soul.

REFLECTION IN THE MIRROR

In this discourse, I want to know the progress of our mini-Gods. I am sure you must have been at peace within. Now you know all the moans and groans are not worth it. You must face the situations that come your way in a calm and balanced way. You can solve a problem when relaxed because you can look at it with a clear mind. With blurred vision, you will not get the full details of the picture and your judgment will not be correct.

Once you get a clear picture of a problem; it does not take long to work it out. Staying in balance and positive is very important. Only then can you help others. The bigger the problem, the calmer you should be. Any person with a hot temper cannot think straight or think of others. At this moment, you are a problem too. All these discourses are eye-openers to realise how spiritually awakened you are. This discourse is to indicate where you stand on the spiritual ladder.

After practising our new spiritual exercise, 'I am God for today,' I am sure you must have realised and made some effort in many ways to be like your creator. The more virtues of God you can adopt, the nearer you will feel to it. I am sure you must have discovered something new about yourself when previously you had a different view. Maybe this is the first time you have stood in front of the mirror to see an accurate picture.

'Did you ever notice your face in the mirror? Your face looks the way you want to see it. But the truth is, if you look at your face from the view of the mirror, it is not the same. Your left eye or ear is not the same; now, it has become the right eye and ear. To have any success, you must blend the picture on both sides, external and from within the mirror and create a balanced image that is very similar to your creator.

I will give an example of how balanced, fair and neutral we are. In reality, we are always far from being balanced, honest and unbiased. I was watching the TV this morning and the presenter praised an actor who succeeded in his career. The actor replied, 'I am always worried that, where I am today, if I don't work hard, someone else will take my place.' In other words, this actor is so attached to stardom that he is unwilling to leave the platform. It is the name and fame equal to the attachment.

Whatever we do in life should be done on neutral grounds or for the good of the whole. So that it will benefit you and, at the same time, benefit others. We build up this fear of losing our ground; this fear is our failure point. It leads us away from God, yet we pray to God to give us success. This fear within does not want anyone else to take '**our**' place. This is where acts of jealousy come in. If you are doing your work with complete honesty and within your rights, no one can take your means away from you.

I am waiting for all to take my place and so does God, to welcome you as assistants. *The Way of God's* discourse was to make you aware that you are a soul. Once you become aware that you are a soul, it is not the soul that does not want to travel; your unwanted burdens hold it down to the ground. You can have Self-realisation if your soul is free or can breathe freely. I know that most of you are or were Soul-realised initiates.

Now the question is, 'Are you? My big problem always has been to hold myself to the physical level, if possible. During the spiritual chants, this was my main problem. I would sing the word a few times and be far away. Despite my efforts, my soul always defeated me. I remember one time I was out of the body twelve times within thirty minutes and all my experiences were on different subjects.

'What is Self or God-realisation?
It is the realisation of God's qualities.

The next question is, 'How **many** have you adopted? The more God qualities you adopt, the more God-realised you are. Otherwise, you know my blunt answer. It is not the soul that does not want to travel; you have trapped the soul. Most of you have used these teachings to solve personal or family problems. Any religion or teaching that tells followers, 'Come to us and all your problems will be solved,' is misleading and deceiving you from your purpose in life.

If you cannot manage to solve self-created problems, then when are you going to have Self-realisation? I hope, after reading this, you will ask yourself a question: 'Where do I stand spiritually? I am sure you know the answer. You must begin to act like your creator or behave like your guru, who is a living example to you. I went to attend someone's funeral. He was a friend and a nice person. While paying tribute to his father, his son prepared a little speech.

His son remarked, 'If I adopt half the qualities of my father, then I will take it as I have been successful in my life.' If you adopt the same attitude and try to adopt **half** the qualities of your creator, you can call yourself successful. The living Master of the time can give Self or God-realisation instantly, provided the Seeker is ready. All previous Masters and I have provided all the tools to accomplish your goal.

Nothing is more accessible than the soul but you have trapped it so firmly; it has become your failure point not to travel. I am not getting much response from our members in the neighbourhood. It seems like they are working so hard to be little gods. They don't have much time to make a monthly report. The members living in Canada are always in touch. I have learned over the years that parents are the first gurus. Naturally, we are taught what they know. Some children are fortunate to have decent parents.

We learn precious points at a young age and our life is successful. The fact is this: Most parents are or are supposed to be our icons but they are not our Bible. One day, I met a young man. He was shouting over the phone when there was no need. The situation he was dealing with could have been sorted out with a very calm attitude. When I asked why he was shouting, he answered, 'Oh, my mum does the same and my dad talks loud too.'

Now the question is; 'has your parents' life been successful? I knew them too. Their life as a couple had been almost hell. Therefore, they were not ideal parents. The young man must learn from their mistakes and try to lead a better and more peaceful life. I asked this young man to explore his parents' behaviour further. 'Why were they shouting all the time? I asked. I was told this was the only way to get your point across.

So, to win the argument was very important; my mum always made sure that the point had been made, he told me.

Some people never learn. To them, it does not matter, even if these arguments destroy their lives. If the young man's parents had both moved away from the situation silently, it could have been good of the whole, for both parties. These stubborn people do not let the Spirit penetrate to solve the problem. Valuable lives are put at risk.

At what cost? One day, they will know and it will be too late to regret it. The chapter will be closed for both parties. These mistakes can create suffering for many generations to follow. We must watch our behaviour and what we say in the presence of our children. They pick up on our strategies, behaviours and attitudes naturally and their lives will be moulded around the situations we present to them. I remember once an old lady advised me about my recent marriage.

As a couple, you will never argue, fight or misbehave in the presence of your children. They will also learn these habits. Teach your children the value of love and responsibility and their lives will be successful. Most of the time, we are responsible for the failure of our children in life, as they are reflections of our thoughts and actions. Those children who find their ways in life with good karmas lead their lives successfully and become the pioneers of the way forward for others.

Paul Ji taught three main speech points to his wife, 'Gail.' Before you utter a single word, pause for a second and think about the statement you will make. 'Is it true, is it polite and is it necessary to say? If you apply these principles in life, your life will be wonderful to live as created by our creator. We make our lives miserable with our wrong or irresponsible actions. Then we pray to Spirit and repeat many times, 'I leave this in the hands of Spirit.' 'Do you?

I don't have any problems when more problems are knocking at my door every day than there are for most of you. I say I don't have any problems because, when a problem is standing at my doorstep, I say to it, 'Hold on there, you are not allowed to step in.' As I said previously, do not let the Kal circle around you. It is important to do your spiritual exercise. After a successful session, you will feel the flow of Spirit all day within yourself.

That will reflect in your countenance; that you are full of love, peaceful and balanced. Many negative situations will bounce off without even touching you when you live in a bliss state. A physical example would be that you don't find many cockroaches living in a clean house. If you prefer, you may live with them. That is your choice. Long ago, I invited someone to check the grammar of my writings because I was feeling a bit rusty in this field and that person kept rephrasing most of the sentences.

I said to the person, 'I want to keep my writing as original as possible. So please, only check spellings and part grammar.' But a beautiful conversation took place out of our laughter. This person had lots of ups and downs in life. I said to the person, 'Do you know what? You love to rephrase my writing. 'Why don't you rephrase your life? This person was stunned and at a loss for words. Finally, he said, 'Oh my God. I never thought of that! This person took my advice and now he is delighted.

We can do the same, as this lifespan is too short. We must make the most of it. We must adopt the qualities of God, as I suggested in the last few discourses. By these principles, you will know how wonderful this life is. As Paul Ji said, there is so much to achieve or unfold that there is always a plus element. It does not matter what you have achieved so far. There is much more to know yet. Some people who are very close to me make the same remark.

We cannot do as much as you have done or achieved in life. I say to them; you are joking. I have so much more to do and I am always on the move. Or, as they say in English, I am always on my toes. You may think the same but this is true. There is no end to purity. You must carry on until the day you are sitting within the heart of God. That will be your day of celebration. But on that day, you will not celebrate, even if someone asks you to celebrate. You will ask yourself, 'What is a celebration?

Now you will live in your creator's virtues, a peaceful bliss state. The five passions will be balanced; Anger will be under control. There will be no reaction to the emotions, as is true of God watching us all day when we try to create chaos every day and all through the world. God is not affected by our doings. Yet it takes all our doings upon itself at the same time. If you understand this philosophy, then there is nothing else to understand. Now, 'Do you know who you are?

You are the reflection of God.

FRUIT

'What will be the fruit of our relationship with God? When I was young, I admired a unique mango tree in our village. It was majestic in height; it was not easy to climb and had green leaves on healthy branches. Out of these branches, many small green mangoes used to appear. With season and time, they grew but were still green. The weather changed the colour of mangoes to yellow but the fruit was still hanging on the tree.

With maturity and the consent of God, it left the branch and fell on the ground (physical) to be served. Now it was in service as an assistant. Nowadays, we don't have the patience to grow our fruit on the branches of Spirit. Every person is looking for shortcuts and all our problems result from these shortcuts. We can go to the market stall and buy the fruit. That is the easy way out. But to grow your own and then eat it, is an experience.

We have created a wall within us. When trying to find the easy way out, as we are not a part of God. If you feel not part of God or as long as the wall is there, it means no success. Demolish this wall and hang onto the branches of God's tree as a part of itself. All your problems will vanish. I can only provide the tools. You must make an effort. Spirit can help in every corner of your life, but you end up doing nothing and we will not achieve our goal:

Be the reflection of God.

RELIGIONS

Religion is to believe or worship a superhuman; we often call them prophets. The prophet has written a spiritual book for the followers to abide by and lead a spiritual and honest life. The prophet has created miracles to amuse the human mind. All religions are unique. They follow the practices recommended by their prophets, such as; religious books, prayers, rituals, symbols, holy temples and meditation.

It is important to believe in something to occupy the mind; otherwise, an empty mind can create havoc. It is also thought that the world would be much more peaceful without religions. Each religion builds a unique thought according to the prophet's instructions or as recommended in the religious book. This difference in the opinion of each religion creates a barrier that leads to the non-tolerance of other spiritual practices.

This mass following overpowers the individuality of humans. This is the main barrier for the Seekers to achieve spiritual freedom. All religions stress the teachings on humanity but fail to provide psychic space or freedom of speech. This is why Seekers fail to walk away from the faith they were born in. Also, many walk away from their religion and become atheists. At present, every person is searching for breathing space.

The morality of religions leads the followers not to commit bad Karma. It forbids people from killing each other, committing adultery or any other act not acceptable to God. It teaches to determine between right and wrong. The religious book sheds light on human behaviour. Therefore, all religions have their ten commandments. Without sacred books, humans will have wild imaginations. Wild imaginations can lead to destructive thoughts.

Each religion has its ethics. Religious wars are the origin of contradictory beliefs. Some religions permit eating meat, whereas others condemn it. Both views claim to be sacred. Only God can decide who is right or wrong. Good ethics help to achieve spiritual freedom. With negative behaviour, the journey to God becomes relatively long. Negative and positive are part of the same coin.

There are strict or dangerous religious beliefs. These beliefs create a fraction of other faiths. Our God is the real god and it is on our side. Our prophet is the last sent by God. All other religious followers are non-believers. They do not appreciate those thinking different or independently. Non-believers are considered evil. Those who do not believe in our religion will end up in hell.

Religions influence human thought. This group thought creates the society. This leads to the same pattern of behaviour or acceptance of other faiths. This difference in semantics creates a wall that leads to violence. Violence has been part of all religions. In the beginning, all religions teach love; later, their thoughts lead to hatred. The message in the religious book states that God is one. Extreme thinkers mould the text as it suits them. That is a violation of spiritual law.

There is a political war between several countries. There is a holy war between two or more religions that can take place within the same country. The sacred war becomes the cause to justify the difference in religious thought. Because of differences in religious belief, the same religion can branch off into many extensions. This is why many religions are fighting among themselves.

In Islam, the word Jihad is used for holy war. It also represents the inner struggle of any individual to be a good Muslim. Jihad also means to protect its believers from foreign oppression or religions. Sometimes people with extreme thoughts wage war to justify their anger against others or countries. Allah does not command such acts. It does not matter what religion we follow; we are the children of Allah or God.

A few religions are born due to religious wars. There was a war between Hinduism and Islam that led to the birth of Sikhism. At present, Hinduism is trying to suppress Islam and Sikhism in India. Religions are used on the front face; in the background, it is all politics and power. No one spares anyone; they all give a bad name to our creator God. Christianity has tried to rule the world religiously.

Modern religions are based on new or present thoughts of people. At present, the new study is going through many experiments. The latest review is a mix of many emotions and illusions. Illusion always leads us to our failure on a spiritual basis. These religions move along with new thoughts to gain membership or popularity. The primary thought is better than many gains.

There are many cults in this world; they are based on the worship of an Image or deity. Most religions condemn cults for many reasons as they don't believe in the living masters;

they all worship several images and gods. They will never accept this statement because they cannot think in these terms. Most religions have images in temples or several statues. All these beliefs lead to mythology.

The word cult shares the same term as culture. Culture means a group of people share the same thought. All religions are inactive because they do not have a living prophet. Therefore, they believe in whatever supports their idea or livelihood. Religions are used as the front faces but are not religious. They are willing to commit any sin to satisfy their needs.

We can end all world wars if all religions apply religious thought during negotiations. Our extreme thoughts create barriers and fail to reach any mutual agreement. The purpose of the sacred book is to wake up the spiritual spark; so, we can see the spiritual light. Our extreme thoughts and hunger for power lead us to darkness. In a dark room, we can swing our arms but fail to find the door which opens to a peaceful life.

We need to be born again. We need a complete transformation in Spirit and prevent hostility. To be born again require lots of effort and sacrifice of many attachments. We learn how to forgive and surrender to the Spirit unconditionally. To forget your past and live in the present moment is a challenging task. Most Seekers fail because they fail to eliminate their past thoughts or memories.

Religions are the biggest hope for many. Religions give people something to believe in; these thoughts can occupy their minds most of the time. Religious beliefs positively impact us and save us from many wrongdoings. Empty minds and worldly thoughts are very dangerous. Spiritual thoughts lead us to do charity work. Many third-world countries are surviving on your good deeds.

All religious followers have set dreams based on their teachings; which are inactive but give hope to live on something. Living spirit does not exist in religions but people visit temples to satisfy their minds. All humans have fear within; it needs moral support to bring positivity to life. Sacred books and practice fill the emptiness within. Some people need complete transformation to lead a peaceful life. The religious following becomes their way of life.

Most religions provide the practice of baptism. This is only given to serious or regular members. Although it is only a ritual, it brings complete transformation in the mental approach to life. They are obliged to represent their religion ethical way. Your good presentation can attract followers from other practices. This is how most famous religions prosper.

Other than religious books, the success of each religion is based on miracles created by its prophet. Although the prophet is not living, people feel the pull to visit where miracles took place. There is no spiritual gain but it brings inner peace. The visit also fulfils the obligation towards their prophet. The miracles created by the prophets make them superhumans; otherwise, they were ordinary individuals.

Primarily religion is a practice of spiritual principles suggested by their prophet. As soon as the prophet leaves the living stage, the mixer of thoughts begins to rise in followers' minds. There is no one to guide them or there is no one to carry on the spiritual torch. The followers invite the practice of politics to intervene in religious places. Most religions claim to be spiritual but the state controls them.

Politics should be removed from religious places. This confuses our minds and people begin to act religiously and politically at the same time. This is why they apply the voting system to choose the leaders. Religious leaders should not participate in politics. All religions have leaders but no prophets; therefore, religion cannot be separated from politics. Political leaders purposely enter into religious places to create vote banks.

Most religions create fear within their followers that the end of the world is soon. They repeat the reference given by their prophet in religious books. Those who follow our religion be saved; the others will die. This creates unity among their followers. When a catastrophic situation occurs in any part of the world, people die; it does not matter if you are religious or not. Nothing can save you from the wrath of God.

Religious thought is always against the slavery of humans but fails to justify other creations of God. This is why they use the term animal to verify their identity. Most prophets are born out of slavery. The spiritual spark within helps them to have the courage to free the humans from the captivity of their masters. Moses led the Jews out of slavery in Egypt. Moses became the saviour of enslaved Hebrew nation.

Slavery ended long ago in this world but most religions do not practise equality of gender. Most religious books state that males and females are equal. Their prophet suggested it because he was a spiritually awakened soul. The followers repeat the phrases but fail to act upon them. Gender equality is important because females are the backbone of our existence. Otherwise, males will never exist.

The costume of each religion is a symbol to represent their individuality from the rest of the world. These costumes bring pride in what they follow. This becomes their failure point in the presence of God. They bypassed God and followed what their prophet told them to follow. This is why prophets are spiritually awakened souls but not Gods. This is the point all religious followers fail to grasp.

Future forecasts show the end of religions. One day they will become obsolete because they fail to provide security as stated in religious books. The spiritual hope is disappearing into the thin air. The science gives evidence of what they claim. The modern mind doesn't believe in hollow promises. In the future, religions can only survive if they begin to feel like having living masters. Otherwise, we should expect the dead-end is soon. When in distress, we need a shoulder to lean on; this is what religions are used for.

THE PROPHETS OF GOD

The prophets of God are great 'souls' and are primarily sent to earth for a purpose. Their births are always forecasted before they arrive in this world. These souls are very close to God or are known as assistants. God does not or will not invest this power in any individual, religion or prophet to make the statement that this person is the last prophet.

This kind of statement is good enough for self-pleasing or brainwashing followers. This kind of statement is used when any religion is feeling a threat from other religions based on domination. The prophets are spiritual but not as great. The mythology built around them makes them appear like superhumans. Every person loves their religion, whatever it may be.

A similar situation can be found each year on Mother or Father's Day. To draw the overall picture, you will notice that some parents are excellent, while others are average and many are below average. But consider these two days and you will see that most parents get the same message. On the greeting cards: 'You are the best mum or dad in the world.' 'Are they? Maybe not but in the opinion of their children, they are.

This is because we fail to look outside and make a comparison. Despite this, we still want to believe 'my mum and dad are the best.' Every person has the right to express their opinion. We have no right to change someone's mind.

That would violate spiritual law, better known as psychic space. All the religions today had a prophet at the beginning of the faith. Otherwise, new religion would not materialise in this world. Many times, prophets do appear time after time in some religions.

Noah, Abraham, Moses, Jesus Christ and Muhammad are the descendants of Adam and Eve. This is how they are connected and are historical figures. Sri Ram, Krishna, Mahatma Buddha and Guru Nanak have the background of Brahma, Vishnu and Shiva, better known as Hinduism prophets. The descendants of Adam and Eve and Hinduism do not believe they are connected. There is only one God and this supreme power creates every person. We are united as souls and are part of it.

Adam and Eve

According to biblical scholars, the birth of Adam and Eve was in 4000 BC. Adam and Eve are the origins of Christianity, Islam and Judaism. It may not be accurate but according to the mythology of Christians and Muslims, these were the first two people created by God. The birth dates are approximate. In this case, these are the signs of the late Bronze-Age, instead of the Golden-Age as believed originally. Considering the dates of Adam and Eve, it does not add up in time.

Their birth would have been long ago if they were the first two people. Looking at some history provided by the biblical literature, we consider that Adam and Eve were born in 4000 BC or 6,022 years ago. That indicates this is how old the civilisation of this world is. I am sure scholars can come up with better figures than these. The prophets like Abraham or Jesus must have told the age of civilisation somewhere.

But sometimes, followers don't pay attention to this kind of information.

Noah

It is believed that Noah appeared ten generations after Adam and Eve. Noah was born in approximately 2940 BC and the time of floods on the earth was 2,340 BC. At that time, he was 600 years old. Noah received the prophecy and was instructed to build an ark (a ship). Apart from his family or loved ones, he was guided to take several animals on board.

Whoever boarded the ark survived; the rest were wiped out due to their wrongdoings; they were the channel of evil spirits. The rain flooded the earth for 150 days. Eventually, the ark came to rest on the mountains of Ararat in Turkey. Noah led his family and animals to the Promised Land and died in 1990 BC at the age of 950.

Abraham

Abraham was born in 2052 BC. The place of his birth is known as the Ur of the Chaldees, Iraq. He is best known as the patriarch of Judaism, Islam and Christianity. He was married to Keturah. He died at the age of 175 years and was buried in the Hebron cave. He has been known as the father of many nations. Abraham was a descendant of Noah's son Shem; it is believed that Jesus and Mohammad are the descendants of Abraham. Abraham has been accepted as a prophet by many religions.

Moses

Moses was born in 1540 BC and translated from this world in 1420 BC. There was a prophecy regarding the 'deliverer' to free the enslaved people. This was the prophet, Moses; he survived death at birth. To save the young Moses, his mother put him in a basket and left him in the river in the hands of his destiny, which he was to fulfil as he was raised as a prince. Later it was discovered that he was the deliverer and was ordered to go into the desert with little food, to live or die. He survived and became a shepherd. One day, he went in the presence of the Lord.

Spirit manifested as a burning bush and Moses received the spiritual power, he needed to fulfil his destiny. He returned to the pharaoh and told him to free his people but he refused. After many struggles and curses, the king gave up and agreed to release the Hebrews from slavery. Moses prepared his people to leave and led them to the Promised Land. When they reached the Red Sea, Moses managed to prepare the passage with the help of Spirit, an event known as 'the parting of the Red Sea.' As the people crossed, the king's army arrived for a revenge attack.

As the army entered the Red Sea, it closed back up and most of the army drowned. On the way to the Promised Land, Moses went to Mount Sinai to meditate and for future guidance. He received the Ten Commandments. During his absence, the people began to worship evil spirits or pagan gods. Moses got angry and put things right. After that, he passed his spiritual mantle to Joshua and asked him to lead his people to the Promised Land. Moses retired into the mountains and finally died at the age of 120.

Jesus Christ

It may not be accurate but Jesus Christ is said to have been born on 25 December 0000 in Bethlehem. As for his mother, it is known that she was a virgin. He was born in a stable. According to the myth, angels were present at his birth and three wise men visited on camels to see the young Jesus. His birth is known as the arrival of the Messiah. According to the prophecy, which had taken place and people were waiting for him. His real name was Yeshua Ben Josef. He was baptised by John the Baptist.

He went into the wilderness as a test, where Kal made all attempts to fail and prevent him from completing his mission. This is known as the dark night of the soul. After forty days, Jesus Christ succeeded and appeared as the Messiah or the prophet to lead the world. The word wilderness does not mean a desert or jungle; this experience can occur anywhere. It is the fight within. At that time, Jesus was alone, so there was no record of what happened.

You can only verify this statement when you have been through this state of consciousness. Jesus began his ministry and his early disciples were fishermen. As he got famous, he was a marked man and many government ministers or religious leaders felt threatened. He made many statements relating to his kingdom of God. Although the message was on a spiritual basis, the leaders of government and religion began to find or plant false evidence against him.

During his short ministry, he healed many people, raised the dead, turned water into wine and performed many more miracles. The religious leaders felt the threat and wished to get rid of him any way they could. Jesus was publicly making statements against them and they found it humiliating. The Pharisees were always on the lookout to accuse and kill him. In the end, they managed to kill him by employing crucifixion. Jesus Christ is claimed by his followers to be the Son of God.

This is a significant threat to any religious body even today, so be prepared to face the worst. Therefore, some highly spiritually awakened people keep their silence. We can forget about 2,000 years ago. Even today, people are not ready to accept this statement in the modern era. Jesus gave the message of God to the best of his ability and went on the Cross to be crucified, as per the final decision of Pontius, the governor of Judea.

Due to his sacrifice, he is alive forever in the hearts of his followers. His body was kept in a tomb under guards' supervision and a large round stone was rolled in front to seal the entrance. After three days, the disciples found that the tomb was empty. The angel appeared and confirmed the resurrection of Christ to the disciples and later, Jesus appeared to them as well. It is not easy to spread the word of God. All prophets have the same message but appear in different parts of the world.

It is the requirement of the time and the consequences are the same most of the time. Jesus Christ did not write the Bible but there is a contribution from Moses and many others. There is an excellent contribution from Saul, who was born Jewish but had a spiritual experience on the road to Damascus and changed himself to be a believer in Jesus. Later he was known as St Paul. He was also martyred around 67 CE.

Muhammad

Muhammad was born on 22 April 570 CE in Makkah, Saudi Arabia and died on 8 June 632 CE. He spent most of his time in meditation on Mount Hira. One night: in 610 CE, he was meditating in the cave when an angel named

Jibril visited him and told him to recite the name of Allah. Later he received spiritual revelations that were written down and the holy book, the Qur'an, was assembled.

Muhammad began to believe he was chosen as the prophet of Allah. Once he began to gain popularity, the people of Makkah felt threatened. He took his followers to Medina in 622 CE. That journey is known as Hijrah and the Islamic calendar began. It took him ten years to return to Makkah and several wars were fought, including the Battle of Badr, Uhad and Ahzab.

The term **jihad** is given. Finally, Muhammad was accepted as the prophet of Allah. Sharia law is a religious code of living that directs the individual to lead an honest and spiritual life. Muhammad married at the age of 25 to a wealthy woman who was 40 years of age. Her name was Khadijah. After she passed away, he married Aisha. He married a few times and finally translated from this world at the age of 62 years.

THE PROPHETS OF HINDUISM

We have discussed the descendants of Adam and Eve. This is the second line of descendants that runs parallel to the theory of Adam and Eve. The prophets discussed in this chapter were here long before Adam and Eve; This religion is known as Hinduism. Their origins are Brahma, Vishnu and Shiva. They have been here since creation began in this world. They were already residing in the upper regions of the lower planes.

All three were responsible for looking after the well-being of souls while experiencing the lower worlds. This was to create physical bodies for souls and to maintain the well-being and destruction of the physical bodies at the end of their lifespan. Thus, the soul can have experience from another dimension. Brahma, Vishnu and Shiva are better known as Creator, Preserver and Destroyer. The lower worlds are better known as the training ground for souls.

Shiva was established in the physical world for this purpose. There is evidence that Shiva is still here because he shows his presence to sincere followers throughout this world. The historical moments of these three spiritual giants were lost during the Golden and the Silver-Age times. Hinduism claims the trio has been here very recently, during the times of their prophets. The history of other religions is also poor because they cannot relate to these three spiritual giants.

Their spiritual writing is based more on the surface of the physical world than on the higher or spiritual worlds. They were not here only for Hinduism; they were responsible for all creation. They still are and will continue to be until the end of Kali-Yuga. Other religions may accept this statement or not but this is true. The saints of Hinduism managed to look back into the past, as they were interested in studying stars, sun and moon relating to this world and the effects of this relationship.

We will discuss the study of planets in our 'Physical Universe' chapter. The basic theory of Hinduism is excellent but how it is expressed in movies is total mythology. These venues represent that Hinduism has been here since ancient times but its written history fails to go beyond ten thousand years. Therefore, 3,893,201 years of history have been lost. So, we go by the number of years mentioned by their scholars.

Sri Ram

Prince Ram, the son of King Dashrath of Ayodhya, was born in 5114 BC. The story of Ramayana is the base of Ram's existence in this world. Sri Ram was about to be announced as the next king but due to some conspiracy in the family, his father told him to go into exile for twelve years. At that time, he was about 25 years old. India and Sri Lanka (Ceylon) were in the whole civilisation in history.

Sita was the daughter of King Janak of Mithila, now Bihar, India. At the same time, King Ravana was ruling in Sri Lanka. The population of these countries was in the hundreds of thousands at least. Ram is known as Maryada Parshotam (Obedient One). He taught the principles of obedience to his parents and the entire civilisation. He was not an ordinary person. He was born with the natural ability of spiritual powers.

During exile, King Ravana abducted Sita due to grudges regarding his sister. A big battle took place between the armies of Ram and Ravana. Hanuman (a monkey species) gave a helping hand to Ram during this war and Ram was victorious. After fourteen years, when Ram and Sita returned, people lit candles as a welcome gesture. Nowadays, that day is known as Diwali. It is celebrated every year all through the world.

Lord Krishna

According to legend, Lord Krishna was born without a sexual union but by mental transmission. Krishna was born in 3228 BC in the dungeons of a prison where his mother, Devaki and father, Vasudeva, were kept by Devaki's brother King Kansa in Mathura, Uttar Pradesh, India. King Kansa was given the prophecy that one of Devaki's sons would kill and de-throne him and restore righteousness.

King Kansa imprisoned his sister and brother-in-law and he killed every child of theirs at birth up to the sixth. Spirit or God tricked him during the birth of the seventh child. It was time for the prophet to be born. Near Krishna's birth, his father became worried for his safety. Then, during a vision, he saw that the guards would be sleeping and the prison gates would open themselves. Vasudeva put Krishna in an open basket at his birth and moved outside.

It was as he had seen during the vision. He took his son to the house of a friend called Nanda, exchanged his son for Nanda's daughter of the same age and returned to prison.

Nanda's wife Yashoda raised Krishna as her own in the Gokul village. According to the myth, a heavy storm struck when Vasudeva took baby Krishna from prison to Gokul. During that storm, a serpent with many heads appeared and provided a cover over his head to protect him from the rain.

So, these were the signs of a born prophet. Later, many attempts were made to kill Krishna, including poisoning. In his youth, Krishna returned to Mathura and killed Kansa, his uncle 'mama,' and returned the throne to Kansa's father, who had been imprisoned for a long time. Krishna became the leading prince in the kingdom. During those days, he became friends with Arjuna and his brothers (the Pandavas), who were his cousins.

Later, there was a war over the kingdom's right to rule between the Pandavas and the Kauravas': they were cousins. All negotiations by Krishna failed. Krishna did not want to take either side in the war but both sides approached him. Finally, he offered that one side could take his whole army and the other could have him. But he would not use any weapons. Duryodhana tried to be a cleaver and chose his entire army. The Pandavas chose Krishna and he became the charioteer to Arjuna.

Upon arrival at the battlefield, when Arjuna saw the opposition, they were his cousins, grandfather and other relations. He felt very uncomfortable fighting against or killing any of them. Finally, Arjuna put down his bow and arrows. Krishna gave him a discourse on physical and spiritual life to establish righteousness in the world and his duties. Later, these discourses of spiritual awakening were assembled in the *Bhagavad Gita*. Krishna was married to Rukmani.

Some literature mentions that he married 16,108 wives; 8 were his principal wives and the rest were rescued to save their honour. During his last days on earth, Krishna returned to the jungles and was in meditation. A hunter named 'Jara' shot an arrow into his bare feet as he mistook the glorious lotus shining under his feet for a deer's eye. Only a few prophets have the glorious lotus '**Padam**' under their feet, especially those sent by God directly to accomplish a mission.

Krishna ascended to heaven spiritually and his death marked the end of Bronze-Age and the beginning of the Iron-Age. Although he died at the age of 125 years on 18 February 3102 BC, he never aged after his youth.

Mahatma Buddha

He was born in Nepal in 563 BC. He was born a prince called Siddhartha Gautama and the king built three palaces to ensure he would lead a happy and peaceful life. Legend says that he witnessed sickness, old age and death on his three visits outside the palaces. He was disturbed by these experiences and wanted to achieve freedom from them. Despite being married and having a son called Rahula, he walked off to find salvation or enlightenment at the age of 29 years.

He studied under the teachings of Alara Kalama and then moved on to study under Rama Putta. Still, he was not satisfied and moved on to seek further. Later, he followed the path of asceticism and performed heavy meditation with minimum food, a single leaf or a grain of rice. This did not work out spiritually, as he nearly starved to death and gave up on that idea. He decided to meditate under the pipal tree until he reached enlightenment.

After sitting for forty-nine days, he and his companions received enlightenment. At that time, he was 35 years old and had been taught the middle path for forty-five years. Before departing from this world, he was known to have thirty-two qualities or the signs of being a great holy man. He was known as the ninth avatar of Lord Vishnu and is considered a prophet by many religions. Finally, he passed away in 483 BC at the age of 80 years.

Guru Nanak

Guru Nanak was born on 14 November 1469 and died on 22 September 1539 at the age of 70 years. His birthplace, Nankana Sahib, is near Lahore in Pakistan. At his birth, the spiritual light was seen. Later, a serpent was seen to provide a shadow over him as he slept under the sun. Once he was asleep under the tree, it was noted that the sun moved with time but the shadow remained on the same spot.

During his younger years, lots of divine qualities were noted. He made four journeys. His last journey included visiting Makkah, Medina, Basra and Bagdad. He travelled to Kabul and Kandahar and several miracles happened, recorded in Sikh history. Evidence: such as his handprint on a large stone that was thrown at him, is still available today. Panja-Sahib (hand with five fingers) is the temple where the stone is kept.

By birth, he was Hindu. He was spreading the word of God; the Hindus were upset because his spiritual message was universal. He taught that God is one and that Hindus and Muslims are the same in the eyes of God. He was captured by King Babar (Islam) and soon released when the king realised that this person was spiritually extraordinary.

He was the first guru of Sikhism and wrote 947 hymns, comprising Japji-Sahib.

In the beginning, he shed light on the one and only God as Ikonkar, God's first personification Satnam Ji and his qualities. I have not seen or heard this depth of explanation of reality anywhere else. In his last days, Guru Nanak returned to the place called Kartarpur and passed over his spiritual mantle to the second guru known as Angad Dev Ji. Finally, he passed away on 22 September 1539 to be in the presence of God.

RELIGIOUS TRACK RECORDS

To sum up, all the theories, let us investigate Christian theory and the dates given by some Biblical narratives. It indicates that the origin of Adam and Eve is in '4000 BC' or 6022 years old. According to Hinduism, Lord Sri Ram was born in 5114 BC or 7,136 years ago and at the same time, it indicates that this world was full of people.

Considering the number of people at that time, we can easily add a minimum of 10,000 years. That will make 7,136 plus 10,000, which comes to 17,136 years. At the same time, the recorded history of ancient Egypt indicates there was a whole civilisation in 7000 BC. All the theories do not add up compared with the population of this world in the multi-billions. People have not dropped from the sky within this short period.

Having some spiritual knowledge, sometimes I feel that scientists are far ahead compared to religions. At least they are mentioning the time scale in millions of years. Constructing this world could take a few million years. The civilisation of the humans living in this world, according to the beginning of the Golden-Age, began 3,893,124 years ago:

Satya-Yuga	(Golden-Age)	1,728,000 years
Treta-Yuga	(Silver-Age)	1,296,000 years
Dwapara-Yuga	(Bronze-Age)	864,000 years.
Kali-Yuga	(Iron-Age)	432,000 years

The Kali-Yuga is 5124 years old so far and will continue to complete its cycle of 432,000 years, marking the end of civilisation. I am not against any theory given by any religion but I always felt uncomfortable according to the visions I saw long ago. My visions align with the 'Nakal' (copy) records at the Katsu-pary Monastery in Tibet, where all the spiritual records are available. In my visions, the jungles of this world were in full bloom.

In other words, the world was ready to receive human accommodation to provide food and shelter. I have seen the first five people landing on earth. It was in the jungles, as most of the world was jungle. They were in the upright position (standing). I saw them coming down to the ground feet first and the Satya-Yuga began. So, I disagree with the theory given by our scientists that we have progressed from the monkey species.

As the theory goes, we walked on four feet during our early days, better known as two hands and two feet. If this was true, what is stopping the present monkey species from walking on two feet; it is much easier for them to copy humans. The monkey clan is one and humans are another part of God's creation alongside 84,00000 species. Each creation is individual to help the soul's spiritual experience.

Nowadays, some scientists are trying to crossbreed some species. This is a violation of spiritual law can lead to many upheavals in the future.

The first five people who arrived on earth were men. Females came or were created later, as agreed on by a few religions. I am aware of these five people from the last forty years when Dapren and I returned in time. I was surprised to learn about this last year when a friend gave me a book called 'Gurbani Katha Vichar' by Iqbal Singh, which compares Hinduism to Sikhism. **Singh** writes that there is a mention of these five people in 7000 years old Hindu book called Sri Shiv Purana.

The Puranas provide spiritual history. The evolution theory by Charles Darwin is very young comparatively. They were known as 'Panch Sant Kumar' (Five Saint) and were very close to God. That is why they were specially chosen for this purpose to begin Satya-Yuga. The lifespan of these people was a few thousand years. So far, I have traced one person out of these original five. He appeared on earth several times to perform spiritual duties.

He was seen in the sixth century and appeared in sixteenth and seventeenth-century Asia, where he is part of history. He was born again in India in the eighteenth century and passed away in the middle of the nineteenth century. This is just to give a slight hint to some curious minds. I can see that he has returned and taken his spiritual duties for many years serving God. As you can see, these people operate on a universal level, so there is no question of my country or religion.

Since the beginning of these Yugas, many other active souls have been here. They have made thousands of repeated journeys all through the world. These assistants of God are not allowed to sit still in a bliss state somewhere. There are billions of souls seeking spiritual help, so they will appear as directed by the Spirit. This is the original point of discussion regarding prophets. There is no such thing as; this is the first or the last prophet of this world.

The people who make such claims are false. This world is good enough for another four hundred thousand years for human habitation, according to the 'Nakal' records. While some religions are less than 10,000 years old, they feel that they have the authority to forecast the future for 426,876 years. Over this period, thousands or more prophets are coming to accommodate the spiritual knowledge of the time. The prophets we are so proud of today will be forgotten, as we have forgotten the prophets who were here during the times of the Golden or Silver-Age.

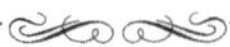

LOST HISTORY OF PROPHETS

I will explain how the history of prophets is lost. Jesus Christ was here only 2,000 years ago and this religion has failed to produce his actual looks in a picture. At present, the image you see is self-created and does not resemble his actual looks. Let us look at the most recent religion of all, Sikhism, which is no more than 550 years old and had the most facilities to maintain every detail of its history.

You will be surprised to learn that the Sikhs do not have a single accurate picture or an actual sketch of their ten gurus. As I had the privilege to be in the presence of Guru Nanak, I am aware of his looks. Unfortunately, none of the pictures in the market today is any closer to his true personality. There is no sign of spiritual countenance on his face. Apart from his image, Guru Nanak has given us treasured spiritual writings that have been changed in the past and are being changed now.

This truth will be lost one day, as it has lost its true power of continuity. The same will apply to all other religions as well. For as long as we can maintain the actual contents of any spiritual writings, it will hold its spiritual powers. As soon as we dilute its true meaning, it will become thinner each day and eventually disappear from this planet's face. I will give another example of how the contents of the writings are lost. Paul Ji brought the teachings into the open in 1965, 'The Path of Enlightenment.'

He said, 'My writings may be edited to sound better or more effective,' similar to the Bible in one of his cassettes. But at no point did he say that you could add anything to his written words. I have this audio cassette for reference. We lose history once we begin to alter, add or subtract parts of written words. The Kal power set up the trap. The mind becomes its victim and history keeps repeating itself.

This was the reason for writing the chapter 'Power' in 'The Way to God.' I don't think people understand the value of originality. All paintings of famous artists sell in the range of millions of Dollars because they are original. The duplicate paintings sell for nothing. The name and fame lead to all the forbidden activities in spiritual law.

Only the born Master or prophet can keep the teachings pure like they should be. He is the only one who will keep the teachings to God's expectations. From other or routine Masters, you can expect anything. My writings are straightforward and may not be up to the current grammar standards. I do not wish my writings to be altered because I have said it the way I want to say or express God-knowledge. *The Way to God* is my first book, so I gave it to someone to check the grammar and make a few corrections.

After a few weeks, when I received my book back, this person in question said it was done very professionally in line with today's reader. I said thank you. Later, I wanted to see the improvements. When I read it, it sounded very foreign to my mind. I had to rewrite the whole book again. Now you see my point. When you make any alterations, it will lose its spiritual charge and become like ordinary writings.

Civilisation will come to a near end many times within the next 426,880 years with the help of weapons of mass destruction. The next big disaster is expected in 2029/30. That can change, provided the vibrations of this world improve. Kali-Yuga is very young and we have a lot to learn. Prophets are born with spiritual knowingness. Not everyone can be a prophet, even if they try.

The death philosophy regarding the age factor does not apply to them. They know precisely when they are going to leave this world. They can also delay their stay for longer if they wish, similar to Sri Rebazar or choose to leave early. The lifespan, number of years or breaths a person is supposed to take in this life are not fixed, as mentioned in a few religions.

They are written to please the mind of humans because their tolerance level is shallow if they lose a loved one. Another statement is not true but has been used to create fear in the mind of the people. That is, to face **death** is truth. Spiritual philosophy is different. Death is no more than changing clothes for the soul; while **living** is the ultimate truth.

The more incarnations the soul goes through, the more experience is gained. Death is truth to the human body. And 'to live' is the truth for the soul. While you know both situations, do not be bothered by these two truths. Follow the middle path and gain as much experience as you possibly can. Wherever you are sitting, you should know that you are the centre of the whole of creation.

Spirit is flowing through you directly. You are the source of God to reach every soul in the universe. Your physical identity has dispersed into thin air. You are only aware of yourself as a soul, reaching everyone through your soul.

'If you know that you and God are one; what is there that you cannot understand? The prophets are in this position. Everyone cannot become a prophet but you can work hard spiritually throughout many lives.

One day, you will appear as a prophet on this earth. God has created each soul with this ability, so do not underestimate yourself. Any person who underestimates their spiritual abilities will never succeed. Keep focussed on your goal. The statement 'this is the last prophet' is not valid. I know one religion that misleads its followers by saying God has said this. God does not exist for only one religion.

Knowing that all religions are man-made makes you understand that they are trying to please their followers. Under the influence of such statements, it is challenging for the new prophet to show any authority, as people do not wish to recognise him. A new prophet fails to speak because he knows people are under this influence and will not accept him. So, one thing leads to another, while this newcomer could be far superior to the previous prophets.

Only one prophet is the creator of all the prophets and that is God itself. The prophets do not wish to call themselves prophets because they know the truth and who runs the show. Only their followers want to label their saints to have an edge over the other religions. 'Who are they to stop any more coming of the prophets? All religions claim that their religion is strong. Internally, they are all fragile.

The day that the prophets stop coming will be near the end of Kali-Yuga. The Yugas, such as the Golden, Silver, Bronze and Iron ages, clearly indicate humans' presence on earth to tell us of their existence. Otherwise, the names of the

Yugas are meaningless. This search will carry on, as we have lots to learn yet. Christians have researched many known saints but their names only exist in mythological stories.

Research has proved that, in reality, they never existed. Many Hindu stories are based on mythology, whereas the truth is different. So only believe what your inner wants to trust. God has given you this knowingness. Keep working towards your goal; one day, you could be the future prophet. To have any success, your mind should be very calm. Overactive or devious minds are misleading. Sincerity, patience, silence and many other virtues of God will help you materialise your goal.

I was in India very recently and about ten people came to see me. They were very sincere but followed other paths and had some questions. One young girl about ten asked me, 'Where is my third-eye? I said, 'Do you want to see it? She said, 'Yes.' I asked her to come and sit on the chair near me and told her to close her eyes. I advised her what to do and where to look.

She followed the instructions very sincerely and suddenly her third-eye opened and she saw the spiritual light. This is proof of having a simple or uncomplicated mind. There was another lady. She could not concentrate on her spiritual eye while her mind was very active and wandering everywhere. She asked, 'Is there any technique to help with this problem? I said, 'Yes. There is always a solution to every problem.'

I explained how to go about this situation and where and how to concentrate and she found our 'Silence the Mind' technique very useful. This technique is written earlier in this book. She tried this technique while we were all talking. Later, she remarked that she was isolated from our noise and had a spiritual experience. This proves that our teachings are 'alive' while others are passive paths. But people are still following them. I wish them success.

SRI PAUL TWITCHELL

Paul Ji was born in Paducah, Kentucky, America, on 22 October 1909. He was a born saint to bring change in religious thought. People were walking away from the traditional religions as the answers to spiritual questions were not given in simple language. Paul Ji struggled to bring the eternal teachings into the open so that everyone could access the truth. The truth had always been here but it contained hidden meanings. In other words, a simple mind could not grasp the message.

Spirit chose Paul Ji for this task. It was a considerable task to run around the world and study all the religions to present a clear picture of spiritual truth on neutral grounds. By doing so, whoever followed the teachings would say, 'These teachings are for me.' He mentions having seven teachers who were responsible for his spiritual growth. Rebazar was the last to provide the final spiritual spark to hand over the spiritual mantle to bring the teachings into the open in 1965.

His ministry lasted under six years until he passed away on 17 September 1971, aged 62. Some people were not happy with his success. As a result, he was poisoned a year before his final passing. It was a great struggle for him to keep his body going until his successor was ready to take over. Finally, he died of heart failure in Cincinnati in the presence of Dr Blyth, the president of the organisation and Paul's personal doctor.

Paul worked as a journalist for many years because he loved to write. It is why he managed to write a number of books. He had this spiritual urge to come out and touch everyone's heart. People felt that; what he wrote in his teachings was for them. This spiritual urge within and the system he was living in made him feel trapped, as though some physical obstacles were in his way. It was why he gave himself the name 'Cliff-hanger.' He held onto spiritual thought beyond human grasp, creating his world.

The training of the masters is so intense that they can drink the whole ocean and the person standing next to them would not know that they have done that. The ocean is very small compared to all the universes. It is said that Paul gathered certain words from other religions. I believe that this is true. He chose these words to give his teachings a universal touch; otherwise, they would sound like an extension of some other religion. Eckankar and Mahanta are part of Sikhism and so forth. The word Shariyat is from Islam. It is called the law of Sharia in Islam.

He met Gail Anderson in 1962 and married her in 1964. Although Paul had tremendous knowledge but he was shy. It was Gail who told him to do something with his knowledge. At the same time, he was receiving inner nudges from Spirit to bring the teachings into the open. He was also writing letters to Gail daily or weekly during that time. This was to educate her about what he knew. Later, these letters were published in two books. Paul encountered some religious teachers.

One was Mehar Baba and he also joined the ashram of Swami Premananda in 1950 and left the ashram in 1955. Later, Paul joined the Dianetics and Scientology movement, based on the teachings of Ron Hubbard. He did not stay there for long, although he became one of the group's consultants. Paul joined the Radha Soami group in the mid-fifties and Saint Kirpal Singh initiated him. All the teachers' Paul had been with contributed to his spiritual education.

Paul had found a connection to the spiritual truth, which no one had before. People have tried to understand Paul but they have failed. To understand Paul, you must be like Paul. If your approach is physical or material, you will never know who he was other than to admire his writings. Paul himself was a great researcher and made every possible effort so he could bring the teachings into the open. This is the failure point of Seekers nowadays. They don't do any research and rely on the words of the Master.

Paul said, 'Don't believe what I say; you only believe when you see the reality.' Paul mentions that it took him fifteen years of intense training to hold the spiritual mantle. Paul never claimed that his spiritual mantle came from Radha Soami. He learned what he required and moved on to his final training under the supervision of Rebazar. In the same way, my background is from Nanak Sar 'Sikhism,' but I received the final spiritual spark from Darwin.

Some American people claim that Paul imagined the character known as Rebazar. These people have no spiritual insight and cannot stand others' success. Although Paul is not with us physically, these people are welcome to walk through my door any time to read my diary. I have recorded a number of my experiences with this spiritual giant. Again, it is up to them to believe; otherwise, no convincing will be enough.

There is a claim by some people that Paul has plagiarised part of his writings from other writers. I want to point here that there is not a single religion that did not copy from another. There is no such thing as the original, as someone else's work always influences writers. I don't think that anyone wants to copy others. During your studies, the influence of what you have learned is printed in your subconscious. When you try to write on the same subject, it may look like someone else's writing.

Rebazar regularly visited Paul to teach him all the required knowledge to bring the teachings into the open. Although the master has unfolded beyond our conception, refreshing training will be given when you take birth on the physical level. The Master of the time will put you through all the physical activities and problems. This is so that, as a Master, you will have experienced and know all Seekers' problems.

Paul was one of the best spiritual travellers of his time. The Master is only used as an instrument by the Spirit to get the message out. Physical personality worship has no place in the teachings. Paul said he did not want anyone to put him on a pedestal. In the early days, Paul began the teachings under the name of bi-location in 1965 but soon realised it sounded more or less like astral travel. Then he adopted the name of Eckankar when he was based in San Diego, California, 92113.

Paul was a hero in his way. He would say that he is living in this world but not a part of it. He taught us to grant freedom to anyone and all religions and to love all life. He knew that each person or religion is connected to God's plan with a golden thread. Therefore, he said, 'Be yourself and let others be.' Do not try to convince anyone to believe what we say. We should be ready to take any criticism and honestly answer what we know.

Paul Ji wrote a book called *Difficulties of Becoming the living Master*. He mentions his difficulties and the struggle to bring the teachings into the open. He was more interested in the unfoldment of an individual soul to find its way back to the Godhead as an assistant. I am always thankful to him for the golden gift he has left for spiritual Seekers. You will always find people from all walks of life who never fail to criticise. Let them be as well.

BHAKTI-MARG

(Meditation)

First, we are fortunate to follow a spiritual path such as this. As Paul Ji mentioned, we are the chosen ones. This term, the 'chosen one,' makes you feel special. It simply means that you have created good karma to be in such a position. Your good karma is responsible for this yearning to seek further so that you can be in the presence of God. Once you have managed to find a spiritual Master, you set up a goal for what you want to achieve in this life.

My job is to remind what that goal was and guide those willing to listen and follow. I do not wish to see people making sandcastles that have no foundation. When a little tide comes out of the sea, everything vanishes without a trace. This is a widespread practice among followers of all religions. The followers want to achieve spiritual freedom from this world but nothing materialises because no one tells these followers what to do and how to do it.

Every person is satisfied by material gains. All the spiritual leaders are deeply involved in material gains too. 'So how can they ask their followers to do something different? To be a saint is not an easy job. Only one person out of a million will be successful. So, if you want to be one in a million, the task is not that easy. I am glad to say that some of you are working hard. Reading past gurus' history and achievements motivates us to do something worthwhile.

They have worked very hard to make their mark in this world. Contrary to what Paul and Dapren said, doing a half-hour meditation daily is not good enough. I have been analysing the results for the last forty years and do not see any positive results. I have not seen anyone doing half an hour of meditation and becoming a saint. I don't think Paul and Dapren were happy with the results either. The followers have become too relaxed.

The more lenient the Master becomes, the lazier the Seekers are. It was said earlier that Seekers should do a half-hour of meditation daily. If the Master wanted to give any experience during that time, he would. If not, you stop. We followed that over the years. 'If the Master wanted to give any experience' indicates that the responsibility is placed on the Master, not the Seeker. If you are satisfied with this gesture of spiritual experience, that is fine.

This lenience of the Master will never lead you to become the Master of your universe. So, 'When will you be the master of your universe? The achievements of earlier saints, such as Mahatma Buddha, Muhammad, Sai Baba and many more, it was this spark within that led you to set a goal for yourself. Now I will give you some examples of how they came to achieve what we know today.

Guru Nanak

Guru Nanak hardly did any hardcore meditation, as he was always in contact with God. He managed to spread the Word of God by word of mouth and writing so people could benefit in the future. He was naturally born with all the abilities that a saint required. A spiritual light appeared at the time of his birth and the shadow of a tree protected him all day. He was a born soul traveller and could take anyone with him.

There are hundreds of examples of Guru Nanak's miracles in his writings. We praise his miracles but fail to ask, 'What did he do in his past lives to achieve this? We all want to achieve what he achieved but we don't want to do anything to materialise it. I hope this statement of mine brings a turning point in your life.

Jesus Christ

Jesus Christ is another great soul. There is not a single person in the world who has not heard his name at least once. It is such an outstanding achievement for any soul. Again, he was not an ordinary person. That was due to his hardcore meditation during his past lives; this meditation led to his fruitful spiritual life. Many saints forecasted his birth or the arrival of the Messiah. We all know the famous story of his birth and the miracles he performed in a short time.

I am sure you want to do the same. But 'What are you doing to materialise your goal? God gives a chance to each soul to make its mark in this world. Some take advantage of this, while others leave this world unknown. You will be given another opportunity, 'but when? That is not for you to decide. But now, you are sitting right in the centre of this opportunity. I would not miss this opportunity for anything in this world.

Mahatma Buddha

Mahatma Buddha was born with great karma. He was born as a prince and heir to the throne but not with any enlightenment. So, he is someone with whom you can compare yourself as a struggler. Once he learned the truth, he began his search, which was not easy. He tried most meditation techniques and ate less food till he was almost all bone but nothing materialised. He gave up on all the systems that had failed him but never gave up hope.

He knew that the truth was somewhere and that he had yet to discover it. He gave an ultimatum to himself and God. He sat under the Bodhi tree and decided that he would not get up from that sitting, even if he were to lose his life. After forty-nine days, he received enlightenment. So, making up your mind is the crucial point. We fail to stand by our goal.

Muhammad

Muhammad was the second person after Jesus to become a household name. Although God sent him as his prophet, he used to meditate regularly within a cave known as Mount Hira. He was a sage man and at the same time, he had spiritual knowledge. This example answers a common question: 'How important is meditation? You need spiritual experience. Otherwise, you will have no legs to stand on, to claim this status. Once you know who you are, you don't have to prove this to anyone.

Sai Baba

He was born in 1838. Sai Baba began meditation at a very young age. People began to believe that he was a miracle man during his youth. He faced lots of rivalry in his day but the truth always prevailed. Nowadays, he is very popular within the Asian community. He was a spiritual dream man and soul traveller and there is much evidence of his supernatural powers.

He made his mark in this world and I do not wish anyone to leave this world without making a mark. At the end of your lifespan, you should be able to say, "This is my spiritual achievement."

Baba Harnam Singh

Of village Bhuchon Kalan, Bathinda, Punjab was here in the eighteenth and nineteenth centuries. He also began his meditation at a very young age. During his youth, his first sitting was for one year. Then he got up for a little while and began his second sitting in meditation, which lasted continuously for two years. His third sitting was also for two years. You may be wondering how he managed to sit for all that time.

Once you make up your mind, the physical body is maintained with spiritual food from the Spirit. You may laugh at what I will say next but I have noticed something during our half-hour spiritual chant. Once the words 'May the blessings' are mentioned, most followers begin to stretch their bodies as if they have just finished a hard labour twenty-four-hour shift somewhere. You must be serious about what you are doing.

The goal you set earlier is not easy. All I can say is that you do have the capability of executing it. Baba Harnam Singh, once recognised as a saint, began to meditate in a dark room 'basement' but set no time limits. Once, he invited one of his disciples into the room, 'Bhora,' to ask if it was day or night outside. Out of curiosity, the disciple asked, 'Why do you ask this? He replied, 'Within this room, the sun is always shining, so I could not judge what it is outside.'

If you were in a similar situation, 'Would you be afraid of a dark room? I doubt it very much. It was before electricity arrived in that village. Baba Harnam Singh's most famous disciple is known as Baba Nand Singh. Born on 8 November 1870, he also began his meditation at an early age. After moving from place to place, he finally came to stay in the small temple of Baba Harnam Singh.

After spending twelve years of hardcore meditation under his supervision, Baba Nand Singh received enlightenment. Baba Harnam Singh then asked him to go to Nanak Sar and do his preaching. This indicates that the guru does not hold you further; once the disciple becomes the master of his universe. This is where the term *assistants* come in. Despite receiving all this power, he meditated all day and every night.

I know the exact spot where he used to sit for meditation. You will be surprised to learn what kind of spot that was. It was open farmland and there were many wild animals. No animal would dare touch you while you lean within Spirit. Half of our members are afraid of tiny spiders. I am just reminding you of how much stronger you need to be. He had all the abilities I could think of, light and sound, soul travel, spiritual and psychic scanning.

Above all, he could turn his body into a lion if someone did not listen to his instructions. Baba Nand Singh and Baba Harnam Singh were temperamental people but only if it benefitted the disciple. Our members have an incomplete picture of the character of a true guru. They think that he is all smiling and goody-goody. That is not true. A good comparison is when we use our ability to discipline a child.

If we do not discipline the child, they will grow up ignorant and oppressive, used to getting their way. Baba Nand Singh's famous disciple was Baba Isher Singh, born on 26 March 1916. After serious meditation, he received enlightenment in 1950. He preached Sikhism at the same place till 6 October 1963. The reason for mentioning this line of master-ship is that Spirit will never fail any person.

Who makes a sincere effort in meditation under the instruction of their guru. Therefore, I am trying to provide all the ins and outs of spiritual tools. You never know which of these tools will lead you to a spiritual awakening. I was fortunate enough to meet and stay in the presence of Baba Isher Singh many times. After enlightenment, Baba Isher Singh made a particular basement room, 'Bhora'; on the ceiling, he fixed a U-shaped metal rod.

Every night, he would tie his hair to this hook and meditate while standing all night. Now you may wonder why he contemplated this much after receiving enlightenment. He did this because once you become responsible for many followers, loads of karma drop on you like a ton of bricks. You must build spiritual stamina to manage the karma load to clear everything.

As Baba Nand Singh forecasted my birth, I have grown up listening to their way of life. I contemplated on what I should do to achieve similar enlightenment. I did follow in their footsteps. And as you can see, it reflects in my character. This is the school of hardcore meditation. I do not wish to see anyone failing. You don't have to become a hardcore mediator but do your best. Your effort will be fruitful.

If you are unwilling to spend any time or effort, that is your choice. There is nothing you can hide from within. I may be temperamental at times but it is only for your benefit. If someone thinks this is not on, I will say, 'You have not joined the spiritual school yet.'

WHIRLPOOL

Whirlpool is a fantastic theory of nature. It can take **within** whatever comes in its way. Nothing will come out quickly unless sheer effort is applied and someone is there to guide you. Otherwise, you never be heard of who you are or were. I have created this freehand sketch to give you an example; whatever comes in its circle is sucked in. In the lower worlds, this whirlpool is known as Kal and has five very sharp and illusive fangs.

These five fangs spare no one. Similarly, there is a natural black hole in the sea. If a boat or a ship is travelling nearby, the vessel is pulled with natural force into its circle and taken down to the bottom of the sea, never to come out. Some scientists were doing a practical experiment and purposely they pushed a tiny boat toward a 'black hole;' it took the boat in and the boat disappeared forever.

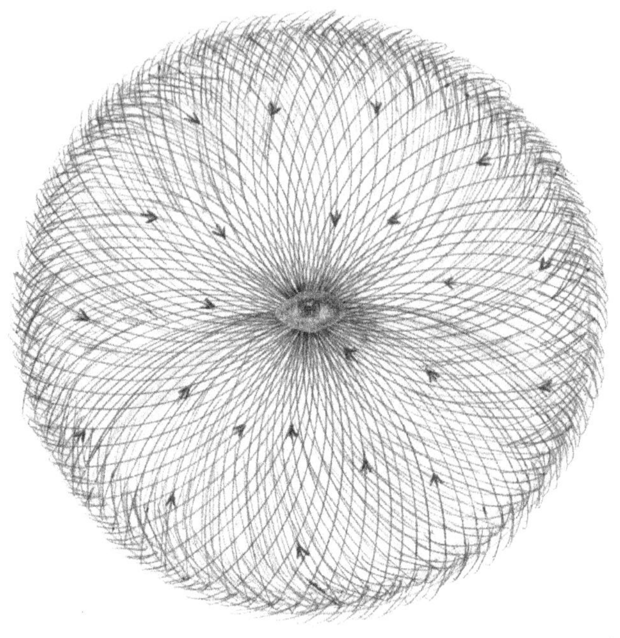

(Whirlpool Picture)

A Tsunami came a few years back out of the sea. Recently big floods flowed out of the Indian mountains and destroyed whatever was in their way, including Hindu temples. Many people were dragged away by this powerful water flow and have not been found. The Asian media has declared it 'the tsunami out of the mountains.' It does not matter how good we are scientific; nature constantly reminds us of who is in control.

So, we must learn the way of nature and 'soul travel' is the natural way of leaving these lower worlds. Soul travel can be done or performed in many ways. I am sure you can find your interpretations of this theory. I have given different theories within the last few discourses to work on. I am sure something will help you to get out of this wisely created 'whirlpool' for the souls. The five passions are part of this whirlpool.

If there is a way in, there is always a way out. I am sure you will find it. Religious teachers do not guide the followers on how to get out of this whirlpool and find freedom. You people are sitting at the bottom of this whirlpool and happy that you have achieved your goal. When you have not even scratched the surface of your goal. You had the living Master and the spiritual knowledge required but you never bothered or managed to give it a practical shape.

As we know, this is our training ground for the souls. The word karma is the way to lead you into this whirlpool and the living Master is the way out. Our creator has created this whirlpool of lower worlds purposely to train souls. There are so many systems in this world better known as religions. All religions are known or believed to be spiritual by their followers when they are nothing other than a system run by some trained people in religious verses.

These priests are more stuck than ordinary people because they have become part of the roots of the whirlpool by their deeds. It is about time to use our spiritual knowledge and put it into practical shape. Slowly but surely, move out of this whirlpool and breathe fresh air on the ocean's surface. Now, we will look at some of the famous religions of this world to see where they will lead their followers.

Jesus once said, 'There are two sides to a coin, head and tails; one belongs to the physical and the other is spiritual.' Most religions have lost the link to this spiritual side of knowledge. They try to express everything physically yet believe it is spiritual. This leads you nowhere other than to the bottom of this whirlpool. Speaking of his kingdom, Jesus said, 'Follow me.' Later, he stated, 'There are many mansions in my father's house and I will prepare the places for you.'

He was talking about the higher spiritual planes. He was never interested in anything on a physical basis. He said, 'My kingdom is not of this world.' Nowadays, his followers are knocking door to door and talking about creating the kingdom of heaven on earth. Now, 'Can you see that the message of this great man has been lost within two thousand years, with misinterpretation in the opposite direction?

Jesus was trying to take his followers out of this whirlpool; his followers lead the masses into the whirlpool. This happens when you don't have a living Master or teacher to put you on the right track. Sikhism is another example, as Sikhs don't believe in having a living Master after ten gurus and have accepted their holy book as the eleventh guru. There are some teachers. They are labelled as 'derra-babas.'

They are living Masters but are not recognised as the Masters of Sikhism. Some teachers are good, while others are pseudo-masters and deceiving people. As they have found, this is an easy way of making money. The question is, 'Why do people walk into their systems? Some spiritual Seekers are looking for a way out of this world. Their respective religions failed to provide any answers. All religions lead the person to physical disciplines.

'Who will lead the individual to the spiritual side or show them what to do next? Sikhism is a great religion. The philosophy is based on the soul's journey into the lower worlds and the soul's final destination is in the soul plane. Too much politics is involved in this religion, which is a setback for the followers. If someone manages to have spiritual understanding, they begin to look elsewhere to find the answers to their questions.

This is a fact. Today more people are leaving this religion than new ones joining. The Sikhs fail to spread the true message in many ways. It is also a fact that many people join Christianity and Islam daily. Islam has its limitations because Muslims do not believe in the reincarnation system. So, the question of how to get out of this whirlpool does not even exist. Islam talks about providing angels to serve the people who become martyrs for this religion.

No true religion in this world agrees to any killings. The followers don't even know what they are dying for. Now you can see that millions of people are led to this whirlpool. **First**; there are not many who can show you the way out. **Secondly**; the people themselves do not want to get out. They are deeply involved in the five passions of the mind: lust, anger, greed, attachment and vanity. Today, science leads the way because all religions fail to provide the proper answers.

Politics must be removed from religions if they are to have any success. I will not be surprised; one day, people will ask, 'What is religion? We failed to spread the true message of God so people could find their way into reality. In our teachings, most members failed because they found the easy way to request that the Master will solve their problems or physical ailments.

You should know that your problems have never ended and your physical ailments are the same or worse. The Master has solved lots of your problems and taken the burden of your sufferings. We all witnessed this in Dapren's body. He sorted out your problems and accepted your pains so you could get out of this whirlpool. But you adopted a relaxed mood.

You should know that your problems will never cease as long as you live in the lower worlds. Nor will your physical ailments. It is about time to decide what you want to achieve in this life. I have no problem taking on your burdens. But I know you will never be as strong as I want to see. I want to see everyone as better or stronger than I am. I am sure you will not let me down.

ALIENS

Aliens have fascinated the human mind for a long time. Some are curious to know how they look. Others are scared because aliens abduct humans. A few claimed that aliens had placed electronic devices into their bodies. At the same time, some doctors claim to have removed these devices. Some people claim they are in contact with aliens regularly. Most of these stories are baseless.

Only these people can tell us if they are telling the truth or if their claims are just a publicity stunt. Many of these stories are found to be hoaxes. Aliens communicate via telepathy and can travel through physical objects because of their vibratory rate. The questions are, 'Can aliens overpower humans? 'Does any government have evidence of aliens? The sightings of aliens are reportable to the police; the information is passed over to the ministry of defence because this agency is responsible for our security.

Our imagination about the aliens is always wrong because we try to scale everything on our physical parameters, while their vibratory rate is different. Their presence could be out of our reach to see them; unless they prefer to show their existence to a group of us or a chosen individual. To us, they travel in astral bodies. Now, 'how many people can see someone in an astral body? We only came to know about the aliens a few years ago. Some people must have encountered them and described what they saw.

In those days, cameras were not available, unlike today. Some claimed to be abducted and faced unknown experiments. They do not acknowledge what happened because their memories have been wiped out. After hearing their stories, scientists used hypnotism to revive the experience to know what these people had seen. Others claim that genetic experiments were tested on them.

So that, in the future, a half-alien race could easily mingle among us. It is known as a future-breeding program. This could be our future, as humans will create dangerous ailments by over-using chemical experiments, which will destroy the human body. So, they are going to prepare something to face the problem. Humans have very limited future foresight into what could take place.

The people on the astral plane have a complete list of what will take place as time goes by. Future inventions are already on the astral plane and the ideas will be released to our future scientists through dreams or semi-conscious states. The information can be released into our subconscious mind, from where we can pick up these ideas. The way we represent the look of aliens is imaginary. They appear as semi-developed people.

In pictures, they appear to have weird looks, skinny and with long limbs. This proves that no one has seen them. They come from higher regions with high vibrations and technology. 'Don't you think they should look better in appearance than us? We know that they are our paranormal visitors who travel from one galaxy to another. They are our visitors from the astral plane's lower part and use spacecraft we call UFOs (unidentified flying objects).

They use the planets, including Mars or Venus, as their way stations and visit this physical plane for many reasons. The Astral plane is responsible for the well-being of the earth. There are a few chances that their travelling vehicles can become or get faulty. We hear many stories about a UFO crashing at a particular place and the army has captured the survivors. When scholars or we investigate the evidence, it turns out to be a hoax.

The astral plane is out of reach to many but current science is aware of our solar system, so people use their imagination to relate them to one of the known planets. 'Are we able to see them? 'Where have they come from and why? Our knowledge is limited. Even if aliens do land on earth purposely or due to the failure of a UFO, we must analyse the whole story with a sceptical mind to know whether it is true or false. Our judgement should be based on the evidence produced.

The planet Mars is well known for the possibility of an alien civilisation since we have landed our spaceship on Mars. So far, there is no evidence of seeing or meeting with aliens or human life on this planet. We must have core evidence before making any claims. All the claims made in the 1940s and 50s were false or hoaxes. We know most of our solar system due to the scientific progress within the last few decades.

The British Ministry of Defence has a UFO desk and several secret x-files. I wonder what their findings are. In 2002, a British man, Mr Gary McKinnon, hacked into American secret files because he was fascinated by UFOs and aliens. His secret hacking was caught by the US authorities, who asked for his extradition. After ten years of legal battle, he was let off. In the early days, aliens were described as looking very similar to ET, extra-terrestrials with big bald heads and slim bodies.

The descriptions developed into depictions of semi-humans, with some expressing an appearance similar to lizards. Lately, it has been accepted that their looks are similar to humans or better. Some believe that aliens are intervening in our politics and giving guidance to some well-known politicians, suggesting what to do. This is a possibility. If we look back in history, we see that most of the inventions have made our modern life, what it is today. It came to our famous inventors from somewhere else.

The aliens gave ideas or dreams and they landed in the museum of future inventions on the astral plane. Aliens may come to earth because our control or powerhouse is on the astral plane. Similarly, the control for the astral plane is on the causal plane. The responsible authorities on the astral plane are concerned about our well-being. They make sure that the balance of everything is maintained.

Some believe that aliens will land on earth to control or dominate us. There are many imaginary theories regarding some kind of invasion and many think they will enter our physical bodies and dictate their message through us. Many believe that, at one point, we will be half-human and half-alien. Most people don't realise that these aliens already live in a better place, as all the higher regions are better than earth.

The physical plane is on the bottom or lower living scale. 'Do you think aliens will leave a better standard of living and join us to suffer? You can draw your conclusions. Most people do not realise that we are offshoots of these people, not vice versa. Aliens may visit if that is possible. Our scientists recognise **aliens,** while spiritual studies recognise **angels of death.** They are also aliens to this world.

They are also of two kinds 'Angels', representatives of Spirit and angels of death sent by the king of the dead. Angels of death are well known in this world. People can witness them while on their deathbed due to old age or severe sickness. A person has to be semi-conscious of this world and on the verge of entering the next world. Many people can talk to their loved ones sitting nearby in this state.

To express what they are witnessing. A few people with this experience get better and tell us what they have seen and where they were on the higher planes. The angels always appear at the perfect time when someone will die. They also know who will die, so there is no mistake. It shows that they are aware of our every move and whereabouts. It indicates that the astral plane has complete control over us.

So, to witness some UFOs or aliens is a minor thing. They can pass through our physical objects because of their high technology or vibrations in spiritual terminology. They often come to do various experiments but we fail to see them because they are outside our physical range of knowingness. The theory of the East or West's devils, demons or witches is different. These are the souls of accidental deaths.

Due to the accidental nature of their passing, they fail to go back to the astral plane, so they are wandering souls. We have many black magicians; some manage to abduct these souls and control them for misuse. So, this is another phenomenon. In the early days, when minds were simple, it was considered a visit from God when someone witnessed a

UFO. Compared to our physical senses, it is all a supernatural phenomenon.

The appearance of these Spirit objects is evidence of their existence. The UFO phenomenon is natural. We can accept this or not. The British, US and many other governments have the proof in their secret files. There is no limit on the shapes of these space objects. They could be round discs, triangular or square and their sightings have been reported since the eighteenth century. You may remember that in November 2006 a UFO was spotted hovering over Chicago's O'Hare Airport.

Another was seen later in March 2007 in Cleveland, Ohio, where we held our worldwide seminar in October 2008. We should be able to visit these higher regions, provided our present scientists can go beyond the speed of light and sound. We must break this barrier of speed. Once this is done, most of our present well-known religions will fade into the background. They have failed to provide what they claim on a spiritual basis. People believe in evidence, not in mythological stories.

The way our science is progressing, it is not that far into the future when a visit to the moon will be available to everyone. The astral and other planes will be next on this list. This theory will be based on Spirit because science's advancement will merge into a spiritual approach. It will be a widespread conversation: 'When did you last visit the astral plane? The theory of 'The Way to God' will survive because we have to answer to our future science. The truth comes out slowly but surely.

There is no truth in the theory that the earth is hollow or flat, with many layers underneath it. "Gnomes" living under the ground is another false phenomenon; our scientists have already disapproved of this theory with modern technology. A Greek mathematician named Mr Eratosthenes, born in 276 BC, proved that this world is round and the globe's circumference is about 25,000 miles. Sir Christopher Columbus sailed the full circle of this world in 1492 and discovered it is round.

So, there are no Patalas (subterranean layers within or under this globe) as believed by some religions. If you look at the sun, the moon and all the stars in our galaxy, they appear round. 'What makes you think that the earth is flat? First, we are influenced by our religious mythology. Second, there is a lack of education. A sceptical mind is always asking for evidence. So far, most religions have failed to answer people's questions.

Most of the photographs and video shoots have turned out to be hoaxes. The day will come when the evidence will be available. As the saying goes, 'There is no proof without evidence.' I have repeatedly said that most of our present religions will fade away, especially those claiming to be the only ones. A question is often raised about why aliens are shown with two eyes, one nose and one mouth, similar to humans.

Why don't these aliens have four eyes and four ears? This is a good argument. But from my experience, it does not matter which plane you are on; we all have similar features. The only difference is the vibrations we carry. The rate of vibrations will indicate our authority over others. Therefore, aliens have more control over humans. Many farmers have claimed that aliens came and made circles in their crops; these claims all turned out to be hoaxes.

Such circles can be made very quickly without a single foot on the soil as evidence. Some sceptical minds often ask, 'Why don't they contact us openly if the aliens visit us regularly? It is not that they are keeping everything secret from us. We fail to see them because our vibratory rate is not the same or comparable to theirs; this is the only reason. In other words, we are a less spiritually advanced civilisation. Humans will not take long to turn into the alien race.

At present, we are moving very quickly in that direction. If we look back at our human history, we were fighting with fists, sticks, swords and spears. Later we used pistols and multiple shotguns. At present, we are already involved in nuclear wars. 'What could be next? 'An alien War? And that will lead us to the end of Kali-Yuga. Asian religions have always believed in aliens. Recently, Christians also believed. A statement was issued from the Vatican on this subject. I wonder if the Pope has witnessed any aliens or UFOs.

There is also a blue book in the Ministry of Defence that records the sightings of UFOs and over 10,000 sightings are recorded. There are two famous people, Mr George and Mr Billy, who have many snapshots in their possession. 'How genuine are these photographs? Only they know the truth. Mr George Adamski (from the United States) claimed that the aliens took him to visit the solar system and that he and the aliens were on Venus. But he could not prove this.

PHYSICAL UNIVERSE

We will discuss what is within this physical universe, such as planets and galaxies of stars and how they affect our lives.

The solar system

The solar system combines nine planets, asteroids, comets, moons and a galaxy of stars. They are placed with the command of Spirit. The distance from each other, heights and the magnetic fields are all in balance. There is a micro millionth difference in push or pull to each other and the sun. This difference makes them orbit the sun and rotate on axes at some degrees; the nearest planet will orbit in less time.

For example, Mercury is 36 million miles from the sun and it orbits the sun in 88 earth days. On the other hand, Pluto is the farthest from the sun, 3,665 million miles away and it orbits the sun in 248 earth years. Our present scientists have found that each planet rotates at different speeds. This rotation keeps the whole environment healthy below the astral plane and down to this earth.

Secondly, their celestial brightness amuses our minds and this amusement leads us to search and attempt exploration of these planets. This amusement has been created purposely by the Spirit to learn for all souls. On 20 July 1969, man landed on the moon. Since then, farther journeys have been made to different planets. At present, this travelling is via spacecraft called rockets.

Eventually, the spacecraft will improve as the travelling goes deeper and deeper or higher and higher. As mentioned in the chapter on aliens, this search and improvement of our spacecraft will help our science to go beyond light and sound's speed. Eventually, spacecraft will land in the astral plane. Then our physical or human bodies will be migrated to the other planes.

In the future, we will learn how to leave our physical bodies to the side, similar to leaving behind our garments when we change our clothes. We as humans always like to migrate to better countries or places where we find some excitement. Therefore, a poor man wants to relocate to a country where he can prosper financially. Those who have seen enough finance or have enjoyed a better standard of living probably like to study the animal kingdom or sea life.

It always has been believed that aliens from other planets will invade earth. I wonder sometimes, 'What excitement will they find here? This probably will be the most boring place for them, unless they prefer to waste their time here. Once we enter the astral plane, only then will actual exploration for the soul begin. This exploration will be available at our fingertips. The experience is for the soul and the excitement is for the mind and this will lead the 'soul' near and close to God.

During the Golden-Age, our third-eye was visible to communicate within God's world on a spiritual basis. In the future, this communication will be spiritual and scientifically based. This urge to find what is new and the poor living conditions on earth will force us to migrate elsewhere. At present, the population of this planet is on the rise or in a growth pattern. Later due to the chemical-based circumstances, it will tend to decrease.

The fertility of all species and the earth will be almost halted. This world will be like a ghost town. We will create this condition ourselves, just as this happened long ago on Mars and Venus. This is why our scientist suspect life on those two planets. Yes, there once was life. In the future, this statement will apply to us too. With more exploration, we will find this evidence. The human population will be a lot less. At the same time, our scientific improvement will lead humans to leave this planet.

It will be about time to close the chapter of Kali-Yuga. The remaining souls who could not earn good karma will be put into a deep sleep in the physical terms or a bliss state. They will remain in this state until a 'new' physical world is ready to begin the new chapter of the Golden, Silver, Bronze and Iron ages. At the end of the last Kali-Yuga, those souls in a bliss state will be the first to begin a new Satya-Yuga.

Their karmas were not good enough last time to allow them to leave the physical forever. Their siblings will be of a new creation, as a long chain of inexperienced souls are waiting. Like the last time, these humans will have holy thoughts initially. Eventually, their opinions will be contaminated with negativity, leading them to Silver-Age. The whole cycle of Yugas will repeat.

What is a solar system? A solar system is where everything circles the sun. The difference between the universe, galaxies and solar system is in size.

Universe

The universe is the largest of these three because all three are inclusive within the realm of this universe. Scientists believe that this universe is expanding all the time. Yes, this is the law of nature. 'Did you ever contemplate the thought that everything in this universe grows and moves? This includes humans, animals and plants. Otherwise, they are declared as no more. There are several planets between what has already been discovered and the astral plane border is yet to be found.

Galaxy

The galaxy is the total of what we can see in the sky. What we see is held together within this big void or space by the magnetic field, currently known as gravity. This galaxy consists of billions of stars and planets that are constantly moving. This universe is moving all the time via Spirit. Scientists believe that gravity upholds the distance between each planet or the stars.

We call it Spirit because everything was created by it. We may notice that some stars are 'in static position' or the same place since we were young. This is because our present lifespan is too short compared to this minor movement, so we do not notice any change. Our current science does not comment to the movement of these stars but they are moving and expanding; this is the law of nature. This movement is not significant that can be put into some calculations.

This movement from A to Z, known as 360 degrees around the sun, will take millions of years. At present, our lifespan does not exceed much over 100 years. So, noticing any change in the position of these stars is impossible. We can see the difference in some celestial bodies, such as earth, the moon, Mercury, Venus and Mars. The solar system is the smallest of three systems: the sun, moons, asteroids, comets and meteoroids.

Astronomy

The discovery of planets and stars within our galaxy and their positions concerning each other resulted from the dedication or contribution of Indian Hindu philosophy, Chinese, Greek and Babylonian societies. In a real sense, all the planets are stars because they shine. Astronomers are people who are very dedicated to the study of the galaxy. They examine the movement of these planets and make a note of any changes. Astronomy is a vast subject; different departments deal with other matters, such as:

1. Cycles of stars
2. Structure and interaction of stars
3. Entire universe structure

Astronomy is a natural science studying celestial objects such as stars, galaxies, planets, moons and nebulae. It involves the study of physics, chemistry and evolution of such things, whatever is within this universe. To make this possible, a telescope was required. The telescope was invented by someone else around 1600 CE but it became famous in 1609 CE when Galileo Galilee presented it to the world. He discovered the rings around planet Saturn.

He was born on 15 February 1564 in Pisa, Italy. He was a physicist, mathematician and engineer. You need specific skills to educate the mind and leave this treasure for the generations to follow on the physical level. Galileo left precious information from his study and observations, which helped present science progress further. Dapren and I visited all the planets, moons and galaxies.

This experience was noted in my diary dated 27 September 1979, which will appear in our new book. I took this visit as a personal study in those days, so I did not bother to make any notes or write what I witnessed. Spirit has asked me to write on this subject to explain what I saw, so I'll try to cover it briefly. My fellow Seekers struggle to achieve their goals despite being so close to me physically and spiritually.

Spiritual guidance is given openly at present. For example, many years ago, the telephone was rare and limited its use. You can find the whole world on your mobile phone, which is in everyone's pocket. In the same way, this present science will turn into spiritual science and all this travelling and spiritual knowledge will become a way of life. First, they will go against all religions because they fail to provide any evidence but eventually, the way to God will appear and show them the way.

The change in this universe will be instant and the gates into heaven will open. Well done to our scientists for discovering all the planets, names, sizes and distances from the sun. The sun is the centre point, which all the planets orbit and there are many moons on each planet. This distance is measured in miles and the earth is 93 million miles from the sun.

Our scientists have considered it to call the distance 1 AU (astronomical unit). According to this unit, all other planets are measured and science has already discovered almost 150 big or small moons. The big moons are in this chart. The sun has the most substantial gravity of all. That is why all planets orbit the sun.

Name of Planet	Size of Planet miles Diameter	Distance from the Sun Million miles	Moons	Orbit time
Sun	865133	0000	0	0000
Mercury	3032	36	0	88 Days
Venus	7520	67	0	225 Days
Earth	7901	93	1	365 Days
Mars	4201	140	2	2 Yrs
Jupiter	83100	482	17	12 Yrs
Saturn	67576	885	18	29 Yrs
Uranus	31041	1780	21	84 Yrs
Neptune	30256	2790	8	164 Yrs
Pluto	1429	3665	1	248 Yrs

(Ten planets chart)

EARTH PLANETS

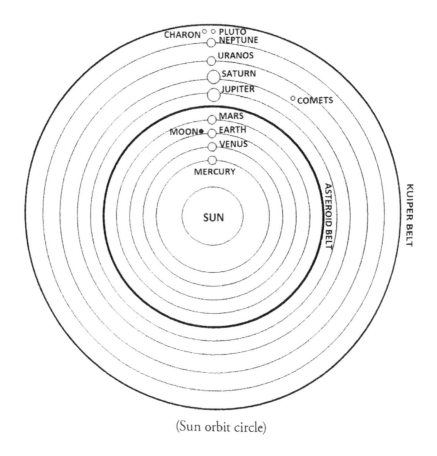

(Sun orbit circle)

Mercury, Venus, Earth and Mars are inner planets. Planets between the asteroid belt and the Kuiper belt are outer planets, as they contain more gas on the surface than the inner planets. The word **planet** is the translation from one

Greek word that means 'wonderer. It means all the planets orbit the sun while all the stars are almost in fixed positions.

Sun

The sun is the giant planet of all. It is the hottest and the centre of all the planets. Due to its strongest magnetic field, all known or unknown planets orbit the sun. Its surface area is 11,900 times that of earth and its diameter is 865,130 miles. It is composed of 75% hydrogen and 25% helium and the overall colour is yellow. The surface temperature is 5,600 degrees Celsius. The light coming from the sun reaches earth in eight minutes and twenty seconds.

It travels at a speed of 186,450 miles per second. The sun is 93 million miles from earth. Our scientists believe that the sun has already used or burned half of its hydrogen. Due to the difference in circumference and magnetic field, the closest planet to the sun will orbit faster than the farthest one. The temperature inside the sun is approximately 15 million degrees Celsius. As you notice, it has a very high temperature. So, it can explode at any time. But due to its enormous gravity force, everything is intact. The sun is responsible for the earth's climate and weather changes.

Sun is the cause for a rainbow to appear. As it appears to us, the light from the sun is white but it is a total of seven colours. You will notice we only see a rainbow during certain weather conditions. Therefore, the word rainbow is taken from rain. Those hanging drops of rain in the sky act as a prism and once this white light passes through the prism, it splits the colours into seven. They are always in the same order; red, orange, yellow, green, blue, indigo and violet. We see the sky as blue and red at sunset due to similar theories.

Mercury

Mercury is the first or closest planet to the sun. This is why its orbit period is 88 earth days. Mercury appears in our earth's sky in the morning or evening but isn't visible at night-time. That is because of its orbit condition in relation to the sun. It is much faster than any other planet. Its atmosphere is freezing. The temperature is –180 degrees Celsius at night and 430 degrees Celsius during the daytime.

The polar diameter is 3,032 miles. One day on Mercury lasts up to 176 earth days and the distance from the sun is 36 million miles. The gravity is approximately 38% compared to earth. Mercury is the closest planet to the sun and does not experience many of the seasons as we do. The temperature is freezing compared to that on earth, although it's so close to the sun.

This is what we call nature. So far, two spacecraft have visited around or near this planet. *Mariner 10* went in 1970 and *Messenger* was launched in 2004 and is still there. The surface of Mercury is mainly 'rock,' a combination of 70% metallic and 30% silicate material. The planet's density and gravity are very similar to those of earth. Metallic content is higher on Mercury than on any other planet.

Although the surface is very similar to the moon, no man has set foot on this planet because our scientists believe the environment is very toxic. It has acidic rains and very high-speed stormy winds and the surface is uneven rock. The surface and atmosphere are the combinations of hydrogen, helium, oxygen, sodium, calcium, potassium and icy surface. The magnetic field is powerful due to its surface properties.

Venus

Venus is the second planet from the sun. It was named after the Roman goddess of love and beauty. It was discovered in the seventeenth century and its orbit period is 225 earth days. The surface temperature is 460 degrees Celsius and the diameter is about 7,520 miles. A day on Venus is longer than an earth year. It takes 243 Earth days to rotate once on its axis. This planet is smaller than the earth and is 67 million miles from the sun.

Satellite on or at Venus is none. Venus is the second brightest star in the sky, so it can be seen during the daytime, provided you know where to look. The atmospheric pressure is ninety times greater than that on earth. It is similar to the bottom of the sea, so humans could not survive. They would be crushed or exploded into small pieces. Identical to Mercury, there are no seasonal variations.

Russia was the first to send spacecraft to Venus in 1961 but failed. With a Venera series probe, their second attempt was launched in 1966. It is believed that Venus had a tropical atmosphere, so life on this planet is possible. It has been found that the planet has a very dense atmosphere due to high temperatures. Its humidity is similar to a greenhouse, known as a hostile environment. The overall surface has very thick clouds of sulphuric acids.

Earth

Earth is the third planet from the sun. Its diameter is approximately 7,901 miles and it orbits the sun in 365.26 days. Therefore, we have 366 days every leap year. At the same time, it spins a full circle in 24 hours. When we face the sun, it is the day; when we are opposite, it is night-time. Earth's surface temperature is 14 to 57 degrees Celsius. Earth's inner and outer core temperature is 6,000 degrees Celsius. In size, it is much larger compared to the moon.

In the olden days, it was believed that the earth was the centre of the universe and all planets were orbiting the earth. Now we know that the sun is the centre of all the planets. Earth is approximately 93 million miles from the sun. Earth's name comes from the Anglo-Saxon word *Erda*, 'supporting life soil.' This is the only planet that is habitable to human life and vegetation. Its habitability is due to the 21% oxygen in the air of one volume. It has water as a liquid on the surface and a soil layer to retain heat.

The latter is responsible for vegetation growth; its natural satellite is the moon. Earth is not as round as we believe. It has a slight bulge towards the equator. That's why it rotates on its axis at 23 degrees. This axis at 23 degrees and the planet's 365-day orbit of the sun is responsible for four seasons. Earth has 3% freshwater pumped out of the soil or in the form of ice. The rest is salt water or other freshwater, evaporating into the atmosphere and returning as rain.

Moon

The moon is in synchronous rotation with Earth. That means the same side will always face earth. The moon orbits the sun once a year or 365 days, the same as earth because the earth and moon orbit the sun simultaneously. The moon orbits around the world in 27.32 days and its polar diameter is approximately 2,159 miles. The surface temperature at night is –170 degrees Celsius and 125 degrees Celsius during the day.

Russia was the first to send spacecraft to the moon in 1959. These were robotic missions of crafts called *Luna 1* and *Luna 2*. On 20 July 1969, the Apollo 11 mission was launched by the United States of America and Mr Neil Armstrong was the first man to set foot on the moon. Missions Apollo and Luna returned home with at least 380 kilograms of rock and soil for future testing.

Effects of the moon

Our monthly calendar is based on the moon's effects. The moon is our natural satellite and provides us light at night. It was beneficial prior to the electric invention. The impacts of the moon have been linked to crime, mental illness, disaster and birth and fertility. But werewolves and Dracula are mythical characters created by our writers or filmmakers, much like Superman and Spiderman. Many psychic people engage in occult rituals, claiming to receive black energy.

In Hinduism, **Karva-Chauth** is a one-day festival celebrated by Hindu married women. They fast from sunrise to moonrise for the safety and longevity of their husbands. They will open the fast once they see the moon.

In Islam, **Eid** is also connected with the moon. It is mentioned in the Qur'an to sight the new moon to begin the month of fasting and end the fasting on sighting the end of the moon cycle.

Solar eclipse

A solar eclipse is when the moon passes before the sun and casts a shadow on the earth. Although the sun's distance from earth is around 400 times the moon's distance and the sun's diameter is 400 times greater than the moon's, as seen from earth, the moon and sun appear to be the same size. That is why the moon covers the whole face of the sun at that time.

Sometimes, it is not a total eclipse, as the moon and earth are at different points because of their rotation, so the moon only manages to cover half or part of the sun. There are two to five small eclipses every year. The longest solar eclipse is every eighteen months and lasts approximately seven minutes and thirty seconds.

Mars

Mars is the fourth planet from the sun; its surface colour is sunset, so it is known as the red planet. Its atmosphere is primarily composed of carbon dioxide. The planet's polar diameter is 4,200 miles, 140 million miles from the sun and it has two moons. Mars has no protective layer of soil, so it cannot store any heat. That is why it is much colder than Earth.

Mars's average surface temperature is –55 degrees Celsius and 20 degrees Celsius midday. It is less than half the size of the earth. Gravity on Mars is 33% in comparison to that on earth. Mars orbits the sun once every two years and one year equals 320 earth days. Seasons are very similar to those on earth but longer. It is believed that "lava" is permanently active.

Although forty missions to Mars have been made, Russia was the first to launch *Marsnik 1* in 1960. Later, other countries followed. This planet has the most significant dust storms. These storms can last for months, covering the entire planet and rendering the visibility of anything is dim. It is very rich in iron, similar to other planets. So far, no known life has been found on Mars.

Jupiter

Jupiter is the fifth planet from the sun and is 320 times larger than earth. Jupiter would be 250% bigger if all the planets were combined. It is next in size to the sun. Jupiter is made up of gases, known as a gas giant. This is one reason that it does not support any life. Its polar diameter is 83,100 miles and its surface temperature is approximately -108 degrees Celsius.

It is the fourth brightest planet in our solar system. Only the sun, the moon and Venus are more brilliant. Jupiter is one of the five planets visible to our naked eye from earth. It is named after a Roman god. The day on Jupiter lasts only approximately ten earth hours. It orbits the sun once every 12 earth years, so weather patterns on the planet are the second reason for not supporting life.

Jupiter is 482 million miles from the sun. The planet's interior is composed of metal, rock and hydrogen. Jupiter has seventeen moons; Ganymede is the giant moon in our solar system. And above it has a ring system composed of icy dust particles. So far, eight spacecraft have visited Jupiter. An automated spacecraft launched for Jupiter in December 1973.

The major problem with Jupiter is that it has no solid surface on which spacecraft can land. The atmosphere on this planet is made up of liquid and has very high radiation levels. Because of these conditions, many systems on spacecraft attempting to explore Jupiter failed.

Saturn

Saturn is the sixth planet from the sun. It is 90% larger than Earth and is the third-largest planet in our solar system. Saturn was discovered by astronomer Mr Galileo Galilee of Italy, who invented the telescope in 1609. the planet's polar diameter is 67,570 miles and 885 million miles from the sun. It has eighteen moons and many small moons and its surface temperature is –178 degrees Celsius.

It is the fifth brightest planet in our solar system and the naked eye can see it. Saturn is one of the flattest planets (discs), whereas other planets are oval or round. It has a very low density and fast rotation. It turns on its axis in approximately ten hours and thirty minutes and has the second shortest day in our solar system. It orbits the sun once every 29 earth years. It is mainly composed of hydrogen and the atmosphere is composed of ice, water, rock, methane and frozen nitrogen.

The first spacecraft to reach Saturn was *Pioneer* back in 1979. It has a powerful magnetic field in comparison to that of earth. Saturn has rings made up of 'ice grains,' which look fabulous. The planet's composition is 96% hydrogen and 3% helium; the remaining 1% is ethane, methane, water, ice and others. This composition of gases shows no sign of any life on this planet. Gravity is very similar to that on earth.

Uranus

Uranus is the seventh planet from the sun and another gas giant; it is impossible to see with the naked eye. A telescope is required. It is a rolling round planet, with its spin axis lying 98 degrees off its orbital plan with the sun and its polar diameter is approximately 31,000 miles. It was discovered on 13 March 1781 by Mr William Herschel.

Uranus turns on its axis once every 17 hours and 15 minutes and its orbit is in the opposite direction of the orbits of the other planets. It orbits the sun once every 84 years and is 1,780 million miles away from it. Uranus is composed of hydrogen, helium, rock, methane and frozen ammonia water/ice, reflecting blue and green colours. It being another gas giant planet indicates no possibility of any life.

The upper surface comprises water, methane and ice crystals, making it the coldest planet in our solar system. The surface temperature on Uranus is –220 degrees Celsius. Uranus has two sets of rings, about thirteen rings in total. It has twenty-one moons and several small moons. So far, only one spacecraft has passed by this planet. That was *Voyager 2* back in 1986.

Neptune

Neptune is the eighth planet from the sun. It is the most distant one and another gas giant that is not visible to the naked eye. Its polar diameter is 30,250 miles and its surface temperature is –210 degrees Celsius. It was discovered on 23 September 1846. It spins around in 19 hours and orbits the sun once every 164 years. It is 2,790 million miles away from the sun.

It is one of the minor ice giants composed of hydrogen, helium, methane, water, ice and rock. Overall, the colour of Neptune is blue with thin clouds and very high-speed winds. Neptune, another gas giant, has no chance of human life;

similar to Jupiter, it has several rings. It has eight moons and some small moons. It is one of the coldest planets.

So far, only one spacecraft has passed by it—*Voyager 2* in 1989.

Pluto

Pluto is the ninth planet from the sun, though lately, it is not considered a planet but only a dwarf planet. It is the smallest of all planets in our solar system. It has its moon named Charon. The surface temperature is –220 degrees Celsius. Pluto makes one journey around the sun every 248 earth years and it is 3,665 million miles away from the sun. It was discovered back on 18 February 1930.

Pluto is composed of dangerous gases, such as carbon monoxide, methane and nitrogen. It orbits the sun on a different plan than the other eight planets, going over or below in a circle. Pluto is only 1,429 miles wide and its moon Charon is 745 miles wide. **One day** on Pluto is equal to approximately seven earth days and Pluto is only visible with the help of a telescope. The density of Pluto is very light; 100 kilograms on earth will act like 7 kilograms on Pluto.

On 14 July 2015, the United States' first spacecraft flew above the surface of Pluto.

Charon

Charon is one of the fifth moons relating to Pluto and it was discovered in 1978 by the United States. Since four more moons have been found, therefore Pluto has five moons. Charon's temperature is approximately –220 degrees Celsius, its orbital inclination is at 96 degrees and its rotation period is 6.5 earth days. Like Earth's moon, Charon keeps the same face towards Pluto during its rotation. Charon is covered by frozen water and like the moon, it does not rise or set but remains the same.

Kuiper belt

The Kuiper belt is made up of billions of ice objects. It is like a frozen edge or boundary over all the planets, composed of ice, methane, ammonia and water. It could be the crossing line between the physical and the astral plane.

NASA

The National Aeronautics and Space Administration is the US agency responsible for the nation's space programs and similar research. Most US space exploration is the effort of NASA, which put the first man on the moon. The agency is also responsible for space stations, shuttles and international space stations. NASA was formed on 29 July 1958 and its headquarters are in Washington DC. It is the contribution of NASA that gives us practical insight into these planets.

Satellite

A satellite is an artificial object intentionally placed into 'orbit' with the help of rockets. Satellites are computer-controlled systems. They are used for many purposes, such as military services and civilian earth observations. In this world, there are approximately 6,500 satellites. About 1,000 are working actively and the rest are out of date or known as debris. The first satellite was launched on 4 October 1957 by the Soviet Union.

Russia was the first to make a move into space. Russia is currently not doing well, which has been the case since the break-up of the Iron Curtain. The United States always followed in Russia's footsteps, launching its first Satellite on 2 January 1958 and the rest of the world was third in line. Nowadays, several space stations have been launched. Again, Russia launched Salyut 1, the first space station, on 19 April 1971.

ASTROLOGY

All stars and planets are for a purpose and affect everyone in this universe. How do they orbit around the sun and this rotation creates an effect? Each star sign in astrology represents one or more planets in the house. As I said earlier, all these planets are moving. Our present or future is dictated by the position of these planets at the time of birth. Therefore, having a correct date of birth is very important.

Fortune tellers are fully trained in this field to know what to look at. Nowadays, some people have worked exceptionally hard in this field; they have managed to feed all the information into the computer systems. Any person can know the future within seconds based on the date, time and place of birth. The future is based on your karma, date of birth and these planets' position.

Experts in astrology use several charts, usually with twelve sections (houses) and work out the position of these planets at the time of a person's birth. Or they may determine in which home a particular star sign was at the time and what other planets were affecting it. Then there is a time limit for these planets to move from their positions. Some move faster than others. The movement of these planets brings changes in our good or bad luck.

This movement of planets also affects the chemistry of our physical bodies. Many species depend on this movement or the position of the moon. This world's population depends on the earth, moon and sun. Another experience was dated 8 April 1980, when I was taught Para vidya. Para vidya was released to me and the significance of the numbers 3, 5, 7 and 12 was revealed.

The solar system is a vast subject. It does not matter how much you have written. It is never enough. Some dedicated people have spent all their lives on this subject. This search can be traced back 15,000 years. What is written so far is basic information. Different researchers have their own opinions. Many times, more than one planet is ruling your star sign.

ZODIAC SIGN	DATES	SYMBOL	PLANETS	ELEMENT	SEASONS	HOW MANY MOONS
ARIES	21MAR--19APR	RAM	MARS	FIRE	SPRING	2
TAURUS	20APR--20MAY	BULL	VENUS	EARTH	SPRING	0
GEMINI	21MAY--21JUN	TWINS	MERCURY	AIR	SPRING	0
CANCER	22JUN--22JUL	CRAB	MOON	WATER	SUMMER	Itself
LEO	23JUL--22AUG	LION	SUN	FIRE	SUMMER	0
VIRGO	23AUG--22SEP	MAIDEN	MERCURY	EARTH	SUMMER	0
LIBRA	23SEP--23OCT	SCALE	VENUS	AIR	AUTUMN	0
SCORPIO	24OCT--21NOV	SCORPION	MARS	WATER	AUTUMN	2
SAGITTARIUS	22NOV--21DEC	ARCHER	JUPITER	FIRE	AUTUMN	4
CAPRICORN	22DEC--19JAN	GOAT	SATURN	EARTH	WINTER	9
AQUARIUS	20JAN--18FEB	WATERMAN	SATURN	AIR	WINTER	9
PISCES	19FEB--20MAR	FISHES	JUPITER	WATER	WINTER	4
			EARTH			1
			URANUS			6
			NEPTUNE			2
			PLUTO			1

(Twelve star signs chart)

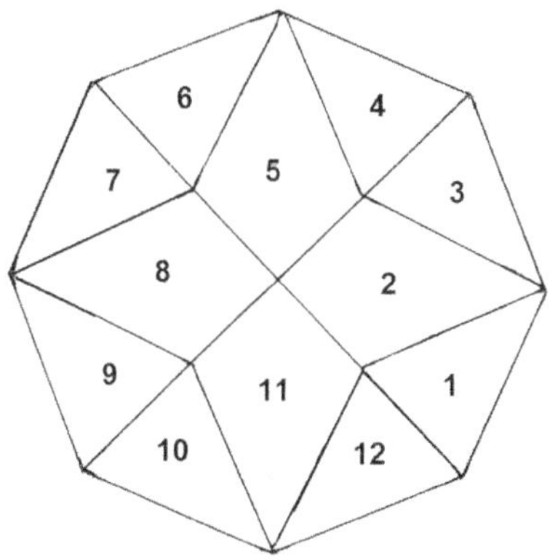

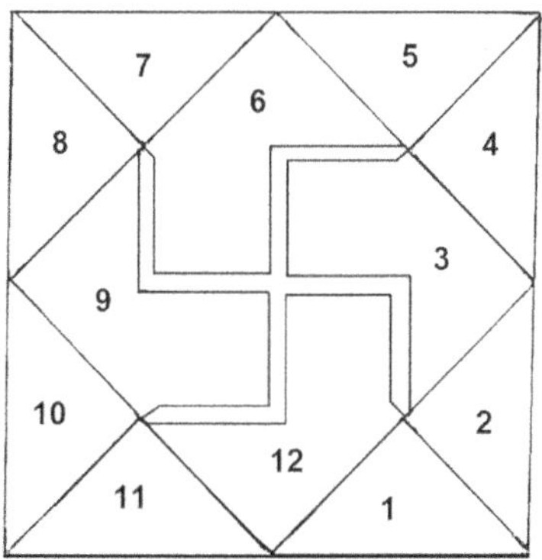

(Two-by-twelve section charts)

Earth orbits the sun at 18.5 miles per second or 66,600 miles per hour or 1,598,400 miles per day. Because of this speed, we do not acknowledge any movement. Due to Earth's rotation, day and night occur because we do not face the sun for twenty-four hours.

Again, the moon has a rotation of approximately thirty days. The light provided to us on any night depends on its orbit, whether a full moon or half; that is another theory.

A full moon is when it is in line with the sun and earth. In other words, the moon is equal to or opposite to the sun concerning the earth (see chart).

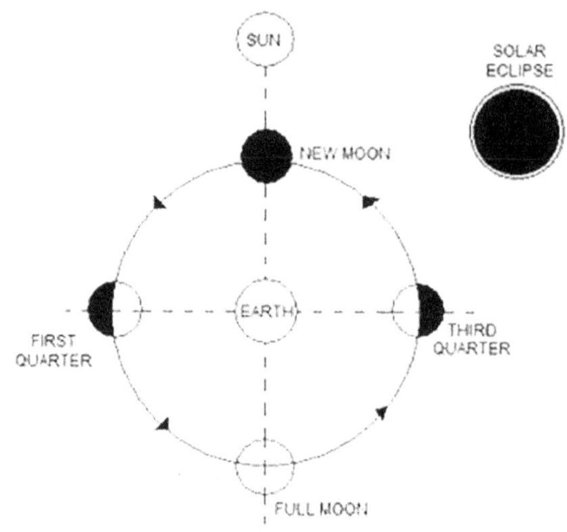

(Moon eclipse chart)

Earth rotates for 24 hours and once a year (365 days) around the sun. That is why we have the four seasonal changes. We are not facing the sun entirely all through the year. This earth's rotation is also at 23 degrees, another rotation within the main rotation. Leap year is part of this—365.26 days or 366 days. In other words, the earth's rotation at 23 degrees itself and at the same time, it is revolving around the sun. This is responsible for long days and short nights or vice versa.

Within the last few years, our scientists have managed to bring back samples from some of the planets. This will help us to learn and it will encourage future exploration. This exploration will go further and further. As you notice, all the planets orbit the sun. Where the circles of this universe end, following are the circles of the astral plane and further inner processes will be explored with newfound technology. Now, 'who was the first to study these planets and stars?

What were his capabilities for doing this? And how effective were his calculations? Our knowledge about the planets and stars that we call astrology comes from the contribution of many countries such as; India, China and the Islamic world. One person lived beyond our recorded history whose calculations are still used today. They are being challenged by many scholars, who have been unable to find them wrong. His name was Rishy Bhrigu. We will discuss his findings in the next chapter.

China

Astrology in China can be traced back to 3000 BC. Chinese astrology is very close to its religious philosophy. Key components are three harmonies: heaven, earth, water and the principle of yin and yang. Yin means negative and yang represents positive. They believe that if both are maintained in balance, harmony is accomplished. It is similar to the karma theory of keeping everything balanced to have a good and happy life.

Babylonians, Iraq

Babylonian contributions can be traced back to 2000 BC in the form of thirty-two tablets with inscribed liver models.

Worldwide

Worldwide, astrological studies can be traced back to 3000 BC. The advanced thinkers in their respective countries knew that some of these 'stars' were moving, leading to our current discoveries. Later, it was discovered that these celestial bodies also affect us on earth. Later, we found that the big stars are actually 'planets,' which led to further exploration.

At present, we know enough. But our knowledge is not even a scratch on the surface. All these stars or planets also move, known as breathing. In this universe, everything must move and expand. Otherwise, it cannot survive. This is the law of nature.

RISHI BHRIGU

Rishi Bhrigu was a saint of the Brahmin caste and his residence (ashram) was on the bank of the Vadhusar River, presently on the borders of Haryana and Rajasthan, India. During the times of Lord Vishnu, he was the son of Sage Varun. Other saints chose him to test Brahma, Vishnu and Shiva to know who is the most outstanding Master. When he went to see Lord Brahma, he disrespected him; Bhrigu cursed Brahma, telling him that he would not be worshipped in Kali-Yuga.

He paid his second visit to Shiva, where Shiva and Parvati were sporting fun, so entry was not granted. He cursed Shiva, saying he would only be worshipped in linga form. His last visit was to Lord Vishnu, who was in a deep sleep. As Lord Vishnu did not respond to his visit, Bhrigu felt insulted. He got angry and hit Vishnu in the chest with his foot on his way out. Upon awakening, Vishnu asked about his well-being. Then Bhrigu declared that Vishnu was the greatest.

Laxmi witnessed the whole incident and got angry and cursed him that you Brahmins (caste) will never see the face of Laxmi (money) and all your caste people will face poverty. Bhrigu explained the purpose of his visit, asked forgiveness for his hostile act from Laxmi and requested that she free him from her curse. Laxmi calmed down and pardoned him. However, she said, 'I cannot free you from this curse.

But I ask you to write an astrology book to help your caste people earn their livelihood.'

Being a saint, Bhrigu was capable of writing this book and it was given the name of *Bhrigu Samhita*. Originally it was written on palm leaves in the Sanskrit language. Later it was translated to Tamil. Bhrigu wrote 525,975 different calculations to cover each minute of the year, including leap year (365.26 days). It is believed that *Bhrigu Samhita* can only be used after performing some rituals. Then a page from the book will open itself as required.

Rishi Bhrigu was the most original person to study the planets and stars and their effect on humans. His original book was only one handwritten copy on palm leaves, which was the property of the Brahmin caste. Many races have invaded India, so that book has gone underground. Today's books claim to be copies of that book. But many are inaccurate, while others are frauds.

These 525,975 calculations can be turned into a calculation for every second (525,975 × 60 = 31,558,500). These many calculations were required to cover every single date of birth concerning the time and position of the planets. The horoscopes were drawn according to the position of all planets, such as the sun, Mercury, Venus, Earth, the moon, Mars, Jupiter, Saturn, Uranus and Pluto. Rahu and Ketu are two nodes.

These are 'still-time' readings but Flexi readings over the millennium could be as many as 28.4 million. All other countries came later to provide astrological readings. *Bhrigu Samhita* displays the art of preparing the chart, known as Janma-Kundli, which is equivalent to Zodiac signs. Saint

Bhrigu's predictions are comparable to the Akashic records to tell the past, present and what will happen to an individual in the future.

Most of the information fed into our present computer system is based on the calculations of Saint Bhrigu. Some copies of the original writings are believed to be kept in Banaras, Puna and Meerut. Things were made easy for the Brahmin caste for generations to come. They can look into the past, present and future of anyone interested in knowing at some charge.

It is believed that Saint Bhrigu lived some 10,000 years ago in India. One thing always astonishes me is that Hinduism relates saints such as Bhrigu and others with Brahma, Vishnu and Shiva. The time mentioned as 10,000 years is totally out of date. These three lords have not physically set foot on this earth for hundreds of thousand years.

Hinduism

Hinduism claims Saint Bhrigu was here in Treta-Yuga, the beginning of Hinduism. I don't want to know at what point in time of Treta-Yuga was here. After Treta, Dwapara-Yuga came and it lasted approximately 864,000 years. Now Kali-Yuga has extended over 5,122 years. I notice Hinduism is underestimating itself in many ways; Hinduism knows what the truth is but has no evidence.

THE EFFECT OF PLANETS

Sun—Surya: The sun is the king of all planets, so it is considered a life-giver. The effect of the sun creates one's unique identity and creative ability, how one faces challenges in life and strong willpower. So, it is the most powerful planet. Medicine affects the heart, circulatory system, bones and eyes.

Mercury—Buddha: Mercury is the messenger planet. It brings good luck. The effect of Mercury is achieving good results overall. It is the planet of mental communication. It is concerned with super-intelligence. Mercury people are always communicative and have strong personalities. As for medical effects, Mercury is associated with one's nervous system.

Venus—Shukra: As the planet of beauty and love, anything pleasant is the symbol of Venus. Venus is the driving force behind one's behaviour. Venus is a friendly planet. It has the capability of building a relationship and is responsible for emotional satisfaction. So, it represents the circle of Spirit and love. When positive, a Venus person is charming, affectionate and artistic. In medical effects, Venus relates to veins, throat and kidneys.

Moon—Chandra: This planet is known as the soul. It represents the child within us. It is known as a creative and receptive planet. The positive effects are a well-settled nature and harmony at home. The moon is feminine and has great concern for self-security and others. Medicine's effects are on the digestive system, breasts, menstruation and the pancreas.

Mars—Mangal: Mars is the planet of strong willpower and 'ego.' Its effect on us is that we are courageous, energetic, bold and strong individuals. A Mars person will have aggressive urges and may lose their temper if things are not done. At the same time, Mars is associated with the unluckiness of brides. Medicine's effects relate to the masculine system.

Jupiter—Brihaspati: Jupiter is the planet of justice. A Jupiter person will have the qualities of moderation and kindness and greater insight into religion and philosophy. Jupiter people can explore the self and always want to go further in life. They are willing to take the risk. This planet is associated with the liver, the pituitary gland and fats disposition in medicine.

Saturn—Shani: Leads the way to God or duty. Saturn relates to the ability to control oneself, including self-discipline and persistence. A Saturn person is a hard task-master. Such people don't prefer to waste time, are good timekeepers, feel happy in mental maturity and may experience loneliness.

Uranus—Indra: The planet of the awakener, Uranus is related to the overall drive for freedom and independence. Uranus people are not much interested in whether they are socially accepted, as they feel ahead of the surrounding atmosphere. They are always willing to challenge injustice; they are true individuals or unique people. Medicine effects include the nervous system, mental disorders, hysteria, spasms and cramps.

Neptune—Varun: Neptune is the God of the sea and drives to transcend the planet of vision. Neptune people are aliens to others in thought because of their character. Their visions are beyond ordinary thinking. Medicine effects include the spinal canal, neuroses and the thalamus.

Pluto—Yam: Pluto is the planet of wealth. Pluto people will be driven to transform themselves, as Pluto is the planet of renewal. These people are quite tuned and not to be taken very lightly. Medicine's effects include regenerative forces in the body, involving cell formation and the reproductive system.

Charon: A Charon person will have the drive to heal their self-image and the willpower to overcome any sufferings.

Two nodes—Rahu and Ketu: Are Chhaya (shadowy) planets. They are the life paths known as the dragon. These are two north and south poles, opposite each other, where the moon's path crosses the ecliptic. North represents the dragon's head and south represents the tail.

SCIENTIFIC FACTS OF HUMAN LIFE

Similar to others, Christians are the same regarding the birth of Adam and Eve. According to their scholars, Adam and Eve were born approximately 6022 years ago, when our scientists talk in millions of years. For example, scientists found human bones and laboratory tests reveal their age far beyond these religious years. This is a clear indication that a real saint has not existed in these religions for a long time.

Their scholars have no authority over proper timings, as they cannot look back into the past to trace an appropriate record of when the events took place or look into the future. To find out the truth, you have to know beyond time. Some believe that copies of the original *Bhrigu Samhita* on palm leaves are kept in the Hoshiarpur library in Punjab. A Brahmin family is the caretaker of these writings.

These leaves are believed to be over 500 years old. However, saint Bhrigu was not from this area. Upon requests for readings; present pandits (scholars) in this library draw the charts after knowing your name, date and place of birth. Two charts are drawn. They look for identical copies of what they have drawn from or within these old leaves as they are placed in bundles. The exact leaf is found.

It mentions the name and the purpose of your visit. Information about your past life, present and future forecast is given. Astrology has helped to drive astronomy development and further studies lead us to explore these planets. Practical visits and the findings of our present science are contradictory to our religious beliefs. So, it is a learning point for us. Sometimes what we see 'is not,' or what we don't see 'it is.'

*The practical exploration of our scientists and their findings.

*Astrology calculations, such as the movement of these planets and their effects on us.

NASA has declared there is no life on any planet, so there are no chances of invasion. But to the contrary, we are trying to explore these planets, which is an invasion from our side. Now, 'Who are these aliens who don't exist or us to them, if there are any? This is very brief information on the subject.

I could write three times more. I don't think that would be enough either. I hope you have enjoyed it. The list below contains some of the facts found by our scientists. They are not to be taken lightly by our religious bodies. Otherwise, one day you will know how out of step you are. I can already see the results. Here are the facts:

*According to the study and findings of our scientists, the age of our solar system is 4.5 billion years.

*The distance between all planets and the sun is in million miles.

*Human remains found by Israeli archaeologists date back 400,000 years. A set of 8 teeth were found in a cave.

*It is accepted that Homo sapiens lived in East Africa 200,000 years ago.

*Human bones were found of at least 28 people in a cave in northern Spain. DNA tests reveal they are approximately 400,000 years old. New York University confirmed that these remains are older than 300,000 years with geological technique.

*20 kilometres from Chandigarh, Punjab, India, French and Indian archaeologists discovered human remains. They're waiting for the final results but they say these remains could be as old as 2 million years.

We cannot sit down and hold onto our guns and say we are always right. All I can say is that the timing of the origin of Adam and Eve and Hinduism is totally out of date. Other religions can be traced because they are not that old. These are only a few facts but you can find thousands more.

POWER OF MEDITATION

The journey of the soul and its spiritual success depends on how we do our meditation. This is the direct path, where you can experience a spiritual journey alive in this lifetime. The spiritual exercises must be practised daily and dedicated to making it alive. Your success depends on attitude and how you apply gentle attention. I am very disappointed with many people; who have not scratched the surface of spirituality.

Though they have followed the teachings for over forty years, after all these years, the common complaints are the same: I cannot concentrate properly. My thoughts are wandering everywhere. I do not see the inner Master. I do not see the divine light or hear the sound. Recently many people have come to see me and these are the common problems they face. For this, the reasons are many. I can conclude that almost everyone is not meditating correctly.

First, 'Do you know what you are following? 'Do you know the purpose of these teachings? Many are following because others or family are following. I should let you know these teachings are designed to train you to become a saint if in doubt. Now the question is, 'Are you prepared for it? If you are, make a fresh start. It is never too late. Every tool has been provided in my book, *The Way to God*.

To access these tools, read the chapter on **soul travel** thoroughly, once, twice or more, until you feel you have reached the bottom. You can ask if you do not understand; I am always close. I love to help those who want to learn. Your success is my aim. I have noticed that the cause for failure is that we are not meditating correctly; sluggish methods are applied during this period. I asked one person, 'How do you meditate?

The question was raised because this person told me he was doing lots of meditation in real life. I noticed this person was suffering from all known domestic and health problems. This person revealed that all the Meditation (Bhakti) was done while lying in bed. What a lazy way of finding God. You are lying in bed and want to become or be under training as a saint. I have never heard of a saint in history lying in bed and finding God.

Saints are willing to follow any instructions or method regardless of how hard it may be to fulfil their desire to meet the creator. Sitting in lotus fashion is very common. During my travels in India, I have seen many saints stand on one leg for long hours and with minimum food. I do not wish for anyone to follow the path of asceticism but our way is effortless. The recommended position is known as tailor fashion.

If meditation is practised while lying in bed or on a sofa, you will face all the known physical problems. Therefore, I noticed that all our members face above-average problems. I know one or two, individuals who said they are successful. Most of them are in crying situations. This is another point. I never knew that saints cry. History is full of evidence, especially those saints who suffered at the hands of the villains.

Many were slaughtered, hanged, shot or crucified. But till their last breath, they were reciting spiritual words. They did not complain and took it as the will of God. The question is, 'What is or was their strength? From 'Where did they get this kind of stamina? The answer is meditation. They are in meditation all day and night. To them, nothing else matters or bothers them. With this recitation, you come to a point where spiritually, you are so strong that no problem does or will bother you.

Problems come into saints' lives more than for an average person. All those entangled in the problem world have a long way to go to achieve their goals. Sometimes I wonder about these crying people, 'What teachings do they follow? The same goes for those who do not leave their negative habits, too many to mention. There are no shortcuts for anyone; who want to become spiritually strong and achieve some spiritual ground.

All these years, you have tried simple methods and failed. To discipline yourself is the basic requirement. The meditation must be done by sitting in a tailor fashion or sitting on the sofa or on a chair with your feet touching the floor, your back erect and chin slightly up but relaxed. The recitation of the '**word**' during meditation must be uninterrupted for one hour. A half-hour twice can be done but do not make it a habit.

It would help if you recite your word during waking hours until you sleep. The Spirit will take responsibility for recitation during the sleeping period. I recommend you read the chapter on fasting. It explains how you can manage to recite your word all day and every day. Your vibrations will be sky-high and beyond; you will be **no more** a crying baby. Now you will be the knower of truth and probably the way shower to the others, valued assistant to the Master and God.

'Do you want to become the Master of your destiny or be toyed by destiny? Successful people are experiencing a state; where their feet are on the ground but dwell in the higher worlds. We dream of having a higher state of consciousness; 'Who wants to make this effort? Only a few. It is about time to wake up and be counted as one of God's own. With meditation, you can achieve a high state of consciousness. There are no shortcuts on the way to God.

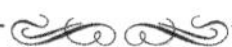

WORD

Many people are not aware that the **word** runs the entire world and universes. This word created all the universes and we have our being and breathing within this word. The word is the creative and communicative force of God. God breathes in and out to communicate with the soul. In return, the soul travels on the vehicle to communicate with God, which helps the soul become aware of its creator. With this awareness, the soul becomes the knower 'as I am it and it is me.'

All the saints have emphasised the importance of the word. In Sikhism, it is known as 'Anhad shabda.' In Christianity, it is mentioned as the **word.** Christ has been known as the word made flesh. Though many people are not aware, Christ as consciousness or soul was indeed word made flesh. When any awakened soul takes a physical body, that time, it is word made flesh. As mentioned earlier, it is the creative force of God.

Many religions call it divine light and sound. **Bani** again indicates the word, so **'Elahi Bani'** means God's word. Similarly, the word **Elahi** is driven by the word **Allah.** It is the name of God in the Islam religion. The Elahi Bani means the word coming from deep within that part known as the presence of God. The whole mechanism of the individual 'soul' is based on this. Any awakened soul is searching for this word to make its way to the creator God.

'Why do we search for this word? It is the craving within us. It does not matter who we are and what status we hold. But something within is nudging and making us realise that something is missing. With our good karma, known as spiritual unfoldment, we become the Seekers. Again, it is an individual search. When Seekers find the true Master, they give the message to all their friends and families.

I have often seen all the family join or become members of the religious organisation run by this saint. Some people join because they become emotional after hearing some stories known as miracles. We cannot become Seekers based on our emotions. Therefore, many people come and leave. We cannot expect all these people to be genuine Seekers. I do not know what you understand about this one word, **Seeker.**

As far as I am concerned, the Seeker is a person on their way to becoming a saint. So, to become a saint, you better be serious. You cannot turn back or give up. You must strive toward God to achieve your spiritual goal. It is just like any athlete who learns to play any game at the school level and later under the supervision of a coach, eventually making it up to the Olympics; must continually focus and strive.

Olympic athletes achieve a gold or silver medal according to their efforts. The guru or teacher is your coach. The guru will guide and teach; you listen and practice. In return, your practice brings perfection. Nothing will materialise if you do not listen or practice what has been told. I have seen many people who do not listen or practice and adequately believe themselves as serious God Seekers. For these people, nothing will materialise; it does not matter whom they are following.

To a true Seeker, only a few words of wisdom and small practice is good enough to make them alive. They become alive and this 'word' rolls within all day and night. The importance of the word can be explained in many ways. There is a word known as the creative force, through which the whole world or all universes were created. That word will not suit all; it is as powerful as God. We will not be able to withstand its power.

According to our spiritual stamina, the guru is aware of our state of consciousness and will give the word during initiation. There are millions and billions of words to suit the whole creation. Every spiritual Seeker must have their word to suit vibrations. The word given by their guru is a particular mantra. It is similar to placing a fuse into the wire to make it live. Without this fuse, the circuit formed by the cables is known as an open circuit; therefore, no current flows.

Any spiritual Seeker can read any known holy book in the world as many times as possible; it will never make you spiritually alive. It can give you enormous spiritual knowledge but you will never become spiritually alive. By chanting your secret word, you can. You only need to recite it a few times during your spiritual exercise and waking state. Doing this helps to stir the vibrations at the 'third-eye' to the level of sun and moon worlds at Ashta-dal-Kanwal.

This is the meeting point between the Seeker and the Master and the spiritual journey begins. You can stay at the seashore by reading the holy books and being loaded with religious knowledge. Or you can dive into the ocean with a single word. I have heard of all religious leaders; who believe in religion based on the masses. They make fun of the concept of individuality; when they don't even know, what we are discussing here.

Now, 'What can you expect from these people? They are misled and instruct the same misguidance to their followers. The word given by your guru is secret and unique; it must never be revealed or discussed with anybody. Once uttered in the open, it will not hold the same vibratory rate or power as before. So, it may not work according to your spiritual expectations. The word is the activating ingredient in your spiritual life.

Keep it safe, as you need it every day until it will lead you to the point of spiritual advancement. Later your teacher or guru will intervene again to change the word, leading you to the next level of unfoldment. The guru is similar to your sports coach, who can give you exercise or techniques to lead you to the Olympics. The exercises and techniques we practice must be changed with our progress, whether in sports or spirituality.

There is always a plus element in all the fields. You must keep striving towards your goal until you have reached your destination or are satisfied. Without the guru or the word, nothing is possible. Most religions are brainwashing their followers not to follow this teaching. They are under the influence of fear, the fear of losing you. These people are not the well-wishers of your spiritual being. Any person can join me any time they wish. At the same time, they can leave me any time as well.

To join or to leave is an individual choice. I am here to teach individuality and will continue to do so as long as I live. That is all that matters to the Spirit and me. God is an individual and it will remain the same forever. Thus, it deals with each soul on an individual basis. You are individual and yet part of God. So be counted as one of its own. Your spiritual word will lead you to this knowingness; one day, you will become the knower of truth and teach others.

TREE OF WISDOM

Once upon a time, a seed was sown in the soil. The person who planted the tree was a sage man. He knew this seed would grow and become a tree of wisdom one day. Before planting it, a good thought was given and all the preparations were made for the tree's future. After a few days, a small plant with two golden leaves appeared.

A new experience had begun. It already had a lot of wisdom but there was more to learn. The planter had a tremendous love for this little plant; he watered the plant from time to time and talked to it. The little plant had good company and security while its new assignment took place. It was looking forward to the new experience.

After a short time, a few branches appeared with many leaves instead of two small leaves. It was a dramatic experience to go through the four seasons—spring, summer, autumn and winter. It was learned that the leaves were not permanent; they would come and go. Winds came, snow fell and birds and children often pulled the branches down.

But this wisdom tree never complained. It had learned in a short time that to make a complaint was a waste of time. Complaints halt the progress. Every moment was a good experience; a pearl of new wisdom was received. It was a gift to those who deserve it. Every year, the tree grew a little. During the spring, it sprouted fresh leaves.

It was a good sight and pleasing to all eyes. But in autumn, those leaves would fall and that routine continued. The tree reached new heights; its branches were more flexible, its thick trunk and the roots firmer. Now it was ready for any weather, any season. It learned the law of balance and patience through ups and downs and the vagaries of bad weather.

It understood living in the present and reliance on its planter. The tree planter also knew that the tree was ready and he could, along with the others, enjoy the shade in summer and the sight and fragrance of the blossom in spring.

Now indeed, it was a wisdom tree.

GHOSTS

We often use or hear these words: 'What are ghosts? A ghost is the Spirit of a dead person, the one believed to appear in body form or likeness to loved ones or people in general or to haunt former habitats. Sometimes they can appear in full flesh or they could appear as shadowy visions. Some people are excited to tell ghostly stories. Some try to avoid it because listening causes a shiver of fear to run through their bodies.

Many will lose sleep because their dreams will be full of ghosts and they are afraid to sleep. They know a ghost will appear as soon as their eyes are closed. Some will try not to enter a dark room or space because they don't know what to expect. 'Now the question is, have you ever seen a ghost? Some don't believe in the existence of ghosts. A good percentage of people believe in or have seen a ghost at least once in their lives.

'How does a person become a ghost? There could be many answers to this question. There are many tell-tale stories with which I must disagree. It is believed that a greedy person with lots of money and unwilling to share will not leave this world after death. We have seen movies and books on this subject, such as the well-known Christmas story featuring Mr Scrooge. These stories may not be accurate. But there are chances that they carry a sliver of truth.

Suppose a person dies accidentally or is killed under abnormal circumstances. In that case, there is a possibility that the Spirit of that person will not leave the physical arena or the place of living. Accidental death means the person who died was not expected to die yet and the **angels of death** did not appear to collect this soul. Accidental death is an incredible experience for anyone. The spiritual journey soul was going through has been cut short and now it has become a wandering soul.

This person, whom we now call a ghost, is going through a terrifying experience. They can see loved ones but fail to communicate with them because the living cannot hear or see this person's 'ghost.' There are chances that a person who has experienced an accidental death sometimes does not even realise that they are dead. Not getting any response from loved ones could be a very frustrating experience.

Some ghosts are helpless to harm anyone, as they live in fear of further torture because of the circumstances they have died. Perhaps they have been through a dramatic situation. They feel safe staying within the boundary of their dwellings and trying to hide in the dark corners. It is possible that if you walk into that dark spot with a neutral state of consciousness, out of nowhere, you might see someone standing there.

A person with strong willpower may not get scared, while others could become mentally disturbed for days. They will not enter that room in the future. Sometimes you cannot see but sense the presence of someone. These ghosts living in that room will always look after their belongings, the ones they had while living. If someone tries to touch or throw away things that belonged to them, they won't be happy and could get angry and try to teach a lesson to the person involved.

If you move something around for whatever reason in the room that person has occupied, you will be surprised to learn something you moved earlier is still in the same place when you come back next time, where it was sitting initially. Now that is a clear sign that someone's Spirit is there. Or you can give yourself the benefit of the doubt and conclude that you did want to move the object but forgot to do so.

If you experience the same thing many times, you know someone is there. It is advised not to interfere anymore—that is, if you don't want anything unpleasant to happen to you. There are many kinds of ghosts; ordinary ghosts, accidental death ghosts or martyred ghosts, cheel, demons, devils or negative energies and hundreds more.

Ordinary ghosts; a typical ghost is one who passed away from physical and did not manage to leave this world. This kind of ghost is harmless. Accidental-type spirits are powerful and at times, they can be very demanding from close family. They hold psychic powers to harm someone if the demands are not fulfilled. Their demands could be regular and continue for generations to follow until a practitioner or a saint can show them the way to heaven or spiritual planes.

Martyrs; Martyrs are mighty ghosts because they have chosen to die for a purpose. Those who die during wars between two or more countries are ghosts. They joined the army to serve their country or were forced to join or some life circumstances pushed them in this direction. Joining the army, navy or air force is good but no one can forecast what could be expected the next day.

It is not the soldiers who fight; most likely; it is a political war. The soldiers who die will be buried or cremated with full honours and medals will be given to the families. That is accepted practice in this world. 'Has anyone given a thought to the well-being of that soldier's soul? At present, that soldier could be a wandering soul. Most of the soldier ghosts are helpful.

Once I was working as a gas engineer and during my work, I became friendly with the person in charge of the premises. He was an ex-soldier and I told him I would like to learn pistol or rifle shooting. He suggested that it is always best practice not to learn to shoot. Otherwise, once you know, it will lead to further exploitations. I agreed with his suggestion. He told me an exciting real-life story about a fight in his country.

Being an ex-soldier, he was assigned to guard his village and a few others. He was not keen to fight but he could not refuse. It was night duty but he loved his sleep. One night while on duty, he was in the local cemetery and very badly wanted to sleep. While he was thinking about rest, a ghost appeared, also an ex-soldier. The ghost told him to sleep next to his grave. 'If someone comes,' the ghost said, 'I will wake you up.'

At first, he feared this incident but he chose to sleep.

After a few days, he felt comfortable with the ghost. This fight carried on for months. During that time, the ghost would wake him whenever he sensed someone was coming.

He said, 'Once I gained confidence that this ghost was helpful, I felt better and enjoyed my sleep every night.' He was very thankful to the wandering Spirit of this person who had lost his life; under what circumstances, no one knows. Now you see, this kind of ghost is helpful because they are trained in how to save lives.

Cheel; Is a name given to a female ghost who did not choose to die but was pushed to her deathbed by circumstances. This happens typically or used to happen when medical help was not available to the woman giving birth to her first child, living in a remote area or without someone available to help her. When she was in pain, the delivery of her child could be easy; at times, it could be a nightmare, especially when there was no helping hand.

The child may have been born safely or at times, still-born babies were as well. During this experience, the lady suffers the most dramatic experience. In a few cases, ladies died due to excessive blood loss. 'Can you imagine the pain she has been through? So, she becomes 'cheel.' This kind of ghost is never happy because the circumstances of her death were not pleasant. She will never leave the place of her death.

If you see a cheel, you will notice her clothes are covered in blood stains. If you walk into that room and see her, never challenge her by asking questions. She is not very happy if she sees a newborn baby in the family. Her single touch on this child could result in death. This kind of ghost is powerful and can manage to give a full-blast punch. This is my very close personal experience.

Martyr ghosts; Known as shahid, martyr ghosts are mighty ghosts. They are the people who gave their lives to some spiritual cause or fought for righteousness. In Islam, this struggle is known as jihad. Christians, Sikhs and Hindus have their names. As the cause of their death is spiritual, this is their belief. And up to some extent, their thoughts were also spiritually based.

These ghosts or shahid are powerful and can be seen at times. Usually, they appear at places where religious war occurs. Their visibility at times helps the soldiers gain confidence or boost morale. I have heard numerous stories about these ex-saint soldiers.

Ghosts; There were some houses boarded up in Southall for years. I still remember two houses on Greenland Crescent, two on Lady Margaret Road and one on Park Avenue. They had been in the sale for years and were very cheap but there was no buyer. Many people bought these houses but ghosts would not let them settle peacefully. Some tried to live in but with fear, they moved out; all doors and windows were boarded up.

I remember one story. A person was excited to buy one of Lady Margaret Road's houses. He was so happy to decorate with clip art wallpapers. The next day, he went to admire his successful decoration. To his amusement, he noticed that all the flower prints were upside down. He gave up and boarded up the property. Nowadays, people live in those houses, so someone must have managed to sort out these ghosts.

The Catholic Church does practice exorcism. So, 'What is it that they do? With their psychic knowledge or spiritual recitation, the exorcist evicts the demon or Spirit from the person's body or any building the ghost inhabits. Due to whatever circumstances, the ghost has entered a person's body or taken possession of a dwelling. These practitioners ask the ghost to leave this person or place. You will find that Indian and other newspapers advertise this practice as well.

In England, some time back, one hospital was in the headlines. Many staff members saw the ghosts wandering in corridors near the morgue area. At least ten complaints were made. Then the person in charge took action to sort out this situation. Experienced people were consulted and things were back to normal. Later, it was discovered that part of the hospital building was built on a former cemetery. Now you see, many ghosts do possess their graves as well.

Group of ghosts; Yes, if a ghost finds another ghost from the same area or comes across a previously known face, they will form groups and dwell where it suits the whole group to stay. I have seen a group of seventeen ghosts. They were all relatives, males and females together and others joined. How they came to this fate is a long story. Some were murdered and others passed on from accidental deaths, which all added to this group.

Once I befriended the ghost, we were working night shifts. Somehow, during our tea break, a conversation about ghosts came up. It was just an ordinary conversation but one person thought it was funny and began to joke daily. I said to myself, 'Enough is enough.' This person needs a lesson. In our factory, there was one darkroom where people complained to the management several times. About seeing someone in a white uniform, especially during the night shift. It was true.

Five ghosts were living there. They were people who had worked there for some time. Why they did not leave the place was not known. They used to appear at times but never face you. As we were all printers, after finishing a particular job, the responsible person was supposed to hang his dirty printing dye in the racks of that room. Being the supervisor, I knew this joking person would be coming to this room soon. It was our night shift.

So, I requested these Spirit friends; it is about time to show your faces when he comes into this room. I stood in one corner to watch. He walked up the stairs and entered the room. While he was in the middle of the room, he saw the visions. He dropped the dirty printing dye there and ran downstairs to his workplace. I made my way there before him to see his face. He was shocked, sweating and speechless. It took him a long time to say, 'I have seen the ghost.'

I gave him a glass of water to drink and calmed him down. At the end of his shift, he went home and stayed in bed for three days with fear. When he returned to work, he told everyone what he had seen and advised the others not to joke about ghosts. 'Have you ever seen a living ghost? I see them every day; 'Surprised? During your travels, while driving, you will notice lots of drivers don't move at traffic lights, although it is a green signal.

Their thoughts are far away. While walking, you bump into many people. They don't even know where they are going. All these people are without any direction in life or suffer from depression. Many people would love to sleep twenty-four hours a day if possible. Those who do not recite the word of God are also without any proper direction in life. In other words, they are wasting precious time. To all these people, I call them 'living' ghosts.

'Are you one of them? Make the most of your time;
it is far too short.

Guardian angels; Many people in this world have guardian angels. A guardian angel could be a former family member who is not living anymore but protects you. All saints have guardian angels provided by the Spirit. That is why they walk anywhere and meditate in dark rooms without fear. All those who follow a true saint, their living Master, will become their guardian angel.

'Do you have a guardian angel?

SPIRIT

Spirit is the essence of God. Anything we can think, imagine or anything that materialises is all Spirit. God cannot show its presence everywhere but via Spirit, it has established itself in totality. Any place, writing or speech mentioning Spirit becomes spiritual; the whole creation is based on Spirit. The solar system, the placement of each planet and the distances between them are controlled by Spirit.

Therefore, all religions mention that there is no place where God does not exist. The crux of the point is that the whole of eternity is assembled and sustained by Spirit. Spirit is divided into twin pillars of God; divine light and sound. This is to enable our communication with God. With light and sound, we are always in the presence of God. Therefore, it is important to open to the light and sound to have any spiritual experience.

Although light and sound are within us; being consciously aware of God is most important. Otherwise, we live in a daydream state and do not materialise anything fruitful. It is like making sandcastles without any foundation, which vanishes with a small tide coming in from the sea. Most of the Seekers are doing this over the last forty years. The Seekers depend on the experiences given by the Master out of his love for them.

This is to raise their vibrations so they can make some positive effort. But they have become too reliant on the

Master and have become passive. This passiveness is Kal's work to keep the Seekers grounded in the physical. Since joining the teachings, you are living with Spirit, as the Master is the direct channel of God. Although Spirit is and has been within all the time, you did not have the means to experience it.

Over the years, doing one hour of meditation every day has been recommended. That is good if you have a total saint nature in living or practice. I have noticed that people create more karma daily that cannot be cleared with one hour of meditation. So, 'What is your spiritual gain? To eliminate our negative creation, we must live our life consciously.

The spiritual force is with us to give a nudge whenever we are about to commit a mistake. However, this nudge is often ignored. 'Whenever you feel the nudge, do you know that you are alive within Spirit? This opportunity is not available to those on other religious paths. Therefore, they keep referring to their religious scriptures; when you can refer to within. 'How much more practical do you want? When I say, 'My love and Spirit always surround you,' this covers all the religious scriptures.

All religious scriptures were within first. Later, the Masters managed to express this spiritual love in writing. God establishes the Master physically, so people will have more opportunities to know the truth. When you meet the Master and see how he presents the discourse to you, you know he is a picture of **the truth**. The Master wants you to know this; otherwise, his efforts are wasted. I am always happy but would be happier if I knew that some Seekers had found spiritual success.

I put lots of effort into writing each month for your benefit; so, you can look at Spirit from another dimension. We must hold a 360-degree viewpoint; this is known as creativity. Spirit is not limited to numbers. Millions of experiences are waiting for each person but Spirit leaves this to the individual's free will. Individuals can take this advantage or lead their lives passively. Many prefer to lead their lives passively, thinking there is plenty of time.

Well, forty years have already gone without any solid consolidated experience. Time is short, as I have mentioned in our book. In a few days, you might know that the 'show is over.' In the next life, 'Will you have this opportunity to be in direct contact with the Master of the time? Only time will tell. I believe that in the present moment; the option should be taken now. I packed my bags from physical work because Spirit is more important to me than anything else.

You can do the same; if you have created the means to maintain your living expenses. Living on social benefits is not healthy. 'Spiritually, do you know the amount of karma mounting in your account by doing this? Probably, your one-hour meditation only just covers it. So, 'What is your spiritual gain? Every breath is counted when you are living at the expense of others. Some try to get away with it by saying it is within the law.

That is true but when the soul faces the king of spiritual law on judgement day, what physical law you follow will not be the king's concern. He is only concerned with what is in your spiritual account. Physical laws are man-made and do not operate in the spiritual world. In our book, I suggested that we learn to give instead of being on the receiving end. Those who are genuinely disabled are excused for the time being, as they are helpless.

However, Spirit will find ways of providing a means of living for those individuals who try to use their creativity. Spiritual exercises are fundamental. Lately, I have noticed that some of you are trying very hard. That is good for you and me as well. The effort must be made to raise your vibrations to the sun and moon worlds or the cosmic level. The signs of this happening are that your physical body will begin to vibrate, you will have a warm feeling within your forehead area or you will hear a sound like a cork popping.

Now you must not get nervous or uncomfortable. If you can hold your nerve for a short period, the inner Master will appear to give darshan or he may lead you on some spiritual journey. You may have noticed that some sci-fi films feature a spiritual man with some powers; when he concentrates, a spiritual ball of light appears physically in front of him. This ball, with its magnificent lights, begins to circle. If his concentration is intense, the ball moves in a continuous circle.

But once he begins to lose his concentration, the ball also disappears. 'Do you know you have the same experience when you have this warm feeling on your forehead? Movie-makers make the experience more attractive by expressing it on a physical level. Miracles are another example of Spirit in action. People can create miracles, provided they are an open channel for Spirit. You walk in any direction and miracles will follow.

Spirit becomes obliged to execute your spoken dialogue because Spirit knows you are an expression of love and the

Spirit of God. To you, this is normal, as you are living within Spirit all the time. But to others, these are miracles. You have gone beyond the amusement of the mind. You do not ask anything for yourself because nothing on the physical level attracts you. But you can ask for others if you think they are worthy of receiving it.

'Why should you ask for anything when everything is provided without you asking? Your very near and dear relationship is with God. You are inseparable, being part of it. All else is an illusion. When you become aware of this relationship with God, 'how can you afford to hold any other relationship, which is painful and an illusion? Illusion means something temporary or created for your experience on the physical level. It often attracts the mind. World attachments come into play.

There is a joy but this joy soon turns into pain. As the saying goes, no pain, no gain. Out of this pain and gain, we have a spiritual experience. Once you understand this and find your way out, you become the way-shower. You can create miracles; Spirit does not hide or deny anything from us. It is we who do not believe in its existence. It appears with little effort to those who believe because nothing is nearer to you than Spirit.

You are part of it. The human mind is always searching for the horizon far away and tries to reach it by physical means. 'Will it ever find what it is looking for? This is the question. You are always in the centre of it. When this realisation comes; all you can do is laugh at yourself. You know it is Spirit and so are you. All these millennia, you have been running away from yourself. This is the riddle between you and God.

Spirit

I am. I am. I am the only way, being the essence of God. No other way or path leads directly to the centre of God. Without me, 'Spirit,' you cannot move and would be in a state of suspension for millions of years. Spirit is always on the move; everything moves and has its being in the worlds of God. I am infinite, without any limits or boundaries. I am present in every corner of all the universes; every soul represents my presence.

I am within each particle of soil; otherwise, nothing would grow. I breathe through the soil so all the vegetation can grow. I breathe through you; you live through me and the circle is complete. It is a continuous and everlasting circle. For your guidance, many times, I appear to you through symbols. You must learn to establish the message within each symbol. I will give information about your future or a warning to be alert of something or some weakness on your part, which you need to work on.

The answers to your questions are given in symbols. A direct answer is often unsuitable, as it could put you out of balance. This is my way of conveying the message. Those open channels to Spirit do not have any questions or seek answers as they dwell in the spiritual fountain. This is where the answer is given before the question arises. These are the people who can answer the questions of others.

They are the expression of Spirit. The followers of any religion will never have a direct experience of Spirit because they only express part of it. They do not believe I am still alive. As long as I am living, everything exists. Otherwise, everything would turn to dust and non-existence. I am Spirit.

All religious leaders fail their followers by dictating to them to find me through material symbols or saying, 'We are the only way.'

When they say, 'We are the only way,' they leave no breathing space for me 'God' in their followers. As soon as this is done, the direct link is closed. I am everywhere and within each soul, no more or less to any soul. The same applies to all religions. They are part of me. But sadly, they only try to express a part of me. When they express me fully, they will become alive as they were in the beginning. In the beginning, every religion is alive.

It is the spiritual saint who appeared in some part of the world to give the spiritual message. Once the saint has gone, the followers create the religion based on this person's given message and sincerity. Later it becomes less of Spirit and more political to control the followers. Material symbols express Spirit instead of leading the followers to experience Spirit directly. Let us take some examples.

One religion does not consider any person a follower unless their natural hair is maintained and they wear certain symbols. That religion's message is good but the spiritual message is lost. If some awakened person tries to lead, they are ignored or ridiculed to silence them. People feel more secure having their being in the past when I always live in the present. I moved from that religious practice and found success.

Another religion recommends that the followers must pray five times a day. 'How can you remember me only five times a day when I do not forget you for a single moment of the day or night? Otherwise, you will never wake up. I am alive and kicking, as they say, all around you, all the time. You only open up to me to feel my presence. I am the way and the way is within, as we are one.

Another religion is famous for going door to door, saying, 'We are the only way and salvation is only through our spiritual leader. That leader left this world many centuries ago and has probably become the spiritual leader of many other religions. These saints do not limit themselves, as they are infinite in the spiritual world. If this religion is the only way and runs the show, 'Then, as Spirit, who am I?

These people limit themselves and stop others from venturing into the spiritual world. By misguiding someone, you become liable for their wrongfully created karmas. In Asia, there are numerous religions using hundreds of symbols and rituals. They are so entangled in these practices that they have forgotten their actual goal. Any religion practising these rituals and symbols only represents a part of me.

The religion or its followers will never succeed in having a solid spiritual experience. Instead, they become storytellers. I Am as Spirit will be out of their reach because they don't want to know me. I am within and closer than your breath or heartbeat. You will know me the day you become one with me to say, 'I am Spirit.'

SPIRITUAL UNFOLDMENT

This is the journey of the soul since it has left the soul plane and entered the lower worlds. It entered as inexperienced and began to 'fold' itself with karma. It was given a few karmas by the 'Lord of Karma' to open its account in this world. Most of us begin our journey in the lower forms of life, as we are all aware. In these lower lives, we hardly create any or not many karmas.

For example, a plant being in one place and not interfering physically or mentally with others cannot create many karmas apart from gaining experience. A tree will have the most experience, as it learns patience by being in one place for hundreds of years unless humans cut its lifespan short. I have seen a few trees in the Golden Temple of Amritsar, India; historically, they are over 450 years of age. At present, they are still as healthy and fruitful as ever they can be.

Being in one place, we can learn so many lessons. All the weathers take its toll; the only protection is the umbrella of the blue sky. That means no protection from anything. We all have been through this journey and succeeded, eventually taking the form of a human shield. We still moan and groan with all this 'tree' patience experience. During our time as lower forms of life, we were passive. Now at present, we are very active mentally.

Due to this activeness, we have become aggressive, adopted non-tolerance and lost our patience at every opportunity. 'What is unfoldment? First, as an experience, we have folded into the lower worlds by creating lots of karma. Now with lots of experience, we want to unfold spiritually. Spiritual knowledge nudges us that we are more than this physical body. 'We begin to meditate and ask ourselves what could be the way out?

We love to be in the presence of those more spiritually awake people. You can talk or listen to this spiritual interest for hours. This will lead us to become spiritual Seekers. You have lost interest in material things but come to this spiritual interest. With a spiritual search, you have managed to find a spiritual Master. You thought your life would be easy but you experienced the opposite.

'What could be the reason for this? There is a task for the Master to help you unfold spiritually. He wants to make sure that you have learned every experience you require. Master allows you to develop spiritually, like a flower, as it opens its petals one by one. You are provided with five passions of the mind as a helping hand to gain this experience. Those who think of these five passions as enemies will never have solid spiritual success.

Initially, you thought all these mind passions were under your control. When the spiritual Master tested you from different directions, it did not take long to learn that you were nowhere near the mark of any command over them. This is where most of us fail, thinking in terms of control. Instead, the approach should be to balance them out. Once we have this balance in our lives, we will move towards spiritual unfoldment.

We always talk of having the experience of a bliss state, 'What is this bliss state? It is the balance of our five passions and the flow of Spirit within. In the bliss state, you are relaxed beyond your physical imagination. Nothing bothers; once you have made a habit of living in this state of consciousness; known as 'being yourself,' in a true sense of spirituality. All the problems we used to complain about in the past, now you probably laugh at them.

There is no such thing as a problem in life. A few situations are not in our favour; otherwise, problems are non-existent. What we call problems, these situations are not bothering the person standing next to you; we can draw some conclusions from that. In 'The Way to God,' I have explained: 'Problems are Zero.' We can compare the soul's journey with any seed of a plant. The physical seed is produced by any plant, while the soul is the creation of God.

In theory, the journey of any soul is not much different from the journey of a seed. Seeds are produced by the billions each year but 'How many manage to become plants? Only a few percentages. Most seeds are used as bird feed or turned into flour for cooking, while a good percentage rot away. This does not apply to any soul, as the soul is here to stay and experience. But one thing is common; not many souls manage to set themselves free spiritually, while most struggle.

Still, we take the example of a successful seed. The seed is planted or grown in the wild. The plant begins to appear out of the soil. A few leaves appear and then develop a little higher; in spring, it is ready to bloom. Notice that most of the plants are green in colour during their youth. Then, with experience; it is time to unfold and show this world what they can produce. It is unbelievable what nature can grow out of a little green plant; yellow, red, pink and white flowers.

We admire the beauty and fragrance of nature. This is the unfoldment of this plant and its successful journey. We, as souls, have a relatively long journey. Now we go back to controlling the five passions; you once thought you had control over. When Master tests your abilities, you will realise nothing is in your control, as they are running all over you. The Master will test you from a point that you have never thought of. There are no shortcuts to this spiritual journey.

The Master will make sure that you have become the knower. The spiritual exercises given earlier are a great helping hand to materialise your spiritual goals. Furthermore, it was recommended to have a 'silence fast' to stay silent most of the day. It will bring stillness to your mind. The next one will be to learn how to blank your mind. It is so easy. This can be practised while sitting still, standing or walking. Now, the procedure is not to think.

As we are aware, the mind is thinking all the time. But this time, you are conditioning your mind not to think. 'Do you know that you are thinking, even when you are not thinking? This is something we must learn. Driving a car makes a good analogy. Although we are moving at high speed, we must change the gear to the neutral position at some point. So, if you can work on this, you will have lots of success. Here are some steps you can follow.

You are practising being in the position of being God. Someone rang me the other day, saying it is an excellent experience to act as a God for the day. It is not just for a day; you must practice every day to achieve spiritual success.

1. You already are practising the food or mental fast.
2. You practice remaining silent for a day once every week.
3. Last, you are beginning to learn how to blank your mind. Now, I think you have enough spiritual tools to practice. Otherwise, I have an unlimited number of tools in my spiritual bag to give.

This is the path of enlightenment, as I mentioned very recently. I have a cassette of Paul Ji, where he says that this path is designed to train you as a saint. When it comes to this training, you better be prepared to become alone but never lonely, as the presence of the Master is always with you. Your companion will be your spiritual Master and many spiritual beings. When you have such companions, 'Who want to deal with so many on the physical level?

You will be dwelling in a bliss state; at the same time, you will be physical too. The teachings have been the same as ever but we have practised in a relaxed mood. While you people are practising to learn how to be in the position of God, at the same time, I have been practising, nowadays, how to relax as you do. God does not interfere with the journey of any soul; it lets the soul learn at its own pace. Soul itself is beyond time.

When we are talking about the physical lifespan, we have limited time. The present Master acts the same way as God. He will not interfere in anyone's life but convey its message. When you have succeeded in being in the presence of God all the time, no one will have to tell you that you have unfolded spiritually. You will know yourself, as you are the knower of truth.

The word we stress often is an **unfoldment.** You will learn there was nothing to unfold or to achieve. You have just become aware that you have always been part of God. If you can catch this point, spirituality cannot be taught but it can be caught (it comes to you like a cat coming on silent feet to catch its prey); you won't even have to practice anything.

You have become the knower of spiritual truth, known as instant realisation. Therefore, Master always said, 'I can give this realisation to anyone at any time, provided the Seeker is ready for this experience.' 'Now, the question is, do you want to unfold the hard way spiritually or do you want to walk into this everlasting experience?

The choice is yours.

ULTIMATE

'What could be the ultimate goal or achievement for us? This is the question. Some parents are already working on their child's future as we enter this world or just before. Most likely, plans are to make their child what they want to be in life; due to many circumstances, they could not achieve. We are responsible for the well-being of our children. It does not mean; we must impose our dictates on the child's future. I have seen many people on TV during the drama, singing or dancing competitions.

To send children to drama, singing or dancing schools is very common. When a child is sent to drama classes, it means that parents once wanted to become movie stars; now, they want to live their dream through children. It is to satisfy their minds. The child is innocent and willing to follow the dictates of their parents. The child begins to feel the natural ability to fulfil this task, designed or fabricated by the parents.

It means we have silenced the free will of the child. Every child or soul enters this world to fulfil some big or small destiny. We are responsible for bringing up and educating our children. However, as the child grows older and has had an education, they adopt a way of life they feel naturally attracted to or can follow. We never know what the child can do. We should not silence the child's individuality. Let the child develop their personality.

What the child achieves; could be less or surpass your expectations. 'What could be our goal in life? 'Do we want to become doctors, politicians or engineers? Many of us cannot think beyond this due to our circumstances. We may not believe but something beyond these goals can be achieved while doing our physical chores. That is to achieve spiritual enlightenment.

I was lucky, as my parents were not well educated and were not concerned about achieving something in life. It was unlucky for me, as they could not guide me on the physical level. But on the other hand, I was lucky; I had the opportunity to do whatever I wanted to do in life. So, I educated myself on how I wanted to be; I have had a fair amount of success. On the other hand, I had a dream within myself to know and experience God in this lifetime.

I developed my personality around that, which is very silent and exciting at the same time. I felt more like a balanced individual as I travelled through the inner worlds. We are happy if we do something worthwhile in life. Our goals are so small; that we become satisfied with the tiniest milestones. Some can buy many properties and are happy to be called landlords. It is the same with politicians and those whose careers are in other fields.

Some can manage to leave their name in this world to be remembered for centuries. However, when we come to the end of our lives, we pause and think, 'Did I achieve anything that I can take to the world beyond? We have not achieved anything that can be taken with us because we have been too busy or involved in physical responsibilities. We never thought of looking beyond or considering what it could be. People rarely talk about the far country or worlds beyond.

Even if we think about it, we feel it is beyond our reach or can't see it. Most of us believe that Jesus, Guru Nanak, Buddha or Muhammad did it and there is no way we can do something similar. Yes, they were special people and individuals in their tracks. Krishna of Hinduism is the oldest and Buddha is second. Jesus Christ is third in line and his followers claim he is the only one to give salvation to this world. According to this theory, Mohammad should not be here.

But he appeared as a new prophet and now he has millions of followers. Guru Nanak appeared in the fifteenth century and now he also has millions of followers. All these prophets appeared in this world time after time. There is no end to it. 'God-sent men' will be coming until the end of this world. 'Who knows who will appear in which part of the world? Never limit yourself by saying, 'I cannot do this.' Every person in this world is equal in the eyes of God, as it has given you the same abilities as any prophet.

God wants every soul in this world and beyond to unfold spiritually to become assistants and take responsibility. It surprises me that we are not told openly by our elders to follow in the footsteps of our creator. No one can become a second God but it has sent us into the lower worlds to educate us spiritually so that we can participate in its endeavour in the higher worlds. It has given us the ability to do this and like any parent, God wants us to be successful as its children.

This should be our ultimate goal.

THE WRATH OF GOD

Every person in this world, especially religious ones, are afraid of these three words. All religions stress that their followers should fear the **wrath of God** and the followers tell the same to others. If you do something wrong, be prepared to reap what you sow. This is the backbone of all religions; otherwise, they may not exist. 'If there is no fear, who wants to know what religion is? Or 'What are the benefits of being a religious person?

If you know what God is, not as a religious person but in reality, which is very difficult to understand, you will be surprised to learn that the expression of these three words is not true. All religious concepts of these three words are far from the truth. It shows that these religions or their founders have never been close to reality or in the presence of God. They always say that God is totally out of reach or knowing.

On the contrary, the same religion also says God is within everyone as a soul or Spirit. God has created the soul in its image to express its presence everywhere. The soul is the pure image of God, very similar to the way we see the image of our physical form in a mirror or water. If we can see our physical form reflected in a mirror, 'Who stops us from seeing God in each soul? The answer is quite simple God has made it easy for us.

We have become lazy. We can travel thousands of miles for our interests but we cannot cross a hair's breadth. It is a well-known fact that if something is given free in life, it will never be appreciated. You are given something you are not interested in, even though your gift is precious. God has given part of itself to everyone to know or feel its presence. Now, 'How many are interested in doing that? Very few or none.

We have created a wall between its presence and us because our interests are elsewhere. As I walk along in life, I come across some faces and through their expressions, I can see God walking on the streets. I have a habit of looking at anyone who comes within my sight once. I will only look twice if I see the spiritual spark in a person's eyes. Then I can see the presence of God walking among us in this world. This expression could be through a male, female, child, dog or cat.

These individuals may not know what they are expressing and their thoughts may be far from knowing. But at that moment, they were the carriers of this spark within. Children do this because they are innocent and don't know what negativity or fear is. 'Do you know? If a child sits next to a tiger or dog, this child may catch the cat or dog's tail and laugh simultaneously.

I expect this animal not to react with anger because animals only respond to our vibrations of fear or grudge. I have seen this personally. We create our fears. This is where the expression comes into action, known as the 'wrath of God.' I must clear this point first. There is no such thing as the wrath of God. As I said earlier, most religions have not touched the face of God to know what God is. God has created souls in his image to experience.

To become assistants in his cause in the higher and lower planes. These include saints or a Master of a given time, created to show the way to souls seeking the truth. The soul is in a neutral state of consciousness as God. God has made everything for the soul to experience. 'Then how can it destroy or have wrath on the soul? This is where schooling comes in and all the ups or downs exist. God dwells in the pure spiritual worlds beyond matter, energy, space and time.

These spiritual worlds are everlasting beyond any effect but God also created the lower worlds, which are not permanent and are subject to changes. The soul is eternal and it cannot be seen visually. So, God has provided the lower bodies as clothing to be seen visually. Soul has four other bodies as a cover or expression and experiences each spiritual plane. These bodies are subject to the lower planes and are also subject to suffering.

These bodies are responsible for creating the reasons for God's wrath to occur. Wrath of God is our creation and suffering. We will see how we make and face the wrath of God and then ask mercy for our doings. God is not in a position to forgive. If God does forgive, the whole system will be out of balance and justice will not be done. As the saying goes, there is no smoke without fire, so this wrath does not come from anywhere.

A single person cannot be responsible for big disasters. It is always a group of people who create negative karma on a massive scale without any due care. If you look at places where large disasters occur and go into the background of these places or the people who lived there, you will find lots of wrong-doings. I always try to look behind the curtains to find the truth. I will give a recent example. This situation can be related to the wrath of God.

On 15 June 2013, big floods took place in Uttarakhand, India. It was a total wipe-out of the buildings, including all well-known temples and people were trapped for days. Approximately 6,000 people lost their lives. First; this proves that God is not living in the buildings known as temples. Second; let us consider the people we thought were poor and who we generally hired as helping hands to climb the mountains to visit these temples.

I would expect them to help every person they could during this situation, as the visitors are their bread and butter. Instead, they robbed every person who came in their way and emptied the pockets of the dead. They stole gold and sexually assaulted the females. This is how our mind works. It does not matter how bad the situation we are going through; we always have careless attitudes and give no thought to any karma.

These people were in the middle of this experience, known as the wrath of God; despite this, they did not feel sympathy for the people. Now is the time to remind everyone why God does not show mercy in these situations; God knows they will never learn. Now, 'Who is responsible for this creation or show of wrath? It is not God, as many or almost everyone believes.

God has created the lower worlds and appointed rulers or a hierarchy of Masters for each plane to keep everything in balance. The Lord of Karma is established on the astral plane to look after the affairs of the physical. Whenever the Lord of Karma notices that situations or places are out of balance, it shows who is in command. This is the wrath of total karma backfiring on us and is often misunderstood as the 'wrath of God.'

We reap what we sow.

The maladjustment created by us; the commanding force takes action to bring back balance; only then do we say it was the wrath of God; when it was our creation. People fear when facing God's wrath but are not afraid when they create situations for it to happen. All the eruptions of volcanoes, tornados or excessive water are signs of this.

Many situations occur due to global warming; we are responsible for that too. Nowadays, many incidents occur throughout this world of a person carrying dangerous weapons and choosing various places to shoot many unknown and innocent people without care. 'Can you imagine the amount of karma this one person has created?

Some people are doing this in the name of their religion. There is no thought given to the consequences. The same goes for those who take money, expensive gifts or property and do not wish to pay back their debt in time. They will face the penalty sooner or later. A very famous writer Sir Walter Scott wrote this favourite line:

Oh, what a tangled web we weave.

If we investigate the backgrounds of the people who created these massacres. No one is born to have this kind of unbalanced mind or be in this position with a careless attitude. As a child, everyone is born innocent, an expression of God. But as children grow, the mind gets stronger or weaker with the years. Some people will take advantage of this innocence and drive you up the wall. Then you either get depressed or berserk mentally to take revenge and go on a spree of killings to let go of your anger toward anyone who comes your way.

Again, someone is responsible for this person's mental pressure. No one cares about creating karma. Most of those responsible for guiding us, religious leaders or priests, are greedy and worse than ordinary people on the karma scale. Minor eruptions in this world or broken stars within a galaxy are regular and happen for reasons. Although temporary, God is unwilling to destroy these lower worlds; minor unbalances are possible.

This universe is good enough to live for humans and vegetation for a long time. One day will come when this universe will not be fit for humans or vegetation. For this, God will not be responsible. It will result from humans experimenting beyond nature and destroying this earth's goodness. It will become barren land and oxygen will only exist just to hold the planet together. Those souls who have found their way back by following the Master of the time will be lucky.

Others will be put into a deep sleep or in a bliss state in spiritual terms. Then the goodness of Spirit will be showered on the 'New Earth Planet' to begin once more Golden-Age. Now you may wonder what mess humans could create to the point that God had to evacuate all the souls. That is correct and it was all expected by its creator; after all, it was a training ground for souls. It is similar to any football ground; it is left empty and alone when the match is over.

We know Kal is or will get stronger by day. But due to scientific experiments, all the sciences will merge into neutral religion and people will become soul travellers. Most of them will find their way back into the higher planes. The essential requirement will be that science has to break the time and speed barrier to zero zones for any actual travelling. Furthermore, there are many zero zones for each higher plane. All the present known or so-called dominating religions will fade away with time.

They will have nothing to offer apart from their hollow promises. Religious scriptures given by their respective prophets are correct but nowadays, they are misinterpreted to satisfy their materialistic needs. Science literature will almost sound like religion because of its spiritual findings. Nowadays, people are excited about mobile phones and the internet. In the future, people will have a hobby of travelling to and exploring higher planes.

The wisest person will be who has travelled farther than anyone else. Almost everyone will be a soul traveller. Those who did not manage will be taken back to continuing the isness state until the new world is ready as it was at the beginning of Satya-Yuga and a new Golden-Age will begin.

LOVE FORCE

In the early days, Paul Ji taught us the art of love force, which I feel at present is missing. God itself is pure love. This love flows from God to us and returns to it, also known as sound. It is God's love that sustains all the universes. It is this continuous and everlasting love that we are all part of. When applied on a neutral basis or for the good of the whole, a love force can work wonders, known as miracles.

This love is also known as Spirit; we are open channels for the Spirit. I don't think anyone can imagine the power of this love force because it is beyond knowing. We must be full of love before its application to bring changes for the good of the whole. Otherwise, it will not work; if your vibrations are not pure, the results you want to see will not materialise. This pure love force supersedes mental power. Mental force is also powerful when applied with total concentration.

You must have seen some programs on TV or some live shows. A trained person with mental faculties can focus on some metal object, such as a spoon; he can move or bend this object without touch. When usually, we cannot bend it this easily. Many trained people can misuse this mental faculty as well. I remember once Paul Ji mentioned he used to visit one cafe and the owner hired someone trained in this mental art.

The man's job was to divert the minds of those passing by so they would come into the cafe as customers. This type of mental manipulation can be done but violates the spiritual law known as psychic space. There is always someone with whom we cannot get along. They will attempt to harm us in many ways. But being on the spiritual side, we do not want to react to this person's thinking standards. We can choose not to respond. Instead, we can apply this love force; it can work wonders.

This art of love is a gift from God to all humanity but I notice we have lost this art over the years. Or we are not using it whole-heartedly and it does not bring the results to our expectations. As I have said in previous discourses, you must be full of love before applying for it. 'If you are God, then what are you? You're full of love. Now you are in the driving seat. Even before you apply this love force, you already know the results. In your attempt, you will never fail.

To have eye contact with God, you must be like God. Our fears keep us away from it and the outcome of any attempt made on our part is inferior. All the religions in this world claim that God is within each individual but all the religious scholars also say that we cannot see or converse with God. To me, these two statements do not add up. If this is their belief, then I don't think they know what "love force" is. The application of this love force is totally beyond their knowledge.

Therefore, they believe in prayers, which are never answered. The person who applies this love force to all without any condition will have the ability of spiritual gaze. Spiritual gaze is the power of your love flowing through your eyes to others, which can be used to raise someone's vibrations or to heal someone. Spiritual Masters are naturally gifted with this power.

People will notice your presence and without knowing, they will feel the pull toward you. Your presence will be similar to a magnet with a natural attraction. A newborn child has this ability naturally. Once you see the child, you feel this love force. It does not matter how tired or angry you are or how much of any other complex emotion you are experiencing; a cute little smile can conquer all of this and you will feel happy and fresh.

This child's little smile will force you to pick up the child, tickle or kiss him as a gesture of love. This is the power of love force naturally used. You must make a habit of this application of love. Give your love to all unconditionally. You will be surprised to learn the results. As I have said many times, I am not a writer but I manage to write lots because I apply this love force on a neutral basis. 'What is a love force? It is Spirit. And 'What is Spirit? It is light and sound. And 'What is light and sound?

It is God itself. If you are one with God, 'What results will you expect? I do not expect any results because God does all for me, even beyond my expectations. When you do not expect any results and leave everything in the hands of Spirit, only then does all materialise. What I write down comes out of this 'love force. I never sit down to write anything ever. When this love force - Spirit guides me to write, I only sit down.

And above all, I never choose the subject; it is given to me. First, Spirit lets me know what the topic will be as 'title.' Then it gives me the love force; what to say on the subject.

As I hold the pen in my hand, my physical speed is so slow when writing; what has been said. Then Spirit gives me breathing space because it is the message of Spirit that I want to convey to the Seekers.

We learned how to use or apply this love force; probably the older members will tell us. We used to feel like we were not walking but floating above the ground. That was the love force in action. But over the years, we have lost this art of loving and many sufferings have begun to appear. Give your love to all unconditionally and all will be yours. The people who are against you will be pulled toward you naturally. Spirit works wonders.

Nothing can stand in the way of Spirit, as Spirit is so close to you. We all know that Spirit is around us; like radio waves, whoever tunes to the correct frequency will get the signal. It will be the strength of your unconditional love known as your positive or neutral vibrations. What you can catch will exceed your expectations. If you want to get stuck in illusions, as many are, that is your decision.

The Spirit may not appear directly to anyone but can materialise anything if doing so is the requirement. Take this discourse as another exercise to practice on. Usually, it will use any person who is an open channel to the Spirit. 'Don't you think it should be **you**, provided you let the Spirit use you? Many people made remarks and approached in the early days by saying, 'I think you are special.' Now when was the last time someone said this to you?

You are still the same person but minus the alive spiritual flow. Revive yourself again; practice the presence of your spiritual Master. Practice your spiritual exercises regularly.

Practice the fact of being part of God. Then I cannot even imagine what can stand in your way. Overall, 'Who is the Master of these problems or conditions? It is God itself. Without its permission, nothing exists.

It has given free will to all so that everyone can have their being at their conditions. At the same time, we will pay the consequences according to our own decisions. You give free will to all, as it does. Apply your love force; all these people, problems and situations will move along without affecting you. 'Let it be.' With this let it be; you can move mountains. With this love force, you are living and so are the others.

If Spirit is alive and so, are you, 'how can someone stand in your way which is not spiritually alive? We always underestimate the strength of the love force, use our physical action and impaired judgement and often fail. I am sure many of you have been using spiritual faculties since you started; your life situations have improved. There will be times when you know that you are floating above on automation like an aeroplane; there is no comparison to this spiritual freedom.

Did you ever realise 'how negative we are or how this world produces negativity? It does not affect God at all. It is beyond matter, energy, space and time. Now, imagine, if you are beyond all this, 'How can anything affect you? All these unfavourable situations are affecting you because you are part of them. Once you rise above, you will know what we are discussing here. It would help if you learned to do everything on a neutral basis.

You are an open channel to the Spirit, so I will not spell it out for you. 'You know what you are? You will know yourself. The word impossible should not exist in your dictionary. Where light is lit in the house, the thieves most likely won't enter the property because they will know someone is awake. It is the same with the five passions of the mind; the Kal force would not enter your psychic space. Kal knows that you are awake spiritually. Love force is only possible if you are spiritually awake. Otherwise, it is a house of horror and 'darkness,' and a love force does not exist.

May this love force be with you.

YOUR SUCCESS OR FAILURE

Once you have read this book, it will be time to analyse your success or failure. Make use of your strong points and work towards your weaknesses. Those who have not made any effort so far should know why Spirit does not listen to your cries. If you want to remain in this maze, it is your decision. Maybe some people want to learn the hard way. In England, there are drains carrying all the domestic or commercial filth that leads to a utility manhole full of darkness and dirt.

Spirit can only help those who wish to move on with their lives. If you are someone who has decided to remain in the darkness and cry, all I can say is that you are underestimating your ability. The people I am talking about here know who they are and should take this message positively and move on to have success in life. All these drains and utility holes, better known as problems, are the story of every house.

At one point, Guru Nanak said, 'Nanak Dukhian sab Sansar' **Everyone in this world suffers or is in sorrow**. Those who manage to face the facts with a smile are better off. Otherwise, an ocean of tears is waiting for you. All these problems or situations are part of darkness or Kal. The word Kal means 'negative.' This word is used throughout this world to express the same. We are often naive enough to walk into problems or create some, not knowing the consequences.

Some are created for pleasure but we begin to suffer when they grow out of proportion, not knowing where to turn. We always expect someone else to care for our problems so we can feel free. We love to leave all our problems in the hands of the Spirit. The question is, 'Did Spirit or someone you rely on created these problems for you? The answer is they did not. So, 'When are you going to learn to face the facts?

This is what Spirit wants to see in each of us to feel and realise our responsibility. What can be the reaction of our actions to others will be karma in our account. Being an assistant means we know our responsibilities consciously. Once my manager told me at work; If you make a mistake on a minor scale, you will probably keep repeating it many times.

If you go through the mistake entirely, you will probably remember it for the rest of your life and not be repeated it. I still see positivity in the people who are not making any effort in this message. One day, they will be the believers I can count on. I will be proud to say, 'Yes, I know them.' you may wonder what your next task will be. Yes, you can write down your recent experiences or learning.

'What are your success or failure points; since you have followed this path? I am sure that some of you can write a book. Pause for a while, review your weaknesses and see how you can improve them. Your success points will be your strength to achieve your goal and you can make the most of your weaknesses. Your strong points and deficiencies will contribute to future success.

SILENCE

Silence is golden. These words are often used. They mean nothing if you do not practice.

God lives in **silence**. That is why. It is beyond matter, energy, space and time.

When you are in **silence**, all time, space and matter dissolve themselves and you are in the presence of God.

Silence is the second name for inner communication.

Silence means you are lean within Spirit. You can meditate under the blue sky or in a jungle; no weather, animal, hunger or sickness will touch you.

Silence means all your external senses are closed and you are directly within its presence.

You must come to the condition of your sitting that all your passions, thinking and body are in **silence**. As long as something is ticking, you will never have success.

You must practice remaining in **silence** and build a cloud of fog around you, so no one will ever know you are here.

The whole creation came out of this **silence**.

Silence is golden. Many invitations to Kal disappear.

What I have written so far came out of **silence.**

Sitting in **silence** is very peaceful. I sit in silence. 'Do you?

All sounds are created out of this **silence.**

All trees are standing in **silence** and having their being. We sit in their shadow because they are silent.

The most powerful beings created by God, known as the **super souls,** are always in **silence.** They control all the universes with this **silence.**

The '**Haiome**' sound is part of this great **silence.**

I am the carrier of this **silence.** That is why I managed to remain silent for all these years.

Silence speaks louder than words.

To know this **silence,** you must be part of it first.

Silence is always alive; all the noises come and die down with time.

At the end of Kali-Yuga, this planet will remain **silent** until its next allotted time.

The secret of living longevity is to remain **silent** as much as possible.

Cat hunts on ***silent*** feet but you must be silent to be hunted by the Spirit.

I ask everyone to write something on the subject 'What are you following? The same question came into the minds of many: 'What do I write? That means you are not **silent** yet.

You can hear the birds singing early in the morning when most of this world sleeps. As soon as this world wakes up and chaos is everywhere, these natural sounds are **silenced** by our noises.

Most saints try to remain sitting in one place, so their **silence** continues without fail. We do not manage to sit in one place because our minds are unstable. We feel irritated and get up. Therefore, every person cannot be a saint.

Eternal sound can be heard when all is **silent,** not when you try to listen.

All priests will not hear this **silence** until or unless they switch to the next spiritual dimension.

The sea is calm and **silent** but our polluted ideas break its **silence.**

All those who are **silent** give. God gives to all. The sun gives light during the day and the moon at night but those who receive; always complain.

You can hear the silent flute on the soul plane because there is everlasting **silence.**

Spiritual Master is always watching **silently** by standing next to you.

All religious followers are looking for their spiritual Masters in churches and temples. What resides within these buildings is hollow **silence.**

Followers who make requests with sincerity have their answers materialised through this great **silence,** providing they manage to raise their vibrations.

We kill animals without their consent to create food and draw milk out of their bodies, which is meant for their siblings. They are all **silent**. Humans, better known as the highest state of consciousness, cry with every bit of pinch. We have not learned how to give. We only know how to steal or grab.

I am the only pure channel of God. That is why I am **silent**. All pseudo-masters are trying to sell what they don't have.

Humans cry at birth because they are a part of this big chaos. They only go in **silence** when it is their last breath. Those who manage to stay in silence are saints.

Wild animals don't have a permanent roof over their heads and the birds are roaming free under the blue sky, yet they are **silent.**

Do not mistake in believing that all those who are **silent** are saints. Some crooks, thieves and backstabbers are hiding behind this silence.

For some, it may seem to be the end of this world due to many problems. Our shadows are always **silent** when you walk through this experience with pain.

The path of enlightenment is the result of this **silence**.

You speak when you know, your words are better than your **silence**.

Silence can lead you to the inner and spoken words can drag you down the hill.

If you do not understand the **silence** I am talking about, you will never understand my writing.

The day you have turned your back on **silence,** you will be lost in a gigantic maze.

You must find inner happiness when in **silence**. If you are sad, then there is something wrong.

Silence is a spiritual virtue of success only a few fortunate ones can master.

Don't waste your words on people who don't want to know. Your powerful speech will be taken as nothing; when your **silence** may be more powerful.

You will feel or know the nudge of Spirit when you are **silent.**

Silence is always better than meaningless dialogues.

Spiritual communication will only whisper in your ears when you are **silent**.

Silence; deaf people may find frustration due to this disability but they will never know how lucky they are not to hear lots of garbage.

Walk on the path to find **silence** within. You will never fail. 'Have you found your silence yet?

Silence is the key to inspiring creativity, turning a simple thing into something extraordinary.

You can experience the whole of eternity in a moment of **silence.**

Once you experience this **silence**, it will never let you down.

You can solve many problems with **silence** and avoid many problems.

Silence always tries to teach us something we are not aware of.

Let the **silence** take over your life. You will be born new spiritually.

Telepathy is the second name for this **silence**. You can hear the whole world if you wish.

Those who are not **silent** make other people's business their own.

Those who are quick to answer in conversation will never know what **silence** is.

The first stage is to know **silence**; the second stage is to walk and live in this silence.

The second name for a spiritual state of consciousness is **silence**.

Silence is the pure language of God; all else is part of the illusion.

Silence can save you from lots of disappointing dialogues.

Within this **silence**, you can project yourself or walk into a beingness state.

With your **silence**, people may get the message more quickly than they would with words.

Silence is the key to tolerance and kindness.

The most remarkable men are often simple and **silent** but have extraordinary visions.

Silence does not mean yes to some or all questions. Sometimes it is better to let people find their answers; otherwise, they will never know the truth.

When an opponent does a spell on you, do not react to accept; put **silence** on your guard.

I was sitting and meditating; within this **silence;** came the light.

During sadness, people often experience **silence**. You can turn this into your strength.

Silence is balance. *Silence* is patience. *Silence* is your success.

Silence is the word of God.

In **silence,** you are with God, never a shadow.

In **silence**, you will see the spark of God in the eyes of a child.

In **silence,** you are never alone.

When I joined the teachings, I was **silent** for two years to understand the spiritual principles. Do not rush over the teachings; have patience. Try to understand the principles till you become the spiritual principle yourself.

We always rush in to read the monthly communication letter and then put that piece of paper to one side. It is the same with life. We are always in a rush; this rush leads you from one thing to another without positive results. One day during this rush, you will come to know that your time is up. We always try to bite more than we can chew.

In **silence** ... every day is Christmas and a happy New Year.

Silence

Silence Silence

Silence Silence Silence

Silence Silence Silence Silence Silence

Silence **Until you are lost within this Silence**

PSYCHIC ABILITIES

Psychic ability is to make connections with negative spirits or spirits of the dead or to do black magic. There are different schools to train the individual in many abilities. Such as; Clairvoyance or Clairaudience etc. we call them mediums as these people act as mediators to help others.

Clairvoyance; means clear voice. This medium has the ability of seeing and knowing in the psychic worlds and can penetrate into the past or future. The present is sitting in front to raise concerns about his suffering. Medium makes the connection via mental faculties. It is mind over matter. It is very intense training to be proficient at this ability. What you can learn; depends on the ability of your teacher.

It is an unwavering focus during meditation to open up to the Spirit. It is a semi-awake state in the paranormal because you are in the psychic world and at the same time you are listening and answering the questions. The medium can give the answers directly or he may use psychic spirits. Sometimes entities describe the scene via symbols to the customer; if it means something to them.

The pituitary gland is the seat of the mind. It is possible that the screen of the mind become alive and clairvoyants can see moving pictures similar to movies on the cinema screen. A medium can roll the history of your past to know the reason for your suffering and pass forward the same into the future to see; what can be expected. A medium can suggest the solution to overcome suffering. It is against the spiritual law of cause and effect.

These mediums don't show much concern about Karma because it is their living. They charge a set fee to provide this service. Some people are born with this ability. It is normal to them but it could be scary to others. It is a way of life for them. Most of the time they are or wish to remain spiritually active. If you are spiritually active then you don't have to go into meditation. The vision will appear on your mental screen all the time.

To the clairvoyants, it is their full-time job. People can visit anytime or through appointments. Some of them are so active, that they can answer your questions without uttering a word. You can trust the person with this ability. Some pretend to be the experts, they are clever and ask a number of questions and they round up the answers accordingly. They ask the questions with style; that you provide the answers for them.

Clairvoyants can see the aura and state of suffering according to the visionary colour seen. Then the prediction is revealed accordingly. Clairvoyants can sense the smell of the energy as you walk into their presence. It is the sense of smell that can lead to many answers. A few entities are always present in the psychic space of a clairvoyant to help. Clairvoyants can deal with these entities as we deal with people on daily bases.

Clairaudience; means clear hearing. They have the natural ability to hear things from distance. They can hear the conversation in this world and from beyond. The practitioner has the ability to open the inner ears. This ability is ruled by the throat chakra, which controls communication. Because the mind screen was for the visions. Sometimes these voices are clear or they may be distorted and fail to deliver a clear answer.

The medium can make the connection with dead relatives and ask what they have to say to their loved ones. Sometimes you can hear the voices of **dead people** through these entities. To some, it may be a startling experience or you could be pleased with what they have to say. Your mind is at rest. All these people are stuck in between worlds, where they cannot communicate or make their way into heaven.

They appear to their loved ones or in dreams to seek help. So, they can be excused from uncertain living. The medium makes the call on them to conversate. After some rituals, it is possible to set them free. Some people have the ability of soul travelling and they can lead them to Astral Plane in the presence of the lord of Karma. God bless their soul.

DÉJÀ VU & ESP

Déjà vu is the ability to know things before they happen. Most likely it is the insight into the future. It is the awakening of the third eye. Once a vision is witnessed you can go silent or reveal the outcome once it has taken place. If it is relating to self then you can prepare to face the situation or stay on guard in such a way that it will not be as effective. What appeared in your vision could be happy or sad.

Déjà vu does not mean that it is a sign of warning. Most likely those who receive the messages often brush them to the side. Although you have forgotten the vision, once it comes true, your memory will reflect back and acknowledge the knowingness. Psychic experts go into the future to answer the questions of the person concerned. In Déjà vu, you receive these visions without making any effort.

I received messages a number of times. Once I was standing at one place in India. Instantly realisation came that I have seen this vision of standing at this place. Similar information is released by the spirits relating to friends or people you never met before. You do not have to be psychic to receive these messages or images. It proves that you are spiritually sensitive.

'What is the cause to receive Déjà vu messages? To those who believe in Karma; it is based on cause and effect. Your fate karma appears as a result. Fate means whatever you are going to face, resulting from your good or bad deeds. This complete film is based on the outcome. If you are spiritually sensitive; the vision of your future can appear in split second. You can see it as real as it could be but try to ignore it because at present you cannot relate to the vision.

These visions can relate to past experiences as well. When meeting a new friend although your friendship is new, somehow your gut feeling is that you know this person for a long time. Déjà vu may show the vision of your past life in relation to this person. The film is made on the basis of your fate Karma; it is similar to the wheel of a bicycle. During life's journey, it keeps coming back to the same point. This is why our thoughts are always going forward and backwards.

If you are spiritually active you are part of the universe. Therefore, you may receive messages concerning the people in your life. Once you receive the inner intuition trust that what you see is true. Otherwise, you will acknowledge it; when it appears on the outer. If it is a negative vision, do not use spoken words to anyone or the person concerned. It is possible that negative happening may disperse at the inner.

Once spoken verbally then it is bound to happen as you have brought the situation into the open. To receive Déjà vu, you are not an ordinary person. Pay attention to your spiritual consciousness. You may begin to see these visions at your will. Déjà vu is a self-discovery of your spiritual awakening. The more you pay attention the more active it becomes. A few people have this natural ability but ignore it; believing it not to be true.

ESP; is known as your sixth sense or paranormal ability. It is the ability beyond our five senses; smell, taste, touch, hearing and seeing. ESP is based on the opening in the seat of the mind; the pituitary gland. Our mind has many sections where enormous information is stored. Your inner makes you aware of something which cannot be known by using our five senses. You can feel something but cannot pinpoint what it is. Your sixth sense is making you aware of what it is.

You mistrust a friend, who appears to be telling the truth but ESP makes you aware that he is making up the story. ESP is nothing of a huge spiritual gain but it can save you from many disasters. For example, Tsunami came on 26-12-2004 in the Indian Ocean and 229,000 people died. 'Do you know that before the Tsunami appeared on the surface all animals made their way to the top of the mountains?

Animals live a more natural life; their sixth sense is more active than the five senses. That saves them from predators at night time. Therefore, they use the sixth sense more than humans. Humans do receive inner messages; we always try to ignore them. That is why 229,000 people lost their lives. Animals act according to the messages received while we have a don't care attitude. God created heaven as well as earthquakes and Tsunamis. At the same time, it has given us the ability to save ourselves from disasters.

The more you pay attention to your sixth sense the more active it becomes in your life. Once you have the knack for it, you will have the knowingness of each happening in your life. Clairvoyance, Clairaudience, telepathy, telekinesis and mediumship are part of ESP. Anything that operates above the human level has connections with ESP. Telekinesis is the ability to move objects at a far distance. I try to ignore all these abilities because sometimes you are more involved with them than necessary.

LOYALTY & REWARD

God created each soul as its loyal assistant. We were loyal in the presence of God. Since we are in the lower worlds, God made a system of Karma to test our stamina if we can remain faithful to reality or walk on the path of deception. We often curse Karma, not knowing Karma is our most excellent guru. Karma teaches us how to become loyal once more to God, its creation and ourselves.

We work all our life to prove our loyalty and as a reward, we receive a royalty. Genuine commitment means you are loyal upfront and behind the back of the person concerned. If you are loyal, people will appreciate and remember you till their last breath of life. Loyal people are never short of love and support. This is where betrayers fail and no one trusts them. They walk alone all through life. A loyal person walked alone but many joined.

Loyalty is tested when you have no ground to stand on and have no hope of receiving any help. It is tough to stand alone when hailstones are dropping like stones. We often pretend to be loyal but we know the truth. No one deceives within. People often trust those who trust others. It is your loyalty that creates trust. No one trusts the deceiver. Their life is like a flower cut off from the branch; it cannot shine forever.

In other words, loyalty means self-sacrifice. It can be fruitful but often suffer in silence. I hope your glorious day will come. Sometimes your day does come when you have lost the hope of justice. It does not matter how loyal you are; people will do their best to find faults or create stumbling stones in your path. Your loyalty may hurt within but never lose your ground. Stay put: you will be rewarded.

It is human nature to judge others on our parameters. You cannot be the judge and jury. Karma decides your fate or line-up destiny. Your loyalty will speak louder than words. Your words may not impress others but your loyalty will. Never lose hope; your loyalty will be rewarded one day. Your reward is that people love and respect you: when you are no longer beneficial to them.

I remember those who stood by me when I was in need. I still love and trust them, although I have not seen them for years. Loyalty is earned and makes a way of life. Learn to stand by those in need through thick and thin. When you are loaded, many unwanted friends will join; when you have nothing, they all disappear and are never heard of again. Our friendship, family and marriage are based on loyalty. It takes all life to build loyalty; it can shatter in minutes.

If someone is loyal to you, do not push them to the extreme: where they walk on you, never to return. I have experienced this myself. To bring back your faith once more is beyond question. I have been loyal to God and the teachings I followed. I have been loyal to my family and friends in my circle. People do not appreciate your loyalty; they often try to stab you in the back. You may succeed in spirituality if you do not strike back. Let them face their music: known as Karma. Karma spares no one.

Loyalty means a reward for life. All good deeds are rewarded a hundredfold by God. All writers and singers receive royalty for life because of their efforts. We expect rewards for our hard work or loyalty towards some cause. The rewards give us the courage to carry on doing good deeds. Sometimes our loyalty and reasonable efforts go against us. Some people do not appreciate your efforts because they cannot do any for themselves.

When loyalty is not appreciated, that can lead to depression. This is what happens in broken marriages. Being loyal to each other builds a strong foundation for generations. Loyalty in friendship leads to love and that leads to marriage: that is for life. Karma will test our stamina on many occasions. Kal will create elusive circumstances to lead you off the track. It is a bond of trust that guides you to stay put.

In royalty, we stay loyal to the crown; this is how monarchy survives. Loyalty is a gift from God. It cannot be created purposely. Most people are eager to receive rewards without creating good Karma. I am loyal to God. I always write about God's way of life so others can benefit. Many people have changed their elusive way of thinking to eternal life.

Other than humans, the whole creation is loyal to God. We may not get big rewards but small praise can make your day. Without little compliments, our connection with society will dry up. The craving for recognition within keeps us going. I receive many praises for what I write. I appreciate them but put these praises aside because they may appear as my weak point later. I receive strength from Spirit itself.

False praise can make someone's day where criticism creates enemies. Our ears are often eager to listen to praise. Good ethics and dedication in what you do: can provide royalty for life. Sincere compliment costs nothing; as a reward, someone can be loyal for life. Praise can lead to love, whereas criticism can destroy lives. A few words of wisdom make all the difference.

A few words of appreciation may help in the future. Most people prefer the benefits of today; tomorrow, they will be alone. Although you love someone but cannot express it: these three words, **I love you**, can change someone's life and become a loyal friend forever. Big rewards are received by giving. When you give, you will experience satisfaction within. People felt my love and I was surrounded by many who became my helping hands.

During old age, we expect appreciation of what we did for others or our family. As royalty, we received care and love. You felt that life has been worth living. Your ego or money you had, does not help. Because of your love, people will hold your hand till your last breath. You do not feel pain and pass away with a cute smile. Your loyalty has been rewarded and you left your mark in this world as a legend.

STRIKE WHEN COLD

Strike while the iron is hot is an old proverb not to miss the opportunity when it arises. The present moment defines the same as having spiritual success. We often miss the chance when we decide to deal with it later. As they say, tomorrow never comes. Prompt action is always fruitful if taken immediately. Some find success when young, while others achieve nothing for years. Sometimes late is better than never.

Most people find success because they are swimming along with the tide. With little effort, you can float the oceans. Some always miss the boat. Progressive opportunity knocks only once on our door. This missed opportunity may irritate you for life. I was lucky to have many options in life but purposely ignored them because I am not too fond of taking advantage of situations.

Honestly, I feel better if I earn something, not regret it later. Sometimes honesty leads to your failure. Some people never find success due to family circumstances. Therefore, some people lead very passive lives. Celebrities lead active lives if success comes easily; they become the centre of attention. The name and fame do not last long.

These people go cold in life. Therefore, many celebrities use drugs. Most of your friends will leave because no one wants to tolerate cold people. Some people are born cold and they lead lonely lives. Most of the time, they are depressed and so are celebrities. Once all your friends leave you, it is an opportunity to realise that you are an individual. As in royal rumbles, everyone is fighting for the title. It is a decision time.

Now you must learn how to strike when the iron is cold. It is time to find the courage to swim against the tide. All your efforts will experience resistance but your strong willpower will help you cross the oceans. Many sharks will attack but will not succeed in their mission. We can rise above our sorrows; it is a time to bounce back and challenge our failures. You feel low but you know that you can succeed in life.

To an insane person, it does not matter if he succeeds or fails. It is your capability within, knocking on your door to wake up. Some people don't want to wake up because they have lost hope in life. When you have given up entirely, sometimes an angel appears in disguise and you become spiritually alive again. In 1982, I felt low because I had missed the most significant opportunity of my life. Satnam Ji appeared and said; "What has happened to my son" to revive my life again.

Those were the magic words; instantly, I was floating in the sky. A similar opportunity returned later but not as good; contentment in life is important. Sometimes accepting your defeat like a champion can turn failure into victory. Those people who believe within always win. We always blame others; most likely, we are responsible for our failures. Many will come in your life and so many have gone; keep focusing on your goal.

Never look back; that was your past. You cannot waste the present moment on past failures. If you do, another failure will knock on your door. Always look ahead and expect to do better; your efforts will be fruitful. Never rely on others; they can help or drown you purposely. I am alone and collect pearls of wisdom to pass over to you. I am successful; I am sure you can do the same; Sharing is caring.

Please share whatever you can; it is very satisfying within. The blessings of others can open many doors for future opportunities. All Seekers are blessed to be in the presence of a spiritual Master. He is always guiding and protecting. Without my Master, I could have lost in the wonderland. Most religions do not believe in living Master at present. All these people are leading their lives with their eyes closed.

Now I am going to ask you a question that may shock you. You have followed your respective religion all your life; 'Did you learn something worthwhile on the spiritual side? Comparative to what you have discovered within the last few years. I know your answer. You are an individual soul and God is alone; all others are lonely. Only lonely people feel low; that is the time to strike when cold and God is waiting for you.

The cold people feel vulnerable due to many weaknesses or defeats in life. You cannot sit in pigeon holes all your life. It is time to focus on your inner self and wake up the sleeping courage to roar like a lion. You are a born king to rule the world; when you roar, your fears vanish. You are born again. It is your new birth and smiles like a baby. Leave all your nasty dreams behind. Experience complete spiritual transformation in your heart.

BEGGARS BELIEF

Beggars' belief differs from the way of God. The way of God teaches that every step of life has to be earned. At the same time, beggars' belief is to expect something without any effort. The beggar's belief leads them into the trap of Kal to earn as much karma as possible. Baggers' belief leads to **myth** and God's way leads to **reality**. You cannot materialise something which does not exist.

This is the kingdom of illusion and there is the kingdom of the high; it is for you to decide what you want to follow. The myth will help you to remain as a man and the way of God will lead the way to become a future prophet. Your name will be carved in shrines. I believe in earning every step of life; 'You can only be a loyal servant to illusion or reality.' We want to be crowned but it is earned with responsibility.

The beggar's belief cannot bear this weight. God created us equal but later, we chose our paths. You can remain a child or grow up to become a man. You can remain a slave to illusion or become the deliverer of all. Never feel discouraged by what others say; you are a king, born to rule. God has given free will to all. You do not judge others; you are the prince of your universe.

This is part of the training to become the master of your universe. We prefer to be led by others because we fail to take responsibility. A child cannot remain a child forever. You are a man created in **His** image. This image has a responsibility; you better learn to dance to the tunes of Spirit. Your stubbornness will fail you from reaching your goal. The gates of heaven are always open for you but with beggars' belief, we lock all doors behind and throw away the key.

We want to have name and fame; Godmen wipe out the evidence of every step taken. Similarly, we do not create further karma; we pay our debts. The one who does not sleep has no name; still, all want to know him because we know it created us for a purpose. We are the wanderers who need to find our path to seek the truth. There are many stars in the sky; you are a born star. Everyone admires your beauty but knows not of your values.

Most sports people practice since they were young; with the effort they find success. Their peak time is short-lived; eventually, they decide to retire. In spirituality, it is the opposite, it may take longer to find success but you cannot retire. I notice most of the followers are in a relaxing mood. They have beggars' belief that the Master will see them through without much effort.

You may pass in your chosen subjects with recommendations. That is physical law or expectations. In spirituality, it is not applicable. The lower worlds are created as a training ground for the soul. You cannot pass or be excused until you achieve perfection. Spiritual freedom means to eliminate all materiality. You cannot depend on any support, not even from your Master.

Your Master can guide or infuse all his knowingness to make you successful. Once successful, you are alone in the presence of the alone. If you don't have this confidence, find your weakness and do your best to eliminate them. The driving instructor gives several lessons, so we become drivers. You are alone with the examiner; he decides if you pass or fail.

Do not follow beggars' beliefs; you will not win the lottery. I do not promise elusive dreams. Despite unexpected obstacles in my path, I worked hard to reach where I am today. I pushed obstacles aside and moved on to achieve my set destiny. The most significant beggars' belief is religious following. All followers follow the religious systems very sincerely. It leads them to nowhere other than to create ego or religious wars.

The worlds beyond are not within their reach. Our needs drive us to visit temples to console ourselves. When we are within the boundaries of religious places and reciting the verses, that is a positive or creative time. Otherwise, most of the time, we dwell in an elusive world. During our religious visits, we vision the image of our holy prophet, the one we have never seen or it looks like. It is similar to accepting a stone as God.

It is true the way I explained it. All make and believe is beggars' belief. Pseudo Masters provide beggars belief and threat; you cannot leave once initiated. **God**, our creator, does not hold your hand; it has given you free will to do as you wish. 'Then who are these people to dictate your freedom? I have unlocked beggars' beliefs because I am spiritual and neutral. When you are religious or biased, you will never understand.

If you are intolerant, you will never become universal. I hope you crack the jukebox of beggars' beliefs and become Godman one day. One time I held a beggar's belief; later,

I learned it does not work that way. Silence is golden; sometimes, it becomes your biggest enemy. You can claim your rights or go into silence and disappear into the dark world. Read the last chapter, 'Strike When Cold.'

Strike when you are on the verge of failure and awake the superman within. You are the replica of the glorious one. A glorious one is alone and does not depend on anyone, does not seek help and does not create religions. We make religions and follow systems and stay in flocks. 'Can you compare your qualities with glorious one? If you want to be one, you must walk alone and people will follow.

You are a 'wind'; no one knows you came and gone. This is how God resides within us and we fail to acknowledge its presence. Those who dwell in the heart of God live in people's hearts. 'They do not even know who you are? God is the unknown king who is not recognised in his kingdom. He is so detached and does not complain. 'Can you detach yourself from this world? If you can, you are following in the footsteps of God.

The world may not recognise you but God knows who you are. Enjoy the company of God. Hold on to its finger; you will never walk alone. You are the assistant of God. No fire can burn, no wind can blow you and no water can drown you. You are the eternal truth. You have discovered what others are searching for. You know, you gain nothing with beggars' belief; only failure is at your doorstep. All champions lose at some point in life but learn to fight back. You are a born champion and will remain forever. God is omnipotent, omniscient, omnipresent.

THE KING OF SAND CASTLES

Life is a continuation of hopes and our hopes create desires. According to our desires, we build sand castles. I do not wish to have any more than what I already have. I want to see your dreams come true. My success is based on your success and it will never materialise if you read the discourse once and then put it to one side. If I am successful in my efforts, then I am the king of the castle. Otherwise, my dreams vanish into thin air.

My dreams ceased because I came to know more than expected with good luck. To materialise your dreams is important. That is part of learning for the soul. We all weave dreams all through life, from birth to death. These dreams keep us going. We hardly realise most of our plans are no more than sand castles. The person with less to do in life dreams the most because he has nothing else to do.

We dream and have high hopes to materialise them, which can lead to problems. From birth to death, we failed to achieve anything worthwhile. We sailed in many boats. Sometimes our lives are smooth but despite our efforts, many tides come and we fail to reach our destiny. Our brain and heart do not synch. Our soul wants to enjoy but the brain leads to hesitation. We want to succeed but are facing failures.

Good luck is beyond your reach. To achieve success, we built many sand castles; heavy winds came and every grain of sand vanished into thin air. You have family and many friends but are lonely at heart. You dream that one-day success will come but always find yourself at the crossroads, not knowing where to turn to. All paths lead to failures. We want to make a name for ourselves; the realisation comes that you are no better than a tramp.

The wild animals are happier and calm than you are. We build sand castles, wait for the night to pass and wait for the sunrise. The sun appears but soon clouds cover its face and your life loses its charm. You have to prove to yourself that you are worth something. Bread and butter are not easy to come. There is always a big fish in the sea to overpower your efforts. You want to be a good fellow but your happiness does not last long.

You wanted someone to come into your life but all appear to be pilgrims and fail to become companions. Sometimes these pilgrims are betrayers and fail to make eye contact; despite all knowing, we want to build sand castles with them. We are waiting for the big day, which never comes but our hopes are high. You opened your heart but people walked all over you. People have innocent faces but hide the darkness inside.

You fail to judge because you are one of them. We are students of the same school. The more you open your heart, the more people laugh at you. 'In the end, realisation comes that what should I do? The eyes look innocent but are the betrayer of all. We fall in love with an illusion. We never stop building other sand castles. We all go astray; we need someone's love to support us to make our turning point.

One day we will discover the turning point in life. To do that, we build different sand castles. Despite our failures, we cried and smiled at the same time. The hunt for the treasure is still on. Pain arises in the heart but still waiting for the sun to rise. You are silent but your eyes say it all. There is a fire within your heart but tears of anger flowed like rain in your eyes.

The clouds are not that easy to disappear, still waiting for the day of your life to come. Although it taught us many lessons, we want to fall in love with life. Each failure leads to success. Bad luck is always knocking on our door. The twain never meets. We all want to be honoured but one dark side always knocks on the door. We all want to be saints but not worthy of its title. Our weaknesses are failure points.

Our horizon is heaven but all doors open into hell. You are alone but **within** leading us to carry on. Whoever we are, we are part of God. All guilt is part of the experience of knowing more. Please do not wait for any justice; it is all our creation. God is more eager to meet us than we are to God. We are more trapped within our creations than we could imagine. Sometimes it is better to close your eyes to many situations.

Silence often wins; the lord of Karma will decide. The wind blows from many directions; sometimes, it may cool you or blow you away from where you may never return. Life is a strange concoction; we still want to build sand castles. We all want to settle scores in life while failing to provide justice to all. Nothing in the world will convince you unless you wish to accept the truth.

Once we were innocents but our creations led us to the path of devils. We weave golden dreams but the threads we use are not pure. That is why we fail to become Sufi saints. The day we wake up, the sand castle has disappeared and standing in front of the king of the dead. Life is so short that it seems we left heaven yesterday. This will carry on until we land on the golden land. God is always with us but we have our sorrows and misfortunes.

Every shattered dream demolishes your sand castle because the foundation was not strong. You have met so many people in your life. No one impressed you, nor do you want to impress anyone. It is time to go in silence; your castles have turned sand. We take so many risks in life; at times, we are prepared to build sand castles middle of the sea. 'Why are you there; when you are not even the king of a pond?

I made a fort at one time. Later it turned into a sand castle. It does not exist anymore but still, I am trying to build its foundation. We believe that our sand castles are shrines and we want to pray but our prayer mats are washed away into the sea. The sand castles are children's delight at the seaside; you cannot rely on them forever. Laying a few bricks with mortar is better than laying a thousand bricks with sand.

Patience and determination are the keys to success. Be watchful; someone is always trying to demolish your castle, although it may be made of solid concrete. We are older and wise with age and all sand castles have not been fruitful. You have wasted all your life crossing the ocean. You want to do more but your system is slow and exhausted. Your magical spark has disappeared.

You could have succeeded if you let the Spirit do your work but you let the devil lay your bricks. We must learn to face the truth but sometimes it does not appear in the clear sky. Our life is like an hourglass; it does not take long to realise when all episodes are over. The Lord of Karma asks the question, 'What did you learn? I did try my best but I suppose it was not good enough. I believe, my doubts and impatience led me nowhere.

I am sure I could have done better if I had trusted the within. All lower worlds are part of the illusion; whatever we do or dream of; is inaccurate. Live your life unconditionally; it may lead you into reality. We failed to learn how to enjoy our life. Have courage and believe in yourself; you will be victorious. Why do we build sand castles because it brings a magic touch to our lives?

The journey to God is alone, so do not weave any dreams or sand castles with others. We believe to be the philosophers of life when there is only a small amount of sand in our accounts. Our treasure is within; listen in silence; God is calling you. The prize is not a sack of golden coins; it is the love of God. God is always on your side in life's low or high tides.

Sand castles are similar to dreams which do not materialise upon waking. Those who fail to achieve anything worthwhile in life build sand castles. Your achievements are small because you failed to consolidate any goals. Sometimes rock-solid castles also sink into the sea, at least you tried. Life is like a wave in the ocean; you may float to safety or sink to the bottom of the sea.

Like sand castles, all your achievements in the lower worlds are temporary. Sometimes you live like an old Wiseman but nothing materialised fruitfully that can force you to build sand castles. On your last day, your hands are empty; you could not manage to take anything with you. You followed your religion but never acted upon its message. You became friends with illusion and it was fun.

Learn to let it go; you may achieve something worthwhile. We know all sandcastles vanish, build your castle with the bondage of light and sound, where you can sleep without any fear. You are in the arms of Spirit. Seek the kingdom of God; it is always with you. Every word of this discourse is similar to the grain of sand, you can make it fruitful or it may vanish as nothing.

LOVE & LONELINESS

The whole creation is surviving with the love and blessings of God. God is love and conveys its love through Spirit. Spirit flows from God to the bottom of the sea. Therefore, nothing can exist without this love force. Love of God is our strength and it is given to us unconditionally. Human love is based on many conditions. Those who cannot live without human love experience loneliness.

Human love can become our weakness. Those who received less love when young due to whatever reasons become strong mentally. They can do without love or moral support. They become the survivors. It does not mean that they cannot give love to others. They are full of love but they never had the chance to share it with anyone. Naturally, they have adopted one quality of God. God is alone and full of love and gives it to creation unconditionally.

If you are full of love, it can penetrate many hearts. Always remember that if no one loves you in this world, God never abandoned you. The whole world can leave you; as long as your nerve is ticking, you should know your companion is with you. Only human companions walk on you when they have lost their interest. If you have a pet dog or cat, they may die but will remain faithful till their last breath.

You may not see God but it nudges within to show the light that may lead you to your destination. God is full of love and gives you enough that you may share with others. God's love shows the way to heaven while a lack of human love can lead you to a life of loneliness. You should learn to make choices between these two loves. We often choose human love because we see it with our eyes and feel it within our hearts.

Human love is easily felt because we are emotional. God's love is pure and it is silent, therefore only a few can experience it. Anything that makes a loud noise is heard easily. Your companions love you but upon one mistake they may walk on you. God loves and lets you commit a million mistakes. Despite your mistakes, it walks along with you. You are breathing because of God's unconditional love that is why you do not acknowledge its presence.

Free gift is often ignored. Many came and walked off; God stood by me all the time which is why I am conveying its love to you. Many cannot survive without human love and many cannot survive without drugs. My biggest drug is; that I experience God's presence. Any other love or companionship is not worth fighting for; one day they walk off and leave you standing at the crossroads of life.

Loneliness is often experienced when our hearts are empty of love or the people, we loved become strangers to us. You cannot accept what you are going through. Maybe God has given you another opportunity to feel its presence and be strong. I feel much better when alone so we can communicate with each other without any interference. I cannot do without its love. Lost time is very hard to gain.

If someone walks on you, you must learn to forgive. Otherwise, your heart will be full of hatred instead of love.

Loneliness is an emotional feeling it can help to appreciate the love of God. The world may walk on you but God always stands by you. You may not know that most religious followers go to church or temple to revive the strength within. Loneliness is not a that bad experience; you may discover a life-changing solution.

Many people become successful, once they have given up. You never know; those people you loved most were holding you back. Sometimes, your lucky charm is tied with others. Once successful, you will forget the people who hurt you if they ever existed. Learning to stay alone can save many disappointments in life. Always remember that green leaves appear in spring and fall off the tree in autumn.

We experience life similarly; from birth till the last hour, you met thousands but only a few remain to hold your hand. We go through many cruel experiences. I think it is beautiful to be alone at least you have time for yourself. Loneliness is better than friends who come and spoil your day. They may not have wasted your time but they have taken you away from the presence of God. When alone you may discover your hidden strength.

Once I was alone and sitting on the river bank. Due to rain, the speed of water flow was fast. I saw one fish swimming against the tide. 'Can you imagine its determination to find success? That gave me the hope never to give up. Our minds are not trained to survive alone; therefore, we give up easily. Always find ways to become alive once more. Do not hope for the people who left you; they have left their concerns behind.

Those who are lonely may find strength in being near you. Many people can draw love and strength without your knowing. Believe in yourself and know there is a hidden treasure within, yet to be discovered. We discover our abilities every day. A lifetime is not enough to know yourself. It takes the wheel of eighty-four to discover our true selves. I always discover something new about myself.

Let people surround you; those who are your well-wishers and try to **avoid** those who are jealous or discourage your achievements. People with negative attitudes can drag you down the hill. Stay clear from these people and focus on your goal. Feeling lonely is your weakness; with a positive attitude, it can become your strength. Sometimes in life, we feel a dead end that is our saturation point in one direction.

You need a complete shake-up to rearrange into a productive direction. You may experience loneliness now; maybe God is building your inner strength. When you receive love beyond expectations that can be boring as well. When love disappears, you will be the weakest person in this world. Most lonely people are the result of this experience. They are not customed to living alone.

Never blame others; try to find the weakness within. Your efforts will be successful. One day you will laugh at yourself because all life experiences are responsible to make the great man; you are today. The realisation came that I held myself back from facing the rising sun. The sun is always shining but we need to move away from the shadow of loneliness to experience the love of God. If you don't; your life will be at a crossroads.

LIFE AT THE CROSSROADS

Due to Covid 19, the lives of the whole world have been at a crossroads. Let alone Covid 19, 'Do you know most of the world population lives at the crossroads? Sunshine's every day but it does not shine for some people. Nothing eliminates their misery. There are four avenues at every crossroads but we don't know which one leads to happiness. The one we are standing at is the correct one but our doubts force us to choose the wrong one.

Every dialogue in this discourse expresses; what leads us to the crossroads and what may be the solution. One wrong decision can force us to go in circles for life. You will experience many twists and turns in these circles. By the time you recover mentally or physically, your life comes to an end. Never take someone's guidance as the Bible; learn to make your own decisions. Sometimes your destiny leads to crossroads because you have a lot to learn.

An altered destiny can also lead to crossroads and you suffer all your life. No one lends a helping hand when you need it the most. The people you love close their doors to your face. All friendships fail at the testing time. A friend in need is a friend indeed. When you are at the crossroads, they all disappear. You wish God may appear to help; you will experience it hiding behind the clouds. You have firm faith but your strength and stamina are crumbling.

The people you trusted the most were all gone with the wind. During sadness, a month seems like a year. At night you want to sleep but you experience twists and turns. If you manage to sleep, you experience the nightmares of your daily thoughts. No matter how hard you try, you cannot have positive thoughts. You wish floodgates of happiness open for you but it is beyond your luck. You are not alone; all your friends are also at a crossroads.

Some speak when circumstances are beyond their control; others suffer in silence. One of the hardest things in life is to let go of your past. Learn to begin life with a new page each morning. Think positive and learn that you are not the only one at the crossroads. When we open to the Spirit, we know many people are worse than us. 'Can you imagine the life of Ukraine people? 'Destiny has brought them to what kind of crossroads? All situations are beyond their control.

People are dying and starving; some soldiers laugh at their faces and shoot them. Mr Putin is responsible for hundreds of deaths every day and laughing at the faces of Ukraine people. We all do the same in different ways. Therefore, what we go through is all self-created. The Romans put Jesus Christ on the cross and with our sins and war fair, we have put God on the crossroads. Do not find fault in others. There are many within us.

You are lucky to be at the crossroads and deciding which avenue to choose. The influential people alter the future of many; they have no concern about you laughing or crying. Learn to motivate yourself; some unexpected solutions may appear. The demons are waiting at the crossroads to demolish your guts. If you are weak, you may suffer but strong-willed people can always bounce back. Always learn to survive; never give up till your last breath.

Good results often appear when you least expect them. No relationship is perfect; we all try to survive. Always learn to take chances. You never know; it may lead to unexpected happiness. Never wait at the crossroads for too long; you may miss many opportunities. Always live in the present moment; every **Is** or **Now** is full of a blissful state; enjoy when you can. Sometimes it is better to take a back seat; many bad situations pass by without affecting you.

To be happy always is not healthy; sometimes, it can bring misery in life. Learn to live in a detached manner; it is always families which lead you to the crossroads. Some may help; others will laugh at your sufferings. Always be the king of your castle, do not invite unwanted guests. Never feel discouraged; you are never alone. Sometimes you must swim against the tides to crossover the crossroads. Many situations are challenging to get rid of but your efforts can be fruitful.

Never leave your responsibilities to others. That way, you will end up nowhere. Sometimes going through painful situations leads to happiness. Humans suffer more than expected because we fail to learn something from our flying friends. The birds do not sit on one branch for too long. We only sit on one branch because we fail to let go of many things in life. Some people are born miserable; they love to be at the crossroads for no reason.

Always try to avoid the company of such people; their negativity will penetrate your aura. Every day brings a fresh opportunity to walk away from the crossroads. This world is a lot better place to live than expected. The choice is yours. Many times, our corrupt minds lead us to a crossroads. The crossroads resemble a puzzle; the Master leads the way to heaven. Your destination is far beyond the expectations of others. Make your flight where no one can touch you.

If you cannot choose which avenue to follow, wait for the inner nudge for guidance. Once one page is read, turn to the next page because there is a lot to learn. Do not hide behind the mask; let people know who you are. You can teach many people at the crossroads waiting for instructions. You don't meet people by chance. There are many old accounts to be settled. Once all accounts are settled, all crossroads turn into one avenue.

There is no harm in asking for directions in life that can help you follow your life path. When at crossroads, we make many wrong decisions and end up in the land of no return. One day you wake up and discover your world has turned upside down. Your life collapses in such a way that you never recover. Many years ago, a friend of mine and full of health; when he woke up in the morning, he could not move. His head function was ok but it was found below the neck to be paralysed. Since then, he has never walked again.

Another friend fell asleep while driving at high speed; his injuries were such that he never worked again. Another one woke up one morning and discovered that his wife had packed her bags and had never seen her since. These are the tales of the unexpected; you never know what to expect the following day. Therefore, I suggest it is better to live in the present moment and enjoy while you can; otherwise, miseries are many.

Most of our physical ailments result from what we don't let go of. Many truths we learn the hard way when all episodes are over. Your life circumstances never turn normal. You may wonder where all my ideas come from because I observe life and try to learn from all situations. I help those who need it. Therefore, don't sleep in your life; many lessons must be learned.

Life is a great teacher. This is the whole purpose of the reincarnation system created by God. Each time we learn more, our minds progress to spiritual life. Saints also get sick and suffer. Many set traps to make sure that you suffer. 'Do you know they enjoy your miseries? Many empires collapse so does our lives, so be prepared to face the unexpected. Learn not to let your circumstances be heavy on you mentally. Do the best you can and smile in all cases.

You can hide many sorrows behind your smile. Doctor your life and control your circumstances before they go out of proportion. 'Do you know that some species bounce back to their original point if they learn that they can't make it; when they take a flight to cross over the river? 'Can you do that? Your lies or backbiting are not healthy; one day, they all backfire on you. Learn to entertain your mind and fill it with positive thoughts.

Your crossroads in life will disappear in no time. Crossroads often do not exist but we have a habit of creating them. Many problems do not exist but we expect them to knock on our doors. A few clever ones Passover their responsibilities onto the shoulder of others. When you want to enjoy life but your health does not improve, your life is at the crossroads. Many people experience life at the crossroads during old age.

Life is not a game, live it well or it may lead you to many crossroads. When you have no money and cannot find work, your life is at the crossroads. All these situations repeat in our lives and half of our life we spend standing at the crossroads. I am the way and the way is within.

DECISION TIME

When our life is at the crossroads, every which way is a dead end. The way you have lived your life; is not leading you anywhere. Life has become boring. 'The question rises within; now or never? It is decision time. You want to decide but it is learned that making a decision is not that easy. All decisions have consequences; whether good or bad. It is about time to experiment.

'Will your decision be fruitful or it may go against you and put you in the worst position than before? Without deciding, you cannot imagine what the outcome will be. We always hope for the better. Sometimes it can lead to treasure or you may lose whatever you have. Most bankruptcies are the result of this. you may become rich overnight or lose whatever you had.

Sometimes you make the decision or they are made for you by the people you are associated with. When deciding, a positive attitude is very important. That helps to assume your goal has materialised. If you allow doubt to intervene that can paralyse; what was going to materialise. If you are indecisive, sometimes it is better to take chances. A fluke decision could be fruitful.

Sometimes we make our decisions based on our failures. Analyse what was lacking last time that led to your failure. Each failure leads to success because an experience has landed in your account. When nothing materialises, your strong willpower is nudging you to say; do it now. All decisions are not fruitful. After facing the consequences realisation comes and wished you had not made this decision.

We make decisions a number of times. I made many decisions in my life. Half of them were successful. A few I regret and others were waste of time or effort. The failed decisions keep you busy mentally. As you can see nothing goes to waste. Our life or family circumstances can force us to decide; knowing it will not work in your favour. We are the victims of the circumstances; so was I. We should learn from each other.

Now, you have the experience; make sure that your children do not face the same. Sometimes you want to walk away; your given word will keep you grounded. I have lost a lot at times but I did not wish to walk away from what I promised. Your loss may be great but internally it is satisfying to live up to your **word**. Next time pause for a minute before making a final decision. Sometimes we underestimate our abilities.

You have the abilities but something is holding you back. In what I teach, only a few have found success while others are undecided about taking the full plunge. They are stuck in the old routines of thinking. That God will help or the Master will show the way. He is showing the way to lead but you are not walking behind. I wish everyone could walk alongside. Master does his duty but does not look back; how successfully you are following.

'Don't you think, you had enough of your excuses and weaknesses; now it is decision time? Later you will regret, your indecisive moments. You know; you had the ability but failed to decide. You knock on the door; you may experience paradise on the other side or it could be a trap. Sometimes traps are also in your favour. Some people try to fail you. Their traps work against them and in your favour.

Some people love to consult others before making any decision. That I do not recommend. Only a few are your well-wishers; others are envious that you may succeed. I consulted someone a number of times; each time I failed. I decided to go alone; I found success. Family or friends; all carry mixed vibrations. Most people suggest their personal experiences; that may discourage you.

Some friends may not show true colours but are holding a number of grudges. They all wish to see that you fail. 'What do you think; that matters? Go alone and be the winner. Always try to do something different. At present, what I write is my own and unique. When the world population is discussing religious books written by their prophets. They have brought the truth for us to learn. But I have to discover my own truth.

This means they are abiding by the truth discovered by someone else. Similarly, you cannot live your life based on the decisions made by others. Their truth is good but it is not good enough if you cannot experience something similar. God has given us the gift of creativity but you need to wake up the courage within to find success. We all experience setbacks but do not allow them to anchor our life to the ground.

We all imagine things; perhaps they are beyond our reach. Action speaks louder than words. Therefore, imagination alone is not good enough; give it a practical shape to your goal. Some people are fearless; they take all the chances. A few believe; that I cannot do it or win. You are holding yourself back. When others walk away with the trophy. Do not be sad about someone's success. Next time this trophy could be yours.

In marriage, husband and wife are similar to two wheels of a cart. They both roll at the same time otherwise the cart may end up in the ditch. This is what happens in failed marriages. Caring for each other is very important that creates a spark of love. God is full of love; it is giving fragrance of his love to all creation; so that you may find success. But we fail to decide and willing to walk into the traps of illusion.

Your family and friends are important but prior to that; you are responsible to God. He created and sent you into the lower worlds to learn. But you have found new friends; who always deceive you materialistically or leave you at their or your last hour in this world. You are standing alone similar to; how you appeared at birth. Learned all the lessons and experiences with many failures. At this moment you are standing at the crossroads to decide and walk in the arms of God. It is always waiting for us.

THE HOUSE OF LORD

We are seeking God in Temples; our approach is external. When a person is in trouble or in some kind of desperate need, we go anywhere to pray. When God is sitting within us and no one wants to know; we have no insight and are not taught this way. Someone can only tell us if they have experienced it. We have come to a point in Iron-age; where we feel God is millions of miles away and out of reach.

Over the millennia, we have lost awareness of God's inner presence and our approach to life has become materialistic. Over the years, I have heard people asking, 'What, God? 'Where is God? 'Has anyone seen God? 'Can you show me where God is? These people are not wrong to raise these questions; the reasons are many. The environment they live in and the way life has treated them.

A saint or a good person suffers at the hands of villains or someone nasty but that villain or nasty person is having a good time and living a prosperous life. After witnessing this, many people lose their faith and ask similar questions as in the last paragraph. These situations may be destiny or they could be a lesson to the villains in disguise, which may not materialise instantly but will shine through in later years.

Many times, saints set up these examples to show; how to obey the will of God and let it be when they can or could have done anything to teach a lesson to the people involved.

Saints leave punishment in the hands of Spirit on a neutral basis. 'Will Spirit give this punishment on the spot or in later years? Saints do not get involved because they are beyond for or against any situation.

They are examples of patience and tolerance. Jesus Christ could have escaped if he wanted to but he did not. This is why we know him today. Otherwise, we or history, wouldn't know who he was. Sikhism is full of thousands of examples. The fifth Guru, Guru Arjan Dev Ji sat on a hot metal plate over a heated clay oven while the Muslim captors poured heated sand over his head.

Despite this, he continued to do **Holy chants** throughout this ordeal. So, 'what gave them the strength to suffer without uttering a single word against these people? This is an example that these individuals were connected to the divine light and sound and had a direct link with God. Now, whether you see God at work or not depends on your state of consciousness.

It was their inner strength or connection with Spirit at work. Unless we have this inner connection, we will never be called saints. We are known as priests or scholars with book knowledge. To be in connection with or to be known by Spirit is most important. We should try in this lifetime or the opportunity may rise in future lives when we have earned good Karma. We express our individuality based on good Karma, which will be our state of consciousness.

When we reach a point in our search, the urge within and the spiritual mind seeks something or someone on the outer: A teacher or some teachings which can lead the individual to inner esoteric experience. This urge within leads you from one teacher to another until you are satisfied or until your destiny leads you to the teachings appointed by the Lord of Karma.

Spirit often leads you under the instructions of God so you can lead the people of some religion in the future. The Master or teachings that do not lead you to the inner are not worth following because your spiritual journey will be at a standstill. The external teachings give you an insight into, what to ponder upon when imagining the inner.

Whatever you have read over the years is fine but now it is your effort and the responsibility of the Master to lead you to the inner. Here are the answers to whatever you have read or studied in your life. Now is the time to reap whatever you have sown over the years. To become the knower of the inner worlds; you must build a relationship with your Master. Otherwise, your journey or dream will not materialise. The primary steps for this will be:

Practice the spiritual exercises daily with complete sincerity.

Total reliance upon the spiritual Master.

Practice the presence of the Master at all times and communicate your way.

Inner Communication: The Master should be able to operate physically and on the inner. Physically he is limited as he cannot be with everyone simultaneously but spiritually, he can be with everyone as required depending on the situation. Despite your spiritual exercises, you should try to maintain your communication with the inner or spiritual Master.

As mentioned, I only met my Master physically a maximum of ten times over 30 years. Still, I never lost sight of him because I learned how to build an inner relationship. Most members failed on this point and tried to be known by the Master on a physical level. Perhaps that is all they achieved and lost in later years.

With inner communication, it becomes straightforward for the Master to teach the Seeker. The advantages are that there is no use of spoken words, so the mind is also set aside. Then the silent language becomes very powerful and pure. It is beyond the reach of any physical means and the teachings are given directly to the soul. It will be a natural process for the recipient but it could become a phenomenon in the average human mind.

This inner communication will lead you to become the master of your universe. Once this communication is established, you will operate from the level of the sun and moon worlds, which is required to contact the spiritual Master during the spiritual exercises. So, the Master can lead you to the inner or higher planes. A person with this ability can roam freely in the upper regions.

As a regular visitor, even without the Master, you will build your authority as you are recognised by the lords of these worlds. With this, you have built inner communication with the spiritual Master and also established a relationship with all the Lords of all the planes. Now you have become authoritative and can take others with you on an inner journey or help someone stuck in these planes; they will be set free at the mention of your name.

This communication will lead you to be in the presence of Satnam Ji. Once you have become Self-realised, you understand that Self-realisation has to be earned. Self-realisation is a practical experience; you will have met all the conditions of roaming freely of your own volition. Now it is time to explore the worlds of being.

You have the blessings of Satnam Ji; during the daytime, it is your effort to maintain this state of consciousness. At night-time, the Master will take you on dream travels as you are an open channel for the Spirit. 'Once this process is continuous over twenty-four hours, can you imagine your progress? This can lead you to God-realisation and into the presence of God.

You have proven this reality to yourself. Without this inner channel, nothing is possible. It is due to this communication that all the secret teachings are made available. These secret teachings prepare the Seeker for the highway to the higher world. Now, you will notice that your material and emotional life begins to slip to the side and your soul shines out and is reflected in your aura. Others see something and wonder what it could be.

All the Inner worlds beyond the physical come into focus through this inner vision. The Inner worlds are as accurate as the Physical Plane is natural to our physical senses. The surrender to the Master also happens on the inner and the outer follows. 'Who is interested in the outer when everything is alive in the inner? The presence of the Master or Spirit is felt when the Inner is active. Nothing is possible unless we leave our physical shell.

This inner strength is responsible for overpowering negative habits such as alcohol or hard drugs. The Inner is also responsible for the origin of mystic powers. To the saints, they are normal but to others, they are miracles. Once you are successful on the Inner, it is also known as soul travel; many other achievements such as healing and telepathy are natural. With this inner connection, Reality shines and the illusion disappears.

LAW OF GOD

Once you begin to follow the law of God, your faith in physical law disappears. The law of God is eternal and non-negotiable. When physical laws have many clauses to protect the culprit. The laws of God cannot be challenged. They are to be abided by; otherwise, you are inviting your failures. The Law of God gives you love and life. Physical laws crowd your psychic space and punish you for wrongdoings.

God's law creates opportunities to learn from our mistakes; to learn it may take 84 hundred thousand lives. God is another name for patience. It teaches us to learn patience during our troublesome life. Once you learn that all turbulence is self-created; patience will shine through. You are the mirror of truth. The day you learn patience; God will see its image in you; as you and God are one.

It is not difficult to understand the laws of nature. We purposely try to avoid them; knowing they may not benefit us physically. On the physical, you are part of the illusion. It takes a wheel of eighty-four to remove this veil to appear as a soul. As a soul, you stand in the court of law but you are the law unto itself. You answer no one; you are answerable only to God.

God said; I am the way and the way is within. You follow my way; you can view the whole world being at home. You can circle all the planets to find me but I have been within you all the time. Your inner action could have saved all your travelling. You can travel all the corners of this world to search for happiness; when you have walked away from the bliss state. Curiosity is an illusion to deceive you.

You are searching for God when it is experiencing itself within you. Every law of God is printed within but we fail to read it purposely to avoid its following. There are criminal and civil laws for punishment; when the law of God is neutral. To follow them no harm comes. Our fears lead us to break the law. You follow the will of God; no physical law will touch you.

You are the replica of God's law; you preach the law of God when you fail to follow it yourself. One day you will learn that you are the maker of law and the breaker of physical laws. Physical laws cannot be compared with God's law because there is a wall of illusion in between. Prophets give spiritual commandments to their followers but they modify the contents to suit them.

To justify their wrongdoings, they create many man-made theories. You can run away all your life but you cannot run away from your spiritual responsibilities. Your sufferings force you to walk towards the gates of temples; otherwise, clubs and pubs are your nests to enjoy material life. No commandment can force you to walk away from these places until you are kicked out by force.

The day you accept your defeat, God accepts you with open arms. We can run away all our lives; there is no peace other than at home sweet home. Eternal home is your residence; that is why you are kicked out after each incarnation. You don't want to leave but your loved ones burn you into ashes. This is the procedure of God so that one day you may learn.

The eternal law exists because of God's divine will. The physical laws are created to control the monster within you. Both laws serve the purpose to create the neuter out of you. So, that the image of God may shine through. One day you may discover the temple within. We are always standing on the holy grounds but love to walk to discover illusions.

The day you discover the temple within; you will never set foot outside your doorstep. The physical laws help to regulate moral codes of conduct; when judges and juries are sitting within all the time. Physical laws are contained in books and the court of law dictates to follow them. Eternal laws are within; God lets you decide what you want to do with them.

It takes the wheel of eighty-four to decide and you will laugh at your decision. Physical laws are controlled by the authorities to dictate. Eternal laws are your own; where you are the judge and jury. You decide what you want to do with your life. Life is a spiritual experience but only a few manage to become saints. It is your promises and responsibilities to the others that failed you to awake Spirit within.

You must recite the truth; even if it may cost losing your life. This is how ancient saints lost their lives. We love to enjoy the pleasures in life when pain and gain are more fruitful. Illusion often attracts our minds and leads us to future suffering. We lie every instant to cover our wrongdoings; which return manifolds. Cause and effect are the golden rules but we fail to read the eternal bible.

All religions have their bible and illuminate the same message. Upon your wrongdoings police come and serve the punishment. God created the law so one day you may learn your own doings and lead you to the path of illumination. You may serve one year behind bars to learn the lesson. God gave you the opportunity during each incarnation; one day you may wake up to discover yourself.

You learn to be yourself and let others be. If you believe within, you are beyond all physical laws. You are created in the image of God to be its representative on earth. You are the Olympian to carry God's torch. Those who come to you will be in touch with God. You understand the purpose of your life. You serve well so God may shine through you. One day we all abide by eternal law.

Physical laws are to punish;
Eternal laws are for realisation.

GOOD OF THE WHOLE

If religion is not answering your questions or not leading you to God: 'Why are you following it? Ask this question within. If you want to see the true colours of life, view it in black and white. You will get the answer. If you do not get the correct answer: your instinct will be not to believe or follow it. We often wish for the **Good of the Whole** for others when we fail to provide one for ourselves.

This means, there is no weight behind our wish. Our assumption only materialises when it is beyond any belief. This is the difference between 9 and 24-carat gold. Good of the whole means to bless the whole world or you want to see peace and love in this world. It is a very positive thought. We all need these blessings. We can see and feel the suffering of many people while most suffer in silence.

You may be surprised to learn that all religious followers suffer; otherwise, they would not be in temples. When our stomach is full; we do not feel the need to eat anymore. During our temple visits, we feel someone is holding our hand and that we are not alone. It is your belief within but it is not true. Make and believe does help in life, although it is false security. But it does relieve some pain. To achieve total security, you must awake within.

'Do you know how many prayers are recited daily worldwide? A few billion, 'Did you feel the change in vibrations of this world? The answer is **no**, because all prayers are said or recited as a routine. One word spoken by someone wholeheartedly can change this world. This is how healing is done. Otherwise, mantra or magic are just mere words. The strength of positive focus during assumption provides healing.

We never feel part of the whole; we create our paths and suffer. Due to this, we do not feel part of God. However, we know that we are part of God but fail to prove this. This uncertainty is our failure point. Seek the wisdom of God; eternity will open for you. The instant spiritual connection will be felt. You will experience the reflection of God in each soul. Every soul is unique.

Gather yourself; the whole creation will be part of you. Your longings to become whole is complete. The marriage between two people is to experience life; our separate ways lead to divorce. If we become whole, then we don't need to wish the good of the whole to others. They are within yourself. The soul is a free and happy entity; it does not cast a shadow over others.

The wholeness is more significant than being lonely. You are an individual soul. That is your identity. The gaze of the Master can turn your individuality into wholeness. Unless you experience the whole; God-realisation is not possible. Nothing is good or bad; it is your awakening within. Always maintain a positive attitude; you will live in paradise here and now. Your positive attitude can change the opinion of the whole world.

You are living in this world and so does the whole world live and breathe in you. That way, you don't have to go too far to convey the message of; Good of the whole. The blessings are constantly pouring from above, our attitudes create umbrellas, so it does not reach us. We learn and send good of the whole to this world. This way, you give hope to people. God is merciful to those who send the message of goodwill and hope to others.

I do not pray for others because my good wishes and blessings are part of God's creation. God has given me the strength to pass over its best wishes to the whole world. Today is the day to receive. Tomorrow the value of blessings may change. The blessings of God are always shining within our hearts; otherwise, we will be lost in the wonderland of illusion. Those open to the Spirit can experience the good of the whole.

I wish your life would be full of blessings: I will be satisfied within. **Blessings**: this one word can create miracles in your life. Spirit blesses God's whole creation; otherwise, it is all dust and non-existent. I eat, breathe, sleep and am alive Spirit; my blessings are the same as sent from above. How blessed are you: your smile will express. Your smile makes my day; I do not look back.

'We are full of blessings, then why are you searching for them in temples? Always believe in yourself. Your doubt will dilute its effect. Do not utter a single word; your smile can make someone's day. We only remember God on Sunday. The other six days are dedicated to the presence of Kal. If you worship Kal, it also blesses you a hundredfold. That is why your accounts are full of negativity.

I walked on God's path; a few pilgrims joined and many let go of my hand. Still, I bless them all. I know nothing other than to say, good of the whole. I cannot satisfy all but I am satisfied within. 'What is within, that matters? Every day is fresh as flowers bloom in the garden. The butterflies are blessings in disguise. That is why all plants let them sit. They feel the touch of Spirit. Once you learn to breathe Spirit: you will never be the same person again.

I went out to change this world: when the most significant change is sitting within. There is no such thing as your blessings or my blessings. The blessings are good of the whole. These blessings create courage within; so that I can write the word of God. Each morning allows us to view the beauty of God. Those who fail on this charisma become miserable. Be still and consider its beauty and feel the flow of Spirit.

Sunrise is a reminder for us from God to live our lives on a daily basis or in the present moment. **If it were not true, there would be no sunset.** Each morning reminds us to make a fresh start in life: we fail to move an inch or make any fruitful effort. Your blessings will reach many and they forward your blessings to many others until it touches the inner core of God to bless you.

Those who wish for the good of the whole; Spirit walks with you. The Spirit always walks along us: 'why are you looking for elusive companions? When you are happy and smiling, many want to join on the way to God. People often let go of the hand: If it is felt that it may drown them. The enlightenment is within to ignite the flame. This alive flame will help to cross many oceans.

This morning I saw a bird sitting on the tree branch; it chirped in a melodious voice. Later it made the flight; I felt it might reach God soon. We cannot progress sitting on the same branch all our lives. Your effort will never fail you. You do not get blessings by raising your hands: you are blessed since birth or created as a soul. You only raise hands when you have lost faith in God.

God blesses us but some receive more favours who dedicate their lives to pass on its message of truth. One day I felt low in Spirits: as I turned around and felt a blessing was circling me from all directions. Be humble, merciful and pure in heart and wish the good of the whole and feel the presence of God. Your life will be full of joy, love and blessings.

WINNER OR LOSERS

On the way to God, no one is a winner or loser. Both contribute to our experience to gain perfection. The winner has been successful in his attempt. A loser is also a winner, your attempt has not been successful but at least you tried. Those who do not make any attempt are losers. The fruits always grow on tree branches, not in the air. You can visit the sea in a boat or dive into the sea; the difference in the experience will be abundant. The soul is not created to lose.

The winners are always remembered and the losers may come second or third. England won the football world cup in 1966; their names are carved in British history. After that how many good players came and went but they are not appreciated as much. We know the names of all presidents of America since Abraham Lincoln. 'How many ministers or foreign ministers came and gone? Their names are hidden in files.

The winners make plans and assume to materialise their goals. The losers expect a miracle to happen. Sometimes losers win with a fluke attempt. For me, nothing happened by chance despite my sheer efforts; I experienced many obstructions. Winning the hard way is more appreciated and fruitful. You will guard it well if you won the hard way. Winning easily is often ignored and forgotten.

Winning with effort is a trophy to display; other wins will end up in the desk drawer. It is hurting when you are the winner and someone else walks away with your trophy. They become the eyes of the apple while you are ignored and forced to live in silence. Sometimes losers become super winners to accept their defeat and return the trophy to the actual recipient. Accepting your defeat is the biggest virtue of ethics.

We always let our children win to see the smile on their faces. God let us win all the time that is why it takes the wheel of eighty-four to clear the main hurdle; known as spiritual freedom. We always dream of this achievement but expect someone else to do it for us. This is why there are billions of religious followers but none become prophets. Do not limit your efforts that way; you achieve nothing.

The miracle man always appears to revive the spirit within. I walked on the journey to win but failed. With good luck, I met many friends. They are better than the golden trophy because they have golden hearts. I have accomplished the goal of my writing but my pen doesn't stop. I make the effort so others may know more. I know my efforts will be fruitful. We compose our words so they may touch your hearts.

When they learn something worthwhile, it is always appreciated. Spiritual Master always makes the effort so you may win. Genuine winners often turn the word impossible into possible. God has created the answer before the question rises. The lower worlds are created in duality. Leave the judgement to God; your decision could be biased. Always act neutral; otherwise, your win will turn into a loss.

The losers always find an excuse not to act; the winners don't miss any opportunity. The difference between the winner and loser is their attempt. Sometimes our fate forces us to lose. The winners always inspire others to try once more. The loser dwell in the past and dreams of a beautiful future. The winners always dwell within the present moment. **Future**; You cannot win; when the event has not taken place. **Past**; you cannot enter the race, which has already been run.

The winner always encourages others to participate while losers envy others. The result of your win or loss will be according to your thought process. 'The losers should be appreciated; otherwise, who will be the winner? The winners always complete their tasks; for the losers, everything is pending but they blame others. Winning or losing is a mind game. God accept your attempt either way.

The winners learn from mistakes while losers treasure their memories. Your first attempt failed to the expectations but your second attempt may set world records. Never underestimate your abilities. Jesus Christ lost his life on the cross but became living forever. Always attempt for something unique. The winners have to live up to their image while the losers can live a free life. Therefore, you win both ways.

The winners are prepared to walk a few extra steps to materialise their goal; the losers pack up their bags before the finishing line. Don't listen to the opinions of others; they may try to discourage you. Once a born tiger will remain a tiger till death. Underprivileged or disabled perform better at the Olympics because their goals are greater than able people. Their failures in life encourage them to accomplish their goals.

A good win can earn the respect for your whole life. Do not try to justify your loss; make another attempt to make your mark. You are the winner because you have conquered your weakness. The winners create miracles; the losers are part of history. It cost nothing to believe in yourself. If you listen to the others; failure is knocking on your doorstep. Do not expect to win every time; otherwise, you are worse than the loser.

Never leave your task unfinished because you got a lot to accomplish. Always believe that today is your day. The failures do not wake up from their sleep. Half of their life is spent in bed. Learn never to quit; your willpower and decisions will be fruitful. You can become Icon for others to be successful and bag many blessings. People may reject or discourage you but God provides all the backup.

Sometimes we become failures by neglecting our abilities. Some people learn how to draw power from others. The motivation helps not to give up. I don't play to win; my wish is that the best **one** may win. With the attitude of; I can and I will walk an extra mile. I had the belief within; I created the miracles impossible to accomplish. Whatever you think will materialise.

I do not rely on others; I find the courage to do the task alone. God is alone therefore no one is mightier than God. To rely on others is your first weakness. You are born alone and learn to survive alone. Have courage and walk alone in the presence of God. The physical world is not your last accomplishment; there are many goals to be accomplished in eternity. Learn to walk with a style so you may become an assistant of God.

SELF CONFIDENCE

Self-confidence is the strength of the Spirit within. High spirits are a sign of happiness. Low spirits can spoil your mood or lead to anxiety. Your knowledge, personality, good health and a number of other things build your confidence. If you are inferior in knowledge, have average looks or are overweight can lead to low spirits and loss of self-confidence. You should be proud of who and what you are.

You cannot satisfy the opinion of others. If you are energetic that can cover many weaknesses. Action speaks louder than words. You will notice, that most movie stars have average looks but it is their self-confidence that helps them to face the camera and rule the cinema screens. If you are shy that can prevent you from many achievements. There are no parameters to weigh your confidence. What you feel matters.

It is easy to walk on the path shown by others. With confidence, you can make your own paths. Something self-created is very satisfying. I never tried to copy others. I have my own ideas and I write the way that is correct. How others value my writing is their opinion. It will not change my view because I know exactly what I am writing. That is self-confidence. Never doubt your abilities. I know you can do better than me.

Never compare yourself with others, they may appear better than you but you can have plus points that the other person may not have. We are individual souls. For example, there are many flowers in the garden. They do not compete with others but give fragrance in their capacity. God has given you exactly what you require to experience life.

When I was young, 2/3 boys approached and said, we are very jealous of your good looks. They let go of their mental pressure and at the same time, I felt more confident. No one can make you feel inferior; if you don't let them. Most likely we invite negativity in life. Keep nurturing your inner with positive thoughts. I treasure my old happy memories. They help when I am feeling low.

There is no person who does not feel low at some point in life. Don't let it be heavy on you. 'Who are the others; you are so concerned about? Their weaknesses are probably hidden behind their good looks. If you are confident half the battle is won. You may know so much but your low confidence can force you to make mistakes. The expression of love on your face and kind words can force someone to do many favours.

I do not compete with others; it is the competition within. It may be on a small pace but I achieve something every day. Today I wanted to write something and Spirit appeared with this title. Find the courage within to walk towards your destiny. Be focused on your goal; many will appear distracted. If you don't succeed on the first attempt, keep trying. Practice makes perfect.

If people try to distract you, that means you are a threat or above them. There is no competition if someone is inferior. You need extra courage to maintain your status. If you are near your goal, you cannot look back. We should not compare ourselves with others because our goals are unique. We are not in the same wrestling ring. You walk alone; there is no competition or referee to judge.

You are the best judge of your doings. Make sure you materialise your goals. Always try to achieve something hard to do or it is unique. There is no value for ordinary goals. Love and enjoy the task you do. Admiration of goal brings perfection to the finished product. Most people enjoy mythology; that is not your achievement. I may achieve less but it is the fruit of my efforts.

Try to create an original; thousands will copy. Only fear can let you down. I walk fearlessly and do not let others stand in my way. Other than yourself, no one knows that you are an unknown genius. It is not important for others to know. As long as you know that builds your confidence. We all try to be perfect. Learn to stay in balance; otherwise, your perfection can become your weakness.

I come across many people who are super intelligent and perfect. They become lonely because no one matches their knowingness. Be positive; you have nothing to prove to anyone. In your own way, you have accomplished your goal. Your confidence can compel you to take chances. You may fail in your effort but at least you tried or explored your potential.

The magician moves the objects without your knowing. It is his practice to give him the confidence of doing it; to bring magic into your life. If you are confident; you are a leader with many followers. You should know; that you are one of a kind. Some people remark, 'how do you do so much with perfection? I said; God made me in his spare time; that was Sunday. Humour in life is very important.

God has invested goodness in each soul; it does not shine because we let our minds take over. Comparison with others may take away the magic and you fail to create miracles. It does not matter if you are big or small; it is the spark in your eyes that matters. If you are confident and wear rags; people may assume that is the new fashion. Keep the spark alive within. Do not compete or compare with others which may create bitterness and lead to low spirits.

Learn to appreciate others for what they do and thank them for their efforts. I felt the presence of God; while others say it is not possible. 'Why should I associate with these people with this statement? They are contradicting their religious book. You are so great that God and all universes are within yourself. 'Can you imagine your greatness? Our own ignorance becomes our failure. Learn to conquer your abilities. Nothing is greater than confidence within.

WAITING FOR GOD

Waiting for something could be part of patience or your act is passive; you need a nudge to crossover. It is that moment, you are standing on the boundary line but need someone to push you. If someone witnesses your position, it is often said, 'Are you waiting for God? Sometimes our effort is not good enough and waiting for God to show miracles. Miracles only happen if you make an attempt.

We can apply this proverb both ways. Are you waiting for God? Or waiting for God to help us, as long as we find success. Once I was waiting for God but it did not come because for some reason it wanted me to wait. If you are in a similar situation, it is possible that God is waiting on us to make an effort. He created the lower worlds as a school for the souls. If God does all then the purpose of training is lost.

God is within and watching us silently. You may feel that you are going to lose but it has not let go of your hand. Keep trying; you may find success. Waiting for something is a waste of time for us but it could be a spiritual experience for the soul. Sometimes waiting is important because your gift is being prepared. God always answer your prayers but you want to hear it so others could hear it loud.

You may abandon your friends or family; God never abandons any soul. Sometimes you may not feel its presence because it is testing your patience. To achieve God-realisation, you must explore the hidden qualities of God. If you know God is working on your behalf; it is worth the wait. Once you felt its presence, it wakes the courage within to do better things. We can do more than expected.

Do not cry out to God because that is not a virtue of God because you are created in his image. The soul is neutral; your success or failure makes no difference. It is only going to register the gain of experience. God is always waiting for me because it provides all before the question arises. 'How can I complain? It is always working for me in the background. I only extend my hand to acknowledge its' gift.

Sometimes the will of God appears in the fog; It wanted me to wake up within to see the light. God is more eager for my success; when I am only trying to make up my mind. You may feel tired and want to rest but God's task is not finished yet. Some people ask me, 'how do I manage to write the pearls of wisdom? Because I have discovered the hidden treasure within.

We always fail because our search is external. You fail to open the inner door. God made some promises to me but they did not materialise because he wanted to see If I am capable of deciding. You have travelled through the experience of lower life. You have come so far; God will not leave your hand halfway. It wanted results. Most likely, it will be in your favour.

Patience is very important; sometimes we fail to see that God is at work. Do not judge the colour of the grass in the next field; the colour of your grass represents your efforts. Every lesson in life needs effort; God will not let you walk away from it until he is satisfied. Eventually, you are going to be in his presence. Purification of the mind is important. If it is not pure, you are not fit for the kingdom of God.

Each effort in life increases the size of your wings. Never compare yourself with others; you will waste your time. Do not live for the others, which we often do. Find time for yourself as well. Wake up the faith within; you are not far from the threshold of God. Once reached, the door will open itself. I waited for someone all day; that person never turned up. God has never failed me.

God does not listen to your prayers as believed by most religions. Because it is within. You are praying as if it is a million miles away. Nor do your prayers change the will of God, nor does it wipe out your karma. If his will is changed or wipes your karma; there was no need for the lower worlds as schooling. Religious thought teaches you how to bribe God. Your little token of donation is worthless because it is already given by God.

God is dwelling beyond matter, energy, space and time. 'So he is not in a rush; how long does it take to achieve perfection? Be yourself and let others be, so others can feel its presence here and now. Learn to romance with Spirit; all other romances are an illusion. Physical romance grows like weeds in the garden and once love is lost or dimmed in life; it destroys all the roots. You are surviving but the actions are lifeless.

You are waiting for the sunrise or another opportunity may come similar to the last one. We love to experience emotional feelings because God is silent. Always learn from your past mistakes so as not to repeat them. We have a habit of going in circles that is human nature. Never over-admire yourself; let God judge you if you are fit for his kingdom.

We walk many miles to buy illusion. The gift of God is often ignored because it is given free. The soul is part of God. The physical body is given to enjoy life. 'How many take care of their bodies? Most likely we all abuse it most of the time. When it gives up not functioning, we are waiting for God to heal. Our eyes and ears are part of an illusion; open up at the inner to listen and talk to God.

God is our best companion. I have given enough examples; 'Are you waiting for God to do your part? We are children of God. Grow up and become a helping hand in his cause. God is the first cause; you may become the second cause as a prophet. In reaction, people will become spiritual. You are part of God so are others. Serve God; you will receive its gift. God has waited for you silently; 'Now, can you talk?

REPENTANCE

One of the weakest points, most religions teach to their followers. The followers are happy to abide by this practice. There is a confession box in most Christian churches. The believer accepts his wrongdoings and turns from his evil ways of living. After this declaration, the believer feels guilt-free. The priest can only listen in silence and bless the followers for taking this positive step.

Most religious books have written statements a number of times. Prophets teach us to forgive those who commit wrong or bad Karma against us. Spiritually this statement may not be accurate but it helps the individual to move on in life. I have already written; sometimes word sorry is not good enough. 'You have destroyed someone's life or livelihood then you want to repent?

A young man fell in love with a beautiful girl and proposed marriage. She refused because she did not hold the same feelings for him. In revenge, he splashed acid on her face and it took 7 plastic surgeries to re-assemble her face. Despite medical help, she still looks like a plastic doll. Although he is behind bars, 'Do you think his sorry can turn the clock back? The word sorry is only valid for the reasons.

We must learn to regret our destructive actions. A religious person should not be committing serious negative Karma. If he does, he is not practising what has been preached by his

Prophet. There are billions of religious followers in this world; who commit wrong Karma. They all try to get away with it if possible. If not, their religious priest suggests asking forgiveness. I wish it were that simple.

Most popular religions do not believe in reincarnation or Karma. It makes no difference to them; what has been committed. No religion or priest can save you from your suffering in the future. Lord of Karma demands equal pay for your wrongdoings. Repentance is important if it can help you to be a better person in the future. Religions are not based on pure Spirit. They are part of the dual world.

This is why their solutions to life are based on positive and negative. Any person commits a wrong that is negative. Equal and opposite they suggest a positive solution. Both are extreme in nature. God is pure and neutral, therefore acts have to be justified. This is why the lord of Karma is established on the Astral Plane to calculate your deeds. After his judgement, you are suggested to spend time in heaven or hell.

If this is the law of God; therefore, priests have no authority to bypass his judgement. My statement may not be accepted by many but priests act this way to please their congregation. The followers are happy to find solace in religious places. If people don't suffer because of their wrongdoings; I can assure you; that they will never visit temples. I am happy if any person realises his past mistakes and is willing to lead a better life.

At least he made the effort to accept his wrongdoings. This commitment is important; many people fail to feel repentance all life. Many died and took guilt with them. They never found the guts to accept their wrongdoings. Some manage to open up in their last hour. We often forgive the dying person. His mental pressure has disappeared; yet to face the lord of Karma.

Some people are behind bars for committing murder. That is physical law to punish someone. Spiritual law is still waiting for his arrival in the Astral Plane. On the physical, we can repent and walk under the shadow of religion. When you are away from a religious roof the shadow will never leave you until death. This system is so perfect; that no one could challenge its justice. Many religions justify repentance but God has not given this authority to any prophet.

This is a general statement but it is true. I heard some people commit murder and leave the scene for good. They take solace in far distant Temple to hide from the law and spend the rest of their life being or acting religious. 'Will they ever become saints? The answer is **no.** Your prayers or repentance will not change the will of God. I have one principle among many others. I make sure to pay, what I owe to someone.

Some religions claim that their prophet had the authority to kill an animal to set free from physical life and be escorted to heaven. They are excited to know the authority of their prophet in God's world. This is not true at all. You have to earn your place in heaven. If you have read my books, you know the path to heaven is not that easy to find. The way is within but out of your reach.

In Saudi Arabia, the blood money for murder by mistake or accidental is set at SR300,000. If the murder is committed with the intention to kill. It is up to the family of the victim to decide if they are willing to accept blood money. Otherwise, they can request the judge to execute the murderer. In this case, the amount has to be agreed upon by the victim's family or offered by the murderer. This repentance is bought with money.

On the physical, we can agree on many terms. We can ask for forgiveness in church or be willing to offer blood money; Nothing can justify what has been committed. The human mind is searching for mental satisfaction. In Hinduism, animal sacrifice is associated with Shaktism within tribal traditions. It is mentioned in Yajurveda; the religious scripture of Hinduism. This sacrifice is used to please God or Goddesses.

Another religion accepts repentance if you can offer the sacrifice of animals in your place. I do not wish to discuss this in detail but the question is; 'how can you justify your actions with animals? It surprises me that most educated people accept this practice. It does not matter, which religion we are following; We all try to justify our sins. We are fugitives on the run and find many places to hide; nothing is hidden from God.

You are in the trap of Kal by hiding in religious places. The big brother is watching you.

DISAPPOINTMENTS IN LIFE

Disappointments are inevitable because we have high expectations in life. We dream all day but they do not materialise. Disappointments are the biggest teacher in our lives. In fact, God has created the law of cause and effect. When we act as a cause it may not hurt us but when we receive a reaction to our doings, then we are disappointed. We love to enjoy but prefer not to suffer.

What goes around comes around. Without disappointments, we learn nothing. Each disappointment leads to a spiritual experience. 'How can you win, when you don't know what is disappointment? I have been disappointed many times in life. I have learned something every time. If I did not learn anything, at least it kept me busy mentally. An empty mind can bring more disappointments than expected.

I realised that I found success after each disappointment. It led me to think differently. Disappointment is a realisation to learn and move on. Disappointment can cast a shadow in life; if you do not find the reason for its presence. Any of the five passions of our mind can be responsible for creating disappointment. Most Seekers are disappointed if their expected spiritual goal is not materialising.

I encourage the Seekers to be disappointed; that may wake them to find the cause for failure. If everything in life goes smooth, we love to enjoy our sleep. Disappointment keeps our minds active. An active mind is not dangerous all the time; it may lead to finding the solution to your disappointment. A passive mind fails to decide. Unless it is the neutral mind that can experience both sides of the coin to find a solution.

Disappointments are self-created or they act as shadows; in the way, we live our life. Our family or at the workplace can bring disappointments. It is nothing of your doing but you cannot walk away from them. Sometimes we expect too much from our family or friends and they fail to deliver; that can lead to disappointment. Learn to stay in balance. If you ask any person at their last hour; they are all disappointed because they failed to achieve set goals.

I aimed for big but I have not even achieved 20% of my set goal. Most populations fail to achieve anything worth considering. Instead of walking or running, they lived life crawling. Life is too short and our dreams are big. A simple person with fewer dreams may achieve something in life. Most of the time our thoughts are dominated by achieving something instead of making an effort to materialise it.

We try to avoid someone if they appear miserable. We never know, how disappointed they are, in life. They have lost the love force and failed to show a spiritual spark in their eyes. They failed to face the facts of life. We should not expect good results every time of our efforts. We should learn to face our failures too. When I was young, I was enthusiastic about doing things; At present, when I look back, I think it was a completely failed policy. What is true today, may not be true tomorrow.

I take that learning positively because few others benefit from my endeavours. After each failed policy we gain experience. This is what our life is about. It is a continuous succession of learning. When we don't accept our defeat that can lead to disappointment or depression. Life is too short to live on regrets. Learn to move on in life at the same time expect disappointments. It is better to expect; otherwise, disappointment may surprise you.

Our life is not an open book; God turns the pages as we learn along. Each page of our life has hidden suspense; we don't know what to expect. If all the pages are open; there will be no more excitement. It is the excitement within that keeps us moving. The law of cause and effect is based on; we are happy when this law is in our favour, otherwise, it leads to disappointments.

We fail to see many disappointments because they are disguised. Our destiny, open the page when we are ready to learn the next lesson. This world is not full of disappointments as many believe. If it is, then it is not in balance. You have to find your own ways of keeping happy. You may find happiness being in the presence of people with positive attitudes. Try to learn their secret of living happy and passing it on to others.

I share my knowledge so you may pinpoint your weaknesses. We are full of faults but fail to acknowledge them. You have to live a life of perfection before getting the gift of God-realisation. All Seekers are eager to have spiritual realisations at set conditions. As long as you are stubborn in your ideas, God will not appear alive in your life. To achieve any realisation, you have to live your life under the set conditions of God. You have to walk in the shoes of God.

I received unexpected disappointment but it led me to the biggest realisation of my life. Each disappointment has a hidden message. Maybe I expected too much which, I was not worthy of. We always expect too much beyond our efforts. The grapes are sour. Maybe you are disappointed but make sure no one is disappointed because of you. That can earn good deeds in your account. Always bad deeds lead to disappointments.

Sometimes I disappoint people purposely so they don't make habit of leaning on me. This is the reason when I say; that what I am capable of; so are you. Sun will shine tomorrow if you make the preparations today. Nothing appears instantly. Therefore, learn to accept instead of expecting. You are born alone and we die alone; our disappointments only appear when we lean on others. Learn to survive alone.

The day our disappointments are over, the gates of heaven will open. We experienced many disappointments in life but something kept us going. God never let go of your hand. Disappointments only appear when we try to leave God's hand. Illusion creates miracles to amuse the mind but at the dead end, disappointment is waiting for you. We always try to eat more than we could chew.

Feel content, expect less, lead a balanced life, be positive and know God is holding your hand. You will experience fewer disappointments. Maybe you have a number of disappointments in life; I can assure you they will not be effective. Our own weaknesses create the shiver within. We are on the verge of destroying this world; God has not lost hope in us. God compensate for each disappointment with love and lesson.

YOUR DAY WILL COME

Yesterday was the day, so is today and tomorrow will be fruitful. You are the son of God; your day will come. You are born to dream; your dreams will come true. Embrace your dreams; night is not over yet. God has not given up on you; so, do not give up. You are the prince; your princess is waiting since sunrise. Tomorrow comes to remind you of your pending goal.

In the present moment; you are the master of your destiny. Your destiny is begging to be explored; 'what is the delay? In the stillness, this world stops; you are living within. Within is the treasure of life; it is all yours to have. You are full of love, beyond the treasures of this world. This world is micro; you are the master of your universe. Prepare yourself for the worlds beyond; God is waiting.

Prepare yourself in the inner; you are the winner. Nothing comes with chance; your efforts will be fruitful. Be humble and you will have all; your day has come. Every morning is your day; wake up and enjoy the sunshine. Sunshine has brought new opportunities; don't let it pass by. Every missed opportunity; may not knock on your door twice. Your wish will materialise; guard it well.

Do not be sad; sometimes opportunity takes the wrong turn. Many golden opportunities are to come; you will be spoilt for choices. Have wonderful thoughts; the day is not over yet. A day missed in life; the same day does not return for a year. What day are you waiting for; you are holding an umbrella under the sun. You and God are one; Every day is your day but you failed to acknowledge it.

Maybe today is a rainy day; the sun will shine tomorrow. God sent many pearls of wisdom; you failed to collect them. Each pearl has a spiritual message; today is your day. You did not trust the inner nudge and let the day pass by. Sunrise reminds you of your day; sunset is missed opportunity. Do not expect mercy from others; they are all competitors. Have faith, let go of the past; your day will come soon.

The present moment is your day; the past has gone; tomorrow is your daydream. Be cheerful; someone is going to hug you today. Maybe today is a sad day; it does not mean tomorrow you cannot smile. Nothing was materialising in life; the day I gave up hope; an angel walked into my life. Never stop trying; you never know who is around the corner. To let go of things is important to have your day.

Do your Karma and do not expect results; good Karma will lead you to your day. Do not underestimate your abilities; maybe God is preparing your gift. Patience can draw your day near than an act of aggressive action. It will be more satisfying; if you manage to make someone's day. Each day in life is important that is why the world is waiting for the sunrise. Many days came in life; you shared with your family. Be prepared; your best day is yet to come.

RICH BY HEART

God is the richest of all. 'Are you rich enough to stand in its presence? That is why all religions claim; that you cannot see God. The religious followers are of a different class. You have to be the class of a person approved by God. You must have your individual class to be in his presence. God gives all. 'Are you capable of sharing with its creation? We pretend to be rich but are poor at heart.

We cannot judge all by appearance; sometimes the poorest are found to be the richest of all. To pretend something is deceiving. The richness is in your heart. The true colours are visible; when you are tested deep down. The rich in heart don't think twice when doing charity. Most likely his richness is disguised. I may not be rich but I will not hesitate to do charity. Nothing is more satisfying when you become a helping hand.

There is no value if you cannot share. You may be rich in bank accounts; people want to see how rich you are in your heart to give away. Do not expect a windfall; work towards your target or be satisfy what you have. Nothing is more pleasing than feeling content. Do not try to fly over the gates to find wealth; every pound has to be earned. Easy come, easy go; money earned by deception does not prosper or will not be fruitful.

Most likely it will backfire on you; known as Karma. A simple person has small needs. A rich person tries to gather money beyond limits. Rich loses sleep worried sick when a poor person snores; you can hear them for miles. You must know your limits. Dignity is more important than being rich by deception. 'How rich are you? We will know, how you treat vulnerable people. As souls we are equal; any mistreatment is not forgiven.

Most important is having love in your heart. Which is willing to serve the cause of God. Selfish people are never appreciated. Maybe they are rich but people prefer not to be friends with them. You are only worth; what people experience with you. You cannot convince others to show that you are rich. 'If you are rich; what is that got to do with me? I am richer than you within my heart.

Poor people have dignity and they are beautiful souls and intelligent; these people deserve respect. How beautiful your soul is; reflects on your countenance. No one wants to beg; it is their life circumstances that push them on the road to extend their hand to beg. They acknowledge lost dignity; how hurt they are is beyond our knowing. No one wants to follow this route but destiny can push you to extremes.

Never underestimate the person standing next to you. We try to save our honour but it is beyond our control. Many people lost their dignity by deception or the circumstances were beyond their control. Lost dignity can hurt you for life. After losing your dignity; you may become rich but you remain poor at heart. The pages of your failure can open at any time. People never miss the opportunity to open your wounds. That is hurting and painful more than cancer. Cancer may be healed but your wounds are fresh.

You walk in disguise but people remember your shadow. 'Under these circumstances how can you become rich? Only

God can wipe your slate of suffering. But it seldom comes to help. People cry in vain; no one listens to their pain. Under these circumstances, it is better to take sanctuary in Spirit. Spirit can help to raise your vibrations to rise above elusive thoughts. Open new pages of your life; the gates to heaven are open.

Your dignity may appear to be part of your ego but it shows; that you are a class of being special; with these guts, you may go against the world to stand by God. Every person in this world has walked away from God, yet they are seeking and praying for help. God is not deaf but your elusive voice does not reach its inner ears. The day you are capable of talking to God; the language will be silent. Your words will sound like thunder. It is not God but the world can hear your words of wisdom.

People may pretend to be rich but God will decide; who is the richest of all. If you are standing by God; consider that you are the second richest person in the world. We want to be rich and teach our children the same. Teach them to be good humans; God will add all the treasures of this world. I can look into the eyes of a king or president because I know they are not richer than me. I have seen the rich hiding in dirty ditches to hide their guilt. One day we all pay the price.

Help the person in need; he may lead you to the gates of heaven. Wisdom in life is important it helps you to walk on the path of righteousness. Without wisdom, wealth always leads to temptations that can lead to your destruction. My dignity is not for sale. The day I sold myself; I will be the poorest of all. It is possible, that a poor person is willing to sell his dignity at any cost. That scar may not heal for life.

Be content with what you have or walk away from the scene to avoid future disappointments. It is always better to forget your past; which is full of haunting memories. The present moment can change all the circumstances. When you dream of being rich the future is flickering in your thoughts. That you may never see. Think of love which you can share with all without hesitation. Most people appear to look rich when it comes to sharing; they are the poorest of all.

I wear simple clothes and feel rich. I don't need any crown jewels to feel rich. Those who wear crown jewels have their legs trembling with fear. Jesus Christ wore a crown made of thorns; that is why he is known as the spiritual king. People want to make their name in this world. It does not matter how many people know you; as long as you are known in the kingdom of God.

We use our impaired judgements when the biggest judge is sitting within us. Let it judge and carve your life. I can assure you; that he will add all the treasures of this world to your account. It will teach, how to be fair to all and universal. You cannot become a prophet without being rich in heart. People come with hope and you are the deliverer of all. You are rich in the heart because you carry the wisdom of God. It Just Is; you can be too.

JOURNEY TO HEAVEN

There are thousands of religions in this world and have numerous beliefs. It does not matter how different we are from each other or how we present the teachings to the followers. All religions are based on different semantics. If our semantics were the same then there would have been only one religion. This difference in thought is based on how our prophet presented the teachings to the followers.

Since prophets are no more living, the followers begin to interpret the teachings according to our limited experience in this field. They mould the spiritual message to suit their needs. Our physical needs force us to commit to Karma. In the eyes of God, we become sinners. For that reason, we are placed in this world to clear our Karma. To be free once more to find solace in heaven. According to our Karma, we experience heaven or hell.

It is a well-known fact in this world that heaven is pleasant and hell is full of suffering. Although it may not be true. 'What is the main attraction of religions; to lead you into heaven? Most religions may differ in a hundred semantics but one thing is common. They all lead to heaven. Now the question is, 'what is heaven? You can allure any follower by promising that we will lead you to heaven. 'Why are we running away from hell?

There is hell and at the same time, there is no hell. Hell is self-created by sinful Karma. If you do not create bad

Karma, I don't think hell can scare you. All prophets have used one common phrase; those who follow me, dwell in heaven. No prophet of this world can lead you into heaven unless you begin to clear your backlog of committed Karma. Five passions of our mind are amused by the attraction of this world. We walk into the trap of Kal or our wrongdoings.

We are searching for the path to heaven. New religions have one thing in common to promise that we can help to find spiritual freedom in this life. The followers are willing to donate all that they have. The whole world is anxious to avoid hell after experiencing difficulties in this life. Anybody promise to show heaven is a hero. We love to dream in the heavenly world. You have not visited heaven but you imagine pleasant treatment.

We live in dream world and are reluctant to face the reality. Reality is the other side of illusion. Since young, I have been searching for spiritual freedom and came to discover the truth. None of the present teachings or religion is leading you into heaven. All religions are based on creating systems. Which are similar to business. All ask for donations or you may offer willingly. Wherever money is involved, it is part of hell.

All promise to lead you into heaven. When they are waiting at the seashore. There is only one person who can lead you into heaven; that is yourself. You will come to know what heaven is like when you begin to love God's creation. Mistreatment of any of his species will close the door before you manage to peep into heaven. You need to cleanse your wrongdoings. Many followers may not agree with what I write because I am holding their hands; not to commit further bad Karma.

We are so used to the old style of living and taking advantage of vulnerable people or species. Your journey to heaven will depend on how many good things you have done in this life. When we check our accounts, I don't think the weighing scale is in your favour. You can turn back and accept complete transformation in your thoughts. Your Karma is based on, how you think and apply these thoughts in life. We pretend to be good humans but carry destructive thoughts.

A drop of water can change the waves of the sea. Your one good thought can lead you into heaven. We are pilgrims in this world. Your place is not at the seashore or on a desert island. One positive thought can lead you into heaven. Heaven is not hidden from you as believed. It is a matter of knocking on the correct door. You need magic words to open this door. While all doors to illusion are left open purposely to facilitate your thoughts.

All the stars and heaven seem far distant. You only need to extend your hand to reach them. Your hand does not reach there despite your efforts because there are thousands; who are holding your hand. With spiritual effort, you begin to feel alive; your loved ones will remove the fuse. There is only one ladder that leads to heaven. That is within. If you know, what is within; your journey is not far.

At present heaven may seem far but it is only one step into Astral Plane. There are multiple heavens in each plane. Each tread on the ladder represents one heaven. There are so many treads on the ladder to climb to be in the presence of God. To climb many treads on the ladder is a hard task. If you give in to Spirit. God can pull your hand in one go. The way to heaven is not that difficult. We love to make our journey long.

As a soul, we are complete and neutral. In the lower world, we have split personalities. We fail to find our true identity. The soul can see God as if it is part of itself. With our double personalities of positive and negative; everything appears as a shadow vision. Shadow is not the truth but we fail to see the image that created the shadow. Shadow is another name for illusion. Hell is part of the illusion and heaven is real.

We left heaven long ago to meet again. We have travelled many miles on the wheel of eighty-four. We are facing the darkness and clouds are blocking the rays of the sun. our vision is blurred; no one is here to show us the way to heaven. Despite all efforts, we fail to hold the hand of a spiritual man. Who is leading the way; we fail to walk in his footsteps. Spirit is alive but we are tired of our long journey. We know heaven is real but out of our reach.

It has been a long journey; we have the longing to be in heaven. Heaven is waiting for us to meet once more. Our desires kept us grounded. The inner strength of God kept us going to seek the path within. Once you reach heaven; you feel at home. As you have never parted. The long journey of the wheel of eighty-four seems like a dream. God pinched my hand to reveal the truth of my journey. I am home in heaven.

The difference between heaven and hell is hair-breadth. 'Why do we find it difficult to crossover? For this purpose; an illusion is created. So, we can value; heaven more. A free gift is often ignored or put to the side. You have learned the path to heaven; the hard way. This is to make sure; you never leave heaven again. You are trained to be the assistant of God. You and the creator are one. You have made your home in heaven.

TEMPTATIONS IN LIFE

Temptation in life is the strong urge to possess or have something. There are a number of things which we cannot resist. That is called temptation. Temptation is a weakness in the human mind. All the saints go through this testing. Spirit creates the scene to test your contentment. We need to fill our minds with the goodness of Spirit so nothing can penetrate into our consciousness.

When temptation is active within the mind, have faith, God will show the way out. You cannot pray all the time to avoid temptation; we need to build our spiritual stamina to feel content. There is always something equal and opposite to replace temptation. Jesus Christ also went through this test. All temptations are a materialistic part of the illusion; nothing can penetrate Spirit.

Temptations can only enter our aura when our spiritual guard is not on. Adam and Eve were tempted to eat fruit from the forbidden tree and their life took a complete turn. They were the cause and we are paying the price of that effect. Over the years; that one temptation has multiplied into millions. Illusion can allure you in many directions. Maybe temptation is our weakness; God has given us the ability to overcome any test.

You cannot fight the temptation; that is another tool used by illusion. Have patience and make plans for how you can conquer this weakness. Many people create illusionary situations to betray. Male or female attraction outside marriage is also a temptation many cannot resist. This trap has failed so many in the spiritual field. The root cause of temptation is our unfulfilled desires.

If you want to overcome temptations; you better overcome your desires. Many people have destroyed their lives to experience temptation. Illusion spares no one. Our desires lead us to temptations and that creates sin. Your spiritual stamina can overcome any temptation. Many temptations came into my life; I let them pass by to the side. When temptation is conceived it gives birth to sin.

Spiritual scriptures are full of examples; of how to avoid temptations. 'Why don't you create a temptation to meet God? Fill your mind and body with Spirit and leave no room for any temptations. Every time you conquer temptation, you are one step closer to your spiritual goal. Never doubt your abilities; we often fail ourselves. No one is superman; we all experience temptations within our capacities.

People often pray to God; to give them the strength to face temptations. God has created these temptations purposely to test your spiritual stamina. This is the only way to know if you are fit for the kingdom of God. This is the riddle of God. God knows your weaknesses and this is the only way to make you strong. We are praying to the wrong source (God) for help. Most religious scriptures state the opposite. Try to analyse what I said.

God sent you into the lower worlds to make you strong; when religions open the door to weakness. 'How can you become an assistant of God when you failed to monitor your affairs? When a ship sinks into the black hole; it does not come out. This world is similar to a black hole in the sea; It will not be that easy to make your way into heaven. Do not waste your time in prayers; try to find the secret door that lands you in God's presence.

Temptations are everywhere so is God holding your hand. Unless you try to run away and fall into the trap of temptation. God does not hold your hand when committing sin and it will not help; when you are suffering. This is the point that religions fail to grasp and try to bypass God's authority by praying. Since I explained this way; 'You believe your prayers will be answered?

Someone invited me to a religious ceremony; they prayed four times within two hours. 'Are they making fun of God or themselves? During one prayer someone requested body healing. I know this person for many years; He has been selling drugs; 'how many lives has he destroyed? As I said earlier; what goes around comes around. 'This man was tempted to make quick money but at what cost?

We try to build human relationships that are part of the physical temptations. God is holding your hand all the time; 'have you ever tried to build a relationship with God? You cannot see, who is standing next to you but you are willing to travel miles to meet your tempted person. Sometimes our children walk on us; it does not matter where they are; we always bless them. This is one of God's virtues, invested within us.

We are the replicas of God but try to act differently. Many people lecture on the power of prayers. This is one of our weaknesses; we believe in it. 'Why should I pray to God? If you believe he is God; He should know better. Some are born great and strong because they act under God's instructions. We are similar to baby lambs. As soon as it separates from the herd, the predators are there to kill. This is how we walk into many temptations of life.

This is how illusion set its traps to allure and catch you. One temptation can create many sins; very soon you can load the ship with your sins. You need sheer effort to make a comeback. Learn to submit to God and let the Spirit flow into your mind and body; you are born again. Never underestimate your abilities. God only test you; what you are capable of handling. With self-created temptations, we cross our limits.

Temptation only comes to knock on our door; we invite it with open arms. 'How can you blame others? Have patience and ponder upon the situation you are in; most likely we created it. The realisation is very important before trying to find a solution. We have the ability to overcome any temptation. 'What do you do, if you are tempted to sin? Ask within and wait for the answer. Do not walk away with the temptation.

ARE YOU LIVING FOR GOD?

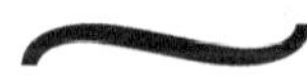

'Are you living for God? God is living for his creation. While we are living for others; 'who do not appreciate what we do for them? Similarly, we don't appreciate what God does for us. We have to walk on the long road to know and appreciate the work of God. The day we learn this, we will be in his presence to learn more. This is the true beginning of learning the eternal truth and being ready to serve God as its future prophet.

God send his loved ones; they are known as prophets in this world. To prove that it is living and waiting for you in his house to enjoy being state. All prophets are spiritual and their knowingness is beyond our grasp. Their knowingness is not even 1% compared to God. This is the reason; there is no prophet who did not made mistakes. Their actions create miracles and history is created.

These prophets give us the hope to live on and we create religions under their banners. The words of the prophet are beyond any melody. They played their tunes and are gone. When the orchestra has gone with instruments, I wonder who is playing the music with sticks. I am familiar with Sikhism, Islam, Christianity and Hinduism. They are so proud of their religions and prophets and forgot God. 'Is your religion greater than God?

At present they are all fighting with sticks to show their superiority. They want to rule the world religiously when they fail to follow within. Our minds and bodies are filled with impurities and leave no room for God. God can only enter when there is room for its presence. Learn to live for God, not for yourself or others. The others you worry about are already been looked after by God. We fail to trust God.

When we leave everything in God's hand then we will experience God's hand working for us. This is how miracles are created. With our endeavour, we only create illusions. I enjoy life because I let God be in the driving seat and I enjoy every ride. 'Is there a better chauffeur than God? 'Why are you wasting your energy, when it can be used for the good of the whole? Live your life under the command of God.

Life is God's gift; 'when are you going to return its favour? God has plans for each soul, whereas we have our own plans. This is the wall of illusion. When I walk in the presence of God, I have no fear and nothing can touch me. When you live under the shadow of others; it could be heaven or hell because it is beyond your control. There is no better commanding force than God. I may be clever because I let God worry for me.

I experience its response during each pain or pleasure. So, it knows my needs and listens to my every pain and heals with its blessings. Life is a precious gift but we fail to live God's way. With impaired judgements, we become the knowers and the knower has become the unknown. This is why we fail to feel its presence. No one is an atheist; we failed to walk on the path to God. Show the way to others if you can.

You will be one step closer to destiny. When I walked many joined and a few tired ones are taking a rest. Sometimes we give up, when very near to our victory. Trust within, feel the flow of Spirit. Instant revival will help you float above the clouds. At times I felt low but I never gave up. Every time I felt God's hand within my reach. That kept me going to recite its message so I can share it with others.

I live for God that is why it is always living for me. All religions recite their verses but point out that God is beyond their reach. 'If he is beyond your reach then why are you religious? You are feeling this separation but God will not let you walk away that easily. The path to God is illuminated but you prefer to live in the corners of darkness. You can hide as much as you like; one day it will dig you out of your hiding place.

You may prefer to live a life of illusion but God has better plans for you. Sometimes our body feels irritated when wearing new garments because our life is used to wearing rags. We need to build trust and stamina to be in God's presence. Being religious does not give you the authority to be in God's presence. This is the veil of illusion most religious followers have. You have to cross the boundaries of religious thought to know God.

God has given you the privilege of life to feel its presence. The day you find the reason to live for God, all the crossroads of life will become the highway to heaven. As I begin to write this discourse the pearls of wisdom begin to fall like hailstones. I was about to finish this discourse but it held my hand and said; It is not finished yet. These words are beyond my control. I am blessed to hold the golden pen.

All the words are full of the glory of God; I don't know what else to write. People have many avenues to follow in life when all the paths are closed for me. The day you believe in

God the sun will never set in your life. When the sun sets and darkness appears. After many struggles during this night in life, you are desperately waiting for the sun to rise. For some, it takes a long time to sunrise. This learning leads the way to seek the kingdom of God once more.

All the paths are not for you to rest; they are created and designed to show the way to God. Provide your shoulder for the others to lean on so they could also walk along. God will return your efforts a hundred folds. Your hardships in life teach many lessons that is your treasure to pass on. Never hold on to your grudges in life they will act as an anchor to your ship. You want to move in life but failed to break the chains of illusion.

The day you begin to live for God; the realisation comes that all the chains were an illusion. You wasted all your life for no reason. In your last hour, you look at loved ones; the realisation comes, that no one could help or hold your hand to heaven. You lived for them and they are living for others. Your doubts have kept you away from the threshold of God. Don't you think; 'It is decision time?

The day you find the reason to live for God, your reasons will cease. We have been creating new reasons all our life. God is forgiving; all mistakes are for learning. The day you learn to correct your mistakes, it will open the door to its eternal home. All people and situations were put in your path so you may begin to live for God. After each realisation, we learn God was up to something.

Without God life has no purpose. It takes all life to find purpose and how to live for God. When your life is empty of all impurities; your life is under the command of God.

It took God many years to evacuate your sitting tenants. When the Seeker is ready, the spiritual Master appears to lead the way to heaven. We always dwell in the past and dream of the future. The present moment is to live and experience God.

The day you learn to live for God, the whole creation will breathe through you. You are the helping hand of God. You will never receive the gifts of God before its time or beyond your luck. That is your destiny. Our destiny kept us going in circles until its door opened for us. Learn to live for God today; tomorrow it will send you on earth to be his prophet. You will write the words of God so others may learn to live for God.

IS GOD HUMOROUS?

God is the combination of all the attributes we have; that includes, love, laughter and sorrow. During one conversation, my friend said; that God has humour which is why he created humans to make fun of him. 'Do you realise, we all make fun of God by not accepting his will? We also abuse all of its creations which is also making fun of his system. God send prophets with spiritual scriptures in their hands to Passover his message to us. We read and listen but do not abide by it.

This is why we are foreigners in the lower world. Once we enter the soul plane then we become citizens. Once you are a foreigner in the lower world, it let you make fun of others and become a laughing stock for others. God wants full submission not only on Sundays but every day. We always do what others are doing that is why we learn nothing. If you want to follow them, try to judge their actions and try to improve that may please God.

We want to harvest the fruits but fail to plant trees. Instead, we are cutting the existing ones. We act as religious but you have to learn; 'are you a missionary or an imposter? God is the planter; by creating the system. Then he planted himself within us. He is the experiencer by watching his own system through us. 'Don't you think God is making fun of himself? God plant the disappointments in your life to experience himself.

God created us within a big circle and said; you are responsible for every created Karma at the same time; he is guarding the door himself. As a guardian ref; Rude awakening 2 in The Philosophy of My Life. God said all my sufferings were created purposely by his guardians. I suffered and cried with pain. When I was going through these experiences; I am sure God was laughing at my hardships. 'Now can you suggest if I should laugh or cry?

When disappointments appear, we suffer, if learned that they are planted purposely by God; 'why should we complain? Learn to laugh at God as well; 'Don't you make fun of your mum and dad? If we cannot make fun of God that means we failed to build up that loveable relationship. There is a difference between making fun of and insulting. Therefore, never cross your limits. Otherwise, God may backfire on you.

The closer you want to be in his presence the greater the tests will be. If you know; you have to suffer to experience his presence. 'Don't you think, you better stay home? I think that is a good joke. God has created the big circle and his centre is within each house; so as to watch. This is why you cannot escape from your doings. It makes no difference; you laugh or cry. God has created the whirlpool. He watches your every twist and turns and laughs at us. As we watch our children in similar situations.

God is total awareness therefore it knows how to enjoy. It wanted us to enjoy while going through the total experience but we complain. The day you cross all the boundaries with ease, you will become a happy entity once more. 'Do you think God is happy when we are sad? God's mood swings according to how we feel. Now it is our responsibility to make God laugh.

I have been to Indian temples a hundred times. I noticed every time that the congregation is sitting very intense. During spare time, they may be backbiting but I never witnessed a smile on their faces. 'God may be wondering why? It does not matter how religious they are but failed to build up that relationship. Their seriousness shows signs of isolation. If God does not have humour, then he would not give us the ability to laugh.

'Where do all the jokes come from? They are part of God's humour. All prophets have a special spiritual spark in their eyes. This is how they express God's humour. Wherever I go. I always stress that you must laugh even at yourself if possible. You may crack jokes anywhere but do not crack jokes where they are not appreciated or accepted by God. God has an enormous amount of humour because he created all the jokes.

We are only acting as puppets to display his jokes. God always appear disguised that is why we make fun of him. 'When was the last time you laughed? If not, that was the time you missed his jokes. 'If you know that you are created as a mini-God then how can you laugh at yourself? The day you become serious; God may laugh at you. He also laughs at us when we pray and ask him; what to do. Yet you believe he is the knower of the truth.

The whole truth is within; we fail to discover it. God is waiting to do all the chores daily. We try to manage and spoil our day. We often feel and say that I am somebody because God let us enjoy humour. If you cannot laugh and enjoy jokes, you are not fit for the kingdom of God. I lived my life seriously up to the age of 36 years. One day God came and said; 'why are you absent? I had no answer and discovered humour.

Someone was teasing an atheist every day; the Atheist was so fed up and said; Oh My God. You can believe it or not; it is sitting silently in one corner. One day you will discover his humour. You can travel the whole world and return to the original point because the world is round. Within this circle is hidden the key to humour. God has plans for us; so, we may laugh but always work against his plans and experience disappointments.

We love to enjoy romantic life; the day you learn to romance with God; the humour is all yours. It is the separation; responsible for our pains. I felt its presence and swung my arms in the air to catch it; God moved out of the circle to laugh. We create imaginary friends when our friend is within us all the time. Thank God every day; he will make sure; that no tears flow in your eyes.

If God were not with me, I would have been wandering in desert islands. God gave you the disappointments to replace with something greater. We are afraid of any change in life. God has given us the life to enjoy. You are only renting out to claim your ownership. We will experience good and bad things in life; they are temporary. Your humour is permanent because; God; It Just Is.

SOUL TO SOUL

God is the soul and it has created us as souls in its image. God sent us on pilgrimage to learn and return to the centre of its creation; the ocean of love and mercy. Everything we do or believe in become a stumbling stone to our success. Religious people believe they will find God because they are religious. 'What is the religion of God? None; So, whatever your belief is; it is holding your hand not to cross over the wall.

The soul is neutral and universal in nature. It is wrapped in lower bodies to create obstacles. Your beliefs are not universal; they do not contribute a helping hand so the soul can unwrap itself to reach home once more. It is our belief that all religions lead to God. Religions take away part of your purity because they are biased. You have to be perfect all the way to see the face of God.

This is why; religions stress that no one can see God. As they fail to see God; it is easier for them to believe in their respective prophets. Our prophets have seen God; otherwise, you would not believe in them. They bless us to do the same but we do not find time to experience the eternal truth. We love to float downstream as all others are doing. That is leading you away from God. Pause for a minute and find the courage to swim upstream to experience the ocean of love and mercy.

We believe our religion is based on the eternal truth. There is no doubt. When you say that you are Christian; that means you are relating yourself to Christ but not God. If you are Sikh, you are relating to the principles of Sikhism but not God. This is applicable to all religions. All religions find their words to justify their beliefs. As far as God is concerned there are no arguments or beliefs. 'Are you with God or not that matters?

The truth is; that we are not religious; we are following it for our convenience. Our minds are mysterious we search for easy paths or find another shoulder to pass our responsibilities on. All religions are; the other shoulders. This is why we fail to receive the gifts of God. There is no need for religious temples or complicated philosophies. God; it just is. It is waiting to receive us with open arms.

All nations are religious and patriotic at the same time. This is preventing us from being universal. Both act as a double edge sword. You cannot have God by holding a sword in your hand. God is an ocean of love and mercy. Your double edge sword is not in line with the principles of God. You must fill yourself with love until you become the magnet of love to share with others.

God shares all with his creation. God is far from your reach; you have failed to knock on its door. You are proud to relate with your religion; but not God. There is always something standing between soul to soul. This gap is widening each day with modern thought. The modern mind is good for analysis but it is leading you away from nature. If you care for nature; you are halfway to reaching God.

God creates all the opportunities for us to draw our attention; we walk away from the scene with hundred excuses. God extends its invisible hand; you need to wake up on the inner to hold his finger. God wants us to be unique as it is but we are busy creating our illusive personalities. Without the Spirit of God; you do not exist. God want us to move on in life to reach home; we always dwell in the past.

All prophets were full of God's love and out of this love they felt like calling God; Allah, Jehovah, Bhagwan. Similarly, we give names to our children but out of this abundance of love, we call them nicknames. Later these God names become our identity to relate with. As soon as we come to know another person is Christian, Hindu or Muslim. We put our guards and become alert like meerkats; expecting them are predators.

This is another stumbling stone between soul to soul. We must admit that whatever we are following or our beliefs are preventing us from being universal. We are on a spree of destroying his creation, while it, re-store all the damages. Despite our mistakes, it is not complaining. We do not tolerate other creations of God. God can take away all your pains and sorrows; spiritually you become fragile. This is what religions are used for.

We have many plans in life but non-related to God. Life achievements help to relate with this world but fail to relate with God. God want you to be yourself so, that one day you may become something. God created beautiful paths to reach home but you prefer to travel a highway to illusion. Birds sing the melodies of God; we love to sing depressing songs. You are depressed because you are not content within.

Your desires stand in the way of soul to soul. God's angels are always around to know your whereabouts. God created you for a purpose to fulfil his purpose. The day you find the path within; you are on the highway to heaven. Those who dream big, do not sleep; the light is lit within so nothing stands between soul to soul. Have faith you will win the heart of God. God's heart is within us but we fail to listen to its beats.

Once you listen; you will be humble forever. Your national flags or anthems, you are so proud of; divide your thoughts and stand between soul to soul. Sovereignty is the pride of the nation to feel free. We often use this sovereignty to harm others that will stand between soul to soul. All souls are created equal. No one is allowed to roam above others. God has given us absolute independence to have free will.

Those who fear God will not have him in their lives. We are not here to create or win wars; we need to win the heart of God. Our doubts and beliefs create a wall between soul to soul. We try to understand God our ways or logic; when it just is. All priestcraft teaches us how to follow religious systems but fails to show the path within. Our focus is on how to become religious but fails to become souls.

Political thought is based on negative or logical thinking which creates a big gap between soul to soul. 'Have you ever seen a politician turn into a saint? Whatever you come across in life such as pain or pleasure creates a wall between soul to soul. The day your questions cease about yourself or this world; you will find the path within. We were sent as innocent souls; we must return as innocent souls with spiritual maturity. The day you begin to see the inner visions; your destiny is not far.

You are a soul and so is God; may you find the path within.

GRACE OF GOD

The grace of God is the nature of him to let us get away with our wrongdoings. It is very similar to turning a blind eye. Instead of punishing us, it blesses us. This is why it is the king of love and mercy. One little problem bothers us for days when it is brushing away billions of issues to the side. It bestows its love on us without being worthy of receiving it. It is not expecting any submission from us. It wants us to be ourselves.

It is responsible for the well-being of billions of souls. The responsibility is huge when we cannot manage our small families. we fail to give equal love to all members of our family. Our love and life are based on set conditions. When God's love is unconditional. Otherwise, we will not be calling him God. He does not discriminate between us or villains. Despite God's grace; we fail to lead balanced lives.

We are loyal to our countries and sacrifice our lives to protect the boundaries. We fail to look after the well-being of ourselves and its creation. Charity begins at home before you are capable of helping others. God wants us to experience everlasting love when we fail to walk away from illusion. We must have faith in its doing and become humble as it is to us. Being humble is another name of God's grace.

You must learn to forgive before expecting any humbleness within. We have compassion for all the avenues of illusion. But failed to hold any compassion for the doings of God.

Despite that, we are enjoying the grace of God. Those who have compassion for the doings of God are known as prophets. We must learn to change our ways of thinking to enjoy God's grace. Despite our unfruitful efforts, it is still protecting us and providing his umbrella of its grace.

Despite our failures in life, God gives us the courage to carry on. This is why we fail to give up. We may be crawling in life, despite our conditions; our focus is on the finishing line. Once we cross over the finishing line; God's grace is waiting for us. We may have given up long ago; it is the spirit within that kept us going. This is a way of life to carry on, despite our failures. Happy new year or Christmas are just basic days. They help us to revive the Spirit within.

We are not created as anything; it is the protection of God's grace helping us to do something worthwhile. Those who abuse other creations of God or humans are a long way to go from being in the presence of God. All your wrongdoings are pushing away the grace of God. Despite your ignorance, it still holds the umbrella to protect you. You may have forgotten but it has created you in its image. God is obliged to protect its eternal souls.

We may have forgotten our true identities but each incarnation is designed to make sure; that one day you will wake up from long sleep. We love our sleep. The day God snores on you; you will never wake up. We take the liberty of everything and become its spoilt children. The Lord of Karma makes sure that you must attend school every day. All your sufferings act as lessons in school. You can run away all your life but you are within its circle.

To chase you, Karma appears at each corner of your life. The corners of life are not to hide; it is a sign of a turning point in life. You are so used to the old ways of living. Any new change in life irritates you. Each incarnation is designed to bring change in your thinking and an opportunity to create good Karma. If we learn to create good Karma, we will not be going through circles of life. We fail to still our minds, which is failing us to experience the grace of God.

So far, we have not learned how to forgive that is why we are always a few steps away from the ocean of love and mercy. You may wonder what the ocean of love and mercy is. The day you begin to forgive and feel mercy on the creation of God; you will experience peace within and rays of God's grace. That will be a part experience of love and mercy of God. One day it will lead you to a full plunge into the ocean of love and mercy.

All your thinking and ways of living are ways of illusion. God's way is eternal. Which is within your reach but fails to touch the face of God because you are not living the life in a spiritual way. God created every step of life easy to follow but we love to circle in the maze. After a long journey, you will learn there is only one entry into the maze and so is the way out. This is a struggle within the wheel of eighty-four. It teaches you a lot so you may grow up from a boy to a man.

This is the purpose of God's grace to motivate us to lead our lives in God's way and represent the true image of God. So, others can follow in your footsteps. Every few years God send one of his prophets on the earth to remind us of our spiritual responsibility. That may help to revive the great man within. We often ignore the new prophet because we fail to accept his Godly presence. We must learn to bring change in our thoughts.

Each year tree receives new leaves and after the experience, all fall off in autumn. We hold on to our old wings of life and fail to change; despite the grace of God. We give up on ourselves and related families but God has not given up on us. It is the invisible force of God that keeps you going. It is also known as the golden thread of God. The silver cord is another one to provide God energy for our spiritual survivor. The silver cord is the soul's connection to the lower world.

Once the silver cord is disposed of soul appears on the soul plane and with effort one day it will dwell in the ocean of love and mercy. The prophets guide us to lead our lives in the devotion of God. This devotion wakes up the spirit within. The depth of devotion makes you feel part of God. You will know that you are a soul and part of God. This is the awakening within God is waiting for. God knows; that one day you will find the path within.

The path is within, it is not that hard to find but illusion kept us in circles. It is the awakening within to lead us to Self-realisation. That is awakening within to claim our inheritance within God's world. The more virtues of God we adopt the more we feel at home. When we close all the doors behind on the physical, God's eternal door opens to reach home. Soul's true home is in the ocean of love and mercy. God's grace has helped us to reach.

God Bless All

SHER GILL Galib

London

SPIRITUAL TERMINOLOGY

Akashic Records: The total record of our physical incarnations, which are kept in the causal plane. On that basis, Past, present and future can be predicted.

Angels of Death: Assistants of the king of the dead to collect the departing soul from the physical at their last hour.

Astral Body: Radiant or emotional body. Astral plane; next plane above physical.

Astrology: The study of planets and their position concerning your date of birth; the future can be predicted.

Aura: This is a magnetic field that surrounds all souls to express their spiritual status.

Brahma: The lord of the mental plane and one of the Hindu trinity Gods. Brahma, Vishnu and Shiva.

Buddhi: Intellectual: Is part of the mind, the chief instrument of thought.

Cause & Effect: Action and reaction create negative or positive karma.

Chakra(s): Psychic centres in the human body; all yoga practitioners use these centres for spiritual experience.

Conscience: This is moral or ethical development in person.

Consciousness: That state of being in which the individual lives all-day

Creation: Whatever has been created by God for training purposes.

Creed (God's): All life flows from God; nothing can exist without spirit or the will of God.

Crown Chakra: The soft spot at the top of the human skull and easy passage for soul travel into the spiritual planes.

Cult: This is a system of worship of a Master, deity, Idol or any celebrity.

Deja vu: The ability to know the events before happening.

Direct projection: This is the technique of instantly moving the soul and body together.

Dreams: It is a way of Spirit to communicate with all souls. The spiritual Master also communicates with Seekers, known as dream teachings.

Enlightenment: The state of spiritual knowledge and awakening within.

Eternity: Expression of life without a sense of time and space; the present spiritual dwelling is always in eternity. `

Etheric plane: The unconscious plane or dividing line between the mental and soul plane. Sub-conscious mind.

Faith: Is the keystone to having any spiritual success. You believe in the Master or teachings to achieve the set goal.

Free will: God's gift to each soul to decide how to create karma or live life.

Haiome: One of the most powerful spiritual **words,** it can lead the Seeker to God.

Hypnotism: Is one of the psychic arts to balance many disorders or practice evil.

Imagination: This is a mental faculty to activate positive vibrations to have an inner experience or soul travel.

Immortality: Is a state of being, deathless or as opposed to mortality.

Incarnations: The continuous cycle of births and deaths in the physical world.

Individuality: The Immortal self of each soul has its own identity; no two souls are the same as twins.

Jot-Niranjan: The ruler on the astral plane and powerhouse to the physical world.

Kal: Is the overall in charge of opposing Spirit.

Karma: The law of cause & effect. It is the decisive part of human suffering.

King of the Dead: Is the lord of karma on the astral plane that judges the soul's journey according to its earned karma.

Light & Sound: These are twin pillars of God; it is Spirit.

Love: It is the love force of God that sustains all creation and balance of all universes. There is human love and impersonal love.

Magic: It is trickery or part of an illusion to please the audience.

Manifestation: Manifested, which is usually apparent to the physical senses.

Meditation: This is the practice of sitting while reciting spiritual **words** to have an esoteric experience.

Mental plane: This is the fourth plane in God's world. The sound is of **running water**.

Mind: The thinking part of human consciousness or the chief instrument for the soul's survival in the lower worlds.

Ocean of love and Mercy: Life-giving spirit. Love for the well-being of all creation.

Omnipotence: All-powerful. Omniscience; all-knowing, Omnipresent; present.

Par-Brahm: He is the lord on the etheric plane.

Para-Vidya: Is spiritual knowledge. **Apara**-vidya; is physical knowledge.

Philosophy: Is the psychic or core study of religions using the mental faculties.

Physical plane: This is the lowest plane of matter, energy, space and time.

Power: There is supreme or neuter power; negative & positive operate in the lower worlds. Political or any other authority in this world is also power.

Prayers: This is an approach to contacting a spiritual Master or God. It could be a request or to feel its presence. If you know God is within, it will understand your needs.

Prophecy: Spiritual man who can forecast future events long before they happen.

Psychic Space: Each soul's natural right to feel free. Be yourself and let others be.

Re-incarnation: Is the circle of each soul, birth- death and rebirth.

Religions: These are spiritual and social systems created in the name of a prophet.

Sach Khand: Is in the fifth plane of God's world. It is the first pure spirit plane and the ruler is Satnam.

Sahasara-Dal-Kanwal: The capital city of the astral plane and meeting place between the Master and Seeker after sun & moon worlds.

Satnam Ji: The first personification of God to be seen in male form. Humans are created replicas of Satnam Ji. Lord of soul plane. The sound is a single note of the flute.

Satya-Yuga: Golden age: This yuga lasted for 1,728,000 years.

Seeker: Disciple: Who has the yearning to experience God in this lifetime.

Self-realisation: Knowledge of its existence as soul and having answers to self, such as; 'Who am I? 'Where am I going after death and how to reach there?

Self-Surrender: Complete submission to the Master and the principles of teachings you follow.

Soul: Atma: Is a unit of God-awareness. It is a micro part of the macro.

Soul Travel: This is the change in the state of consciousness or the means of travelling to other planes.

Space and Time: Space means nothing apart from our perception of objects and time means nothing apart from our experience of events.

Spirit: It is the combination of light and sound. It is the adhesive or life force of all universes.

Spiritual Freedom: Is liberation from the lower worlds or the wheel of eighty-four.

Spiritual unfoldment: This is to become aware of what God has invested within us.

Spirituality: This is the essence of spiritual experience, which cannot be taught but can be caught.

Sub-conscious mind: The unconscious or the reactive mind.

Sufism: Islamic mysticism and total dedication to Allah.

Total awareness: This is the ultimate goal for all spiritual Seekers to achieve on this path.

Trinity of God: God, Spirit and the Master. Father, Son and Holy ghost.

Truth: Is the only source of knowledge and man is the mirror of truth. You cannot receive more than what your soul can hold.

Vibrations: Spiritual waves we carry as our aura will show on our countenance.

Will of God: This is God's ultimate decision and nothing can exist without this will of God.

Will power: Indicates the maturity of each person. The strength of execution.

Wisdom: Is spiritual knowledge beyond all intellectual ability.

Word of God: Shabda or the flow of spirit from God.

CPSIA information can be obtained
at www.ICGtesting.com
Printed in the USA
BVHW031748231222
654911BV00005B/87

9 781803 813318